DIONE LUCAS GOURMET COOKING SCHOOL COOKBOOK

Welcome to my cooking class – and bon appetit ! Dione Luca

DIONE LUCAS GOURMET COOKING SCHOOL COOKBOOK

Classic Recipes, Menus and Methods as Taught in the Classes of the Gourmet Cooking School

BY
Dione Lucas
WITH
Darlene Geis

BONANZA BOOKS

NEW YORK

This 1982 edition is published by Bonanza Books, distributed by
Crown Publishers, Inc., by arrangement with Bernard Geis Associates, Inc.

This book was previously published as
THE GOURMET COOKING SCHOOL COOKBOOK.

Manufactured in the United States of America

Illustrations by John Alcorn

Designed by Arthur Hawkins

Library of Congress Cataloging in Publication Data

Lucas, Dione, 1909-1971.
    Dione Lucas Gourmet Cooking School cookbook.

    Reprint. Originally published: The Gourmet Cooking School cookbook.
New York. B. Geis Associates, 1964.
    Includes index.
    1. Cookery, French.   I. Geis, Darlene.
II. Dione Lucas Cooking School.   III. Title.
[TX719.L79   1982]   641.5944   82-1354
                            AACR2

ISBN: 0-517-3760611

h g f e d c b a

To Mark and Peter Lucas

There is no spectacle on earth
more appealing than that of
a beautiful woman in the act of
cooking dinner for someone she loves.

Thomas Wolfe

A NOTE
FROM THE
SORCERESS'
APPRENTICE

This is not a cookbook. It is a how-to-cook book. Its recipes are much more than a mere listing of ingredients and directions. Each one is an actual lesson, fully detailed, in the preparation of a classic dish of French *haute cuisine*, based upon the teaching methods of the Dione Lucas Gourmet Cooking School. To go into your kitchen armed with this book is to learn how to prepare food under the tutelage of a sorceress, who was also a master French chef.

For Dione Lucas was a diplomate of the famed Cordon Bleu in Paris. She trained and worked under some of the great chefs on the Continent, and in this country taught her culinary arts and skills in her own famous Gourmet Cooking School.

These are the Cordon Bleu recipes as presented in her classes, adapted to American measurements and equipment. These dishes have been prepared countless times in Mrs. Lucas' restaurant and in her classes, under her direction, by students who run the gamut from professional cooks to amateur "I-can't-even-boil-water" housewives. The experienced cooks learn scores of little tricks and secrets they never knew before; the novices start from scratch and discover that even the most complex dish is still prepared one step at a time, and each step in itself is simple.

Where most recipes only give you the know-what, Mrs. Lucas' cookbook adds the know-how. And this is what sets it apart from most other cookbooks. Anyone who has ever prepared a dish from one of these cooking-class recipes has had a phenomenally successful result. We asked a number of people who had never even taken the Dione Lucas course to try some of these recipes, and the magic worked for them. The directions are precise and explicit, and the know-how is fully as important to a good recipe as the ingredients.

For example, a *crème caramel* is a caramel custard no matter how you slice it. By and large, the ingredients are pretty much the same from cookbook to cookbook—eggs, sugar, cream, milk. But a *crème caramel* made according to this Dione Lucas recipe turns out better. Why?

It is her method, carefully explained, that makes the difference. If you add the hot milk in a slow, steady trickle to the beaten eggs and sugar, if you bake the custard in a very slow oven, in a pan of water that is never allowed to come to a boil, for a longer period of time than is usually recommended, you will have not only a satin-smooth dessert, but a conversation piece.

So pay very careful attention to the instructions, as well as to the ingredients, in each recipe. They are the magic formulas of this culinary sorceress. They are what separates the wizardry of a great chef from the mere adequacy of a good home cook. And these fine points of method have all too rarely been presented, *as in a cooking lesson,* with every recipe.

Starting with the basic kitchen equipment necessary for turning out her Cordon Bleu specialties and the basic materials to keep on hand in pantry and kitchen, Mrs. Lucas goes on to tell you how, when and why to use each. You will learn how to organize your preparations before starting the actual cooking of a dish—a procedure that simplifies *haute cuisine* so that it can be performed in the most compact of kitchenettes.

As you follow each of these recipes step by step, you will find every doubt resolved, every question answered along the way. How to stir a sauce, how to beat an egg, how to fold in a soufflé, when is an omelet done—these questions have all been raised before many times by students. Thus, not only have the recipes been pretested but so has the method of their communication been tested for clarity and for ease of follow-ability. Mrs. Lucas also tells you, most importantly, how and in what to serve up each dish, for the presentation of fine food is as much a part of the recipe as the materials and preparation that go into it.

Finally, these recipes are grouped in suggested menus to give you a definite idea of what dishes go well together—no small contribution to a successful dinner. There is even a recommended wine for each meal.

But the really remarkable and exciting thing about this cookbook is that it enables the home cook, however inexperienced, to turn out the kind of food that was heretofore found only in fine French restaurants. Thanks to Dione Lucas' genius as a teaching chef, you too can make a beautiful *Caneton* à *l'Orange* or *Filets de Sole Joinville* at home on your range, with ease, distinction—and with a success beyond your happiest expectations. I know, because that's exactly what happened to me.

—Darlene Geis

CONTENTS

CONTENTS

CONTENTS

CONTENTS

CONTENTS

Chapter 1

WELCOME TO MY COOKING CLASS

For nearly thirty years, in England and in the United States, I have been teaching classes in cooking at my own school. During these years thousands of students have bustled around my kitchen classroom, some of them adept, some of them—at least their first few times —inept. It is to the inept ones that I owe the inspiration for this book.

People who are not experienced in cooking techniques can learn very quickly and simply under direct tutelage. Not one of my students, I am proud to say, ever walked out of a class without having cooked a very creditable dish, no matter how complicated the recipe. Students were able to succeed in class when they were sometimes unable to follow a recipe successfully at home, because they were told exactly *how* to do each operation, and each step was explained in detail.

And I have learned, from the questions students asked and the problems that developed, just what apparently obvious points needed more careful explanation. It would never have occurred to me, for example, to give directions on how to stir a sauce that was simmering in

1

a saucepan—let alone what to use to do the stirring with —until the day I saw a charming young woman blithely paddling a rubber scraper around in a hot Mornay sauce. From her I learned that it was necessary to come right out and say, "Use a wire whisk or a wooden spatula and scrape the bottom of the pan each time you stir." From me she learned how *not* to scorch a cheese sauce or have it taste of burned rubber—in no uncertain terms!

So my cooking classes have become, over the years, a kind of informal and happy collaboration between students and teacher. Any shared creative enterprise is fun, and one of the great pleasures I have found in the Gourmet Cooking School is seeing people not only learn to cook well, but watching them perform with delight tasks that they had previously regarded as drudgery.

When I was asked to put into a book the sum and substance of the Gourmet Cooking School I leaped at the opportunity—and then boggled at the difficulties. But actually each recipe is a lesson, just as it is in school, and the reader need only choose one as a beginning and start from there. Every step is carefully explained, and you will learn by doing, just as my students have.

When you open this book, imagine that you are one of five students in a typical Gourmet Cooking School class. Your first step will be to familiarize yourself with the equipment of our kitchen. In the next chapter you will find a list of the equipment necessary—or at least helpful—for the creation of the gourmet dishes to follow. Read it and get acquainted with the different utensils, their uses, and some hints on their care and feeding. Please imagine that you hear me speaking with great emphasis here, as this is a subject very dear to my heart.

The basic ingredients and staples—items that occur again and again in the recipes—are in the next chapter as well, with explanations of their uses and abuses (the latter, of course, to be studiously avoided!).

Following the kitchen, cupboard and pantry tour, you will find suggestions for what to do before you actually start to cook. That chapter is the equivalent of the first forty minutes of class.

2

My five students arrive equipped with aprons, comfortable, low-heeled shoes and—something you readers won't need—a notebook and pencil. Each student has chosen a dish or a menu the day before, so the food is all on hand.

I dictate each recipe, and the students take them all down—the others, as well as their own. As I dictate, I chop any vegetables or raw ingredients that have been called for, so that when it is time to start cooking, each chef has his or her own tray with the raw materials ready to use.

We do this because of the exigencies of time in class. But it is such a good technique that I suggest it for all cooking. You will find that each recipe in this book has a marketing list and a preparation tray outlined at the beginning. If you make sure you have everything on hand in the former and prepared in advance on the latter, you will breeze through the actual cooking.

The recipes are arranged in suggested menus with recommended wines. Naturally, you do not have to use them in those combinations. But very often a student will want to learn to cook a *coq au vin*, say, or a hot strawberry soufflé, "and what shall I serve with it, Mrs. Lucas?" I have tried to give some answers to those questions, too.

Because no dish can be considered finished until it is properly served up and presented, each recipe includes directions for how to serve and garnish, and what kind of platter or dish to use. The master French chefs of the eighteenth and nineteenth centuries worked like architects or sculptors, and something of their decorative skill survives even in the simplified French cuisine of this century. That, too, is a part of each lesson.

But most of all I hope these lessons in book form will give you the joyous sense of creative accomplishment that is as much a part of a good kitchen atmosphere as the fragrance of fine food cooking.

Chapter 2

THE
COMPLETE
KITCHEN

Every piece of equipment that finds its way into your kitchen should pass one fundamental test: *Does it help you to do really good work?* This simple touchstone would immediately eliminate dozens of ingenious gadgets, quaint vessels and coy accessories that seduced you whenever you passed a housewares display. Get rid of them, and you will gain uncluttered kitchen drawers and cupboards in which to store the basic utensils for good cooking. Your kitchen will be more efficient, and so—it follows as the night the day—will you.

The tools that you use are as important as any of the edible ingredients in a recipe. The wrong saucepan can spoil a sauce as surely as rancid butter; a good tight-fitting lid will help you make fluffy rice, though the rice itself, the amount of liquid and cooking time are the items that generally get top billing in the recipe.

And while we're on the subject of kitchen equipment, I should like to say something about its care. Naturally, everything used in the preparation of food is to be kept scrupulously clean. But above and beyond that, good cooks have a reverence and respect for their tools, as any

4

fine craftsman must. These are the implements by means of which a cook creates what amounts to works of culinary art. They become her friends.

If you have a selection of knives for every purpose, keep them well sharpened and use them only for their specific purposes. Do not cut string or twine or open packages with your kitchen cutlery. Use scissors. Don't pry open jars or tins with the delicate point of your paring knife, because you will miss the point when you need it most—in paring. Always cut on a wooden board, any other surface is death for a keen blade.

Wash your pastry bags and brushes well in warm water and soap after each use and you will get many more years of use from them. Wash your chopping and carving boards, but never dry them near heat or they will crack.

And remember that your own two hands are your most valuable kitchen tools. Handle sharp implements with a healthy caution—"well tempered" when applied to knife blades does not mean that they don't bite. Always use pot holders if there is a suspicion that a handle or pan is more than warm. Never touch a hot pot with a wet cloth just because it is closer to hand than the pot holder. Wet conducts heat like mad, and you'll get a nasty burn.

Your well-tended utensils are all you need by way of kitchen decoration, by the way. A gleaming copper pot is a veritable Tiffany jewel for beautifying your kitchen —and far more practical, though nearly as expensive. But there is absolutely no substitute for tin-lined copper when it comes to making a perfect sauce. You would do better to splurge on a quart or quart-and-a-half copper saucepan, which will make your cooking *better*, than on an electric blender, say, which will only make it quicker. And you will have a kitchen ornament in the bargain.

The following list of utensils is basic. If you have them, you will be able to prepare all of the gourmet dishes in this book, and many more. With a well-equipped and bright, clean kitchen, you will find it a pleasanter task to turn out better and more creative food.

BASIC COOKING EQUIPMENT

ASBESTOS MAT

To use under earthenware pots.

BLENDER

Not really a must, but a great time-saver.

BOARD

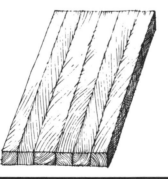

For chopping, a large, very thick one is best, with tongue-and-groove 'joins that will not separate and allow dirt to collect in the seams.

BOWLS

One large metal bowl for whipping cream.

A wooden salad bowl.

A large earthenware crock.

Nested mixing bowls of graduated sizes, from 1 pint to 3 quarts, made of oven-glass or stainless steel.

CAKE RACK

For cooling cakes and pastries.

CAKE TINS

Layer cake pans, 9-inch spring form, loaf tin—1-pound and 2-pound sizes, can be metal or oven-glass.

CAN OPENER

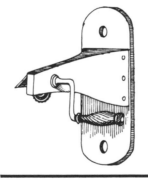

A good wall model is recommended, but don't, please, waste your money on an electric one. Invest it instead in a fine copper utensil.

CARVING BOARD

A large wooden board with grooves for catching the juices.

CASEROLES

Oval and round in several sizes, with lids. The enameled cast iron casseroles are best, as they can be used over direct heat and in the oven. These are for braising and stewing.

COLANDER

For draining liquid from food.

COOKIE SHEETS

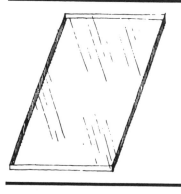

Cookies are the least of it! These are most versatile pieces of equipment. But be sure to get good heavy ones or their surfaces will buckle.

COOKING CHOPSTICKS

For turning small pieces while cooking.

CUSTARD CUPS

Oven-glass ones are useful, too, for keeping small quantities of chopped garnishes, herbs, and other ingredients until you are ready to use them in your recipe.

CUTTERS

Round and fluted, in several sizes. Be sure you get tin ones, not plastic!

DISH CLOTHS, DISH TOWELS

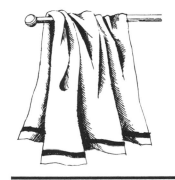

To be used for washing and drying, not as pot holders. Always have one damp and one dry cloth at hand for wiping up table or board on which you are working. After each use, wipe knife blade first on damp cloth then on dry.

DOUBLE BOILER

Oven-glass is good, because you can see the level of the water in the lower pot, and whether or not it is boiling—sometimes it is disastrous if the water is boiling and is in contact with the upper pot.

FISH SLICE

A perforated disk on a long handle, for lifting food from deep fat.

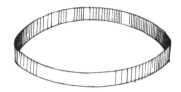

FLAN RING

This circular strip of metal is placed on a cookie sheet and lined with dough for a pastry crust. The ring is removed after baking, so that there is no necessity for a pie plate to come to the table with the dessert.

FOOD MILL

For sieving and puréeing. The French mouli-légumes is excellent.

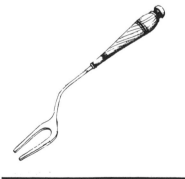

FORK

This utensil has only three uses in a kitchen—to fold an omelet, to prick pastry shells and to eat with. A large, two-pronged fork is a necessity when carving meat, but that is the only time food should be pierced by fork tines.

FUNNEL

You might not use it often, but when you have to pour into a narrow opening, there is no substitute.

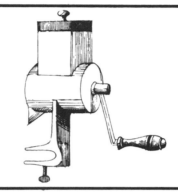

GRATER

Never, never buy cheese that has already been grated. Always grate your own fresh for each recipe. Get a grater that varies from fine to coarse.

ICE PICK

For testing vegetables for doneness; breaking up hard chocolate.

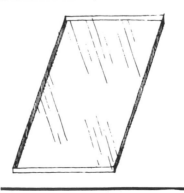

JELLY ROLL TIN

This is also a handy tray for assembling numerous ingredients in their separate cups and bowls when you have a complicated recipe. Excellent to use for the "preparation tray" mentioned at the beginning of each recipe. Be sure you get a heavy metal one, as it will warp and buckle otherwise.

KETTLE

Get a good sensible kettle for boiling water, and leave the whistling to canaries and truck drivers. There is no cozier touch of home on the range than a jolly, fat kettle steaming away on the back burner.

KNIVES

Ah, here I could write a book! Suffice it to say that inferior cutlery is an expensive economy. Get fewer knives, but good ones, and keep them in a safe if necessary. Stainless steel is easier to clean, but harder to sharpen. Industrial steel or carbon steel make the best blades. Let your butcher do a professional sharpening job on your knives about once a month, and in the interim you can touch them up with a Carborundum. Clean your knives immediately after you use them, and keep the blades dry. They will repay your most meticulous care by being most accurate and dependable tools.

Chef's knife — 8-inch blade. The most versatile of all, it chops, cuts, slices, minces.
Paring knife—for cutting and trimming vegetables.
Boning knife—used on fish, poultry and meat.
Flat cleaver—the best possible implement for smacking veal or beef slices really thin.
Swedish fish scaler.
Filleting knife—for skinning and filleting fish.
Carving knife—10- to 14-inch blade.
Serrated knife of stainless steel—for cutting fruit, tomatoes.
Cake knife—stainless steel or plated.
Narrow bladed slicing knife—for very thin slices of ham, roast beef, etc.

LADLE

For soups, stocks.

LARDING NEEDLES

These should be used a lot more than they are; less expensive cuts of meat can be tenderized by threading a few pieces of fat through them with a larding needle (you'll need several sizes). If you are married to Jack Spratt, remove the fat before serving him the tender roast.

LEMON SQUEEZER

Useful when your recipe calls for small quantities of lemon juice.

MANDOLINE

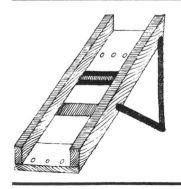

An unmusical instrument for quick, regular slicing—even paper thin—of potatoes, cucumbers and various fruits and vegetables.

MARMITE POT

The tall brown earthenware marmites are best, but they take a bit of special care. Earthenware cannot be exposed to direct heat, so an asbestos mat must come between it and the top-of-the-stove burner. If the marmite is hot, don't expose it to sudden cold or it may crack. Use warm water and be gentle. On the plus side, an earthenware pot holds heat admirably and needs only a small flame beneath the asbestos. The glazed surface and rounded corners are easy to keep clean.

MEASURING CUPS

One set of aluminum in 1-cup, ½-, ¼- and ⅓-cup sizes. Oven-glass measures in 1-cup, 2-cup, 4-cup and 8-cup sizes.

MEASURING SPOONS

Don't use the measuring spoons that come in sets. They vary appallingly, and will throw your recipe off. Use instead an ordinary kitchen tablespoon and teaspoon. Woolworth's are just dandy—I've checked them myself.

MEAT CHOPPER

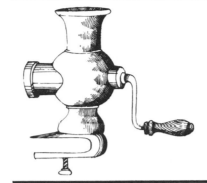

A hand grinder — the Swedish meat chopper— that screws to the edge of the table is adequate. But if you have an electric mixer, you'd do well to buy the grinder attachment, too.

MELON BALLER

For melon balls, tiny potato balls.

MIXER

An electric mixer is not an absolute necessity for actually improving the quality of your preparations. It is a time-saver, however, as you can be doing something else while your mixer is at work. If you do buy one, you may as well buy a good one, capable of performing heavy work, with a deep bowl rather than a shallower, wide one.

MOLDS

Charlotte mold, brioche tins, coeur à la crème baskets, Savarin (ring mold), baba molds, boat molds, madeleine molds, dariole mold, hinged raised-pie molds for certain dishes cooked in a crust, cornucopias.

**MORTAR
AND PESTLE**

For grinding quantities too
small for the blender or
mixer.

**NEEDLE
AND THREAD**

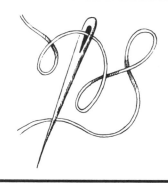

Keep a large needle and
coarse white thread in the
kitchen just for sewing
poultry, meat and fish. If
you use a thimble keep
one in the kitchen.

PAPER TOWELS

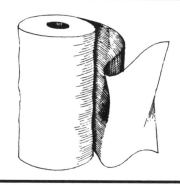

Foil, wax paper—keep
these essentials in one of
the convenient dispensers
that holds all three.

**PASTRY BAGS
AND TUBES**

Buy fairly large canvas
bags with plastic lining—
Atco size number 10.
They are the easiest to
keep clean. You will need
these tubes: Round—¾-
inch and #7, star—#10,
rose—#2b, #4 and #6b.

PASTRY BOARD

If you have a formica counter top you can use that. Otherwise you need a large thin wooden pastry board for rolling out dough.

PASTRY BRUSHES

Don't buy a regular pastry brush. Get several good badger-hair paint brushes instead, and wash them thoroughly in soap and warm water after each use.

PASTRY PINCERS

Indispensable for giving a beautiful and professional edge to your pastry shells.

PEPPER MILLS

One for whole white, one for whole black pepper-corns. Don't ever use commercially ground pepper; you might just as well throw sand in your food.

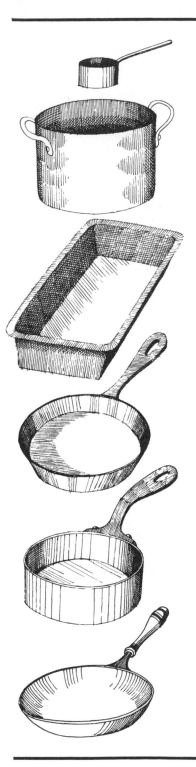

POTS AND PANS

Choose covered pans that have flat, tight-fitting lids. There is less condensation with a flat lid.

Aluminum saucepans—series from 1 to 5 quarts.

Copper pot—toy-size—for flaming brandy. This is a good one to start you off on your copper collection.

Stewpans—essential for soups. Copper is best, but cast iron or heavy cast aluminum will do. You need one for cream soups, one for stronger flavored meat or onion soups. You can use them for other dishes, but cook the mild and the highly flavored dishes in their respective pans.

Roasting pans—uncovered shallow aluminum rectangular pans in several sizes.

Frying pans — heavy cast aluminum or iron, in several sizes. One for deep-fat frying with a basket.

Sauté pans—deeper than a frying pan, with straight sides.

Omelet pan—heavy cast iron or cast aluminum with a rounded base. This should be used exclusively for omelets, and water must never touch its cooking surface. After each use it is wiped out with a clean, dry cloth.

POTS AND PANS

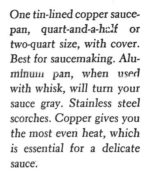

One tin-lined copper sauce-pan, quart-and-a-half or two-quart size, with cover. Best for saucemaking. Aluminum pan, when used with whisk, will turn your sauce gray. Stainless steel scorches. Copper gives you the most even heat, which is essential for a delicate sauce.

One unlined copper sauce-pan for working with sugar and syrup. This gets so hot that it would melt tin.

POT HOLDERS

Good thick ones with asbestos backing.

POTATO PEELER

One gadget that really does the best job of peeling thin-skinned fruits and vegetables is this one with the floating blade.

POULTRY SHEARS

The best tool for disjointing poultry, especially uncooked poultry.

REFRIGERATOR JARS

You can use glass, china or plastic, as long as they have tight covers. Best of all are the square plastic containers which take up least room and can be used to freeze things. Never freeze in glass jars. They crack when the food freezes. Nothing should ever go into a refrigerator uncovered, because air, even cold air, affects food and dries it out; the odors permeate the refrigerator, and all in all it is a slovenly practice. Bowls should be stored with a tight covering of transparent wrap.

ROASTING RACK

For holding meat up out of its juices so it roasts rather than stews.

ROLLING PIN

The long thin French rolling pin is best. It is easiest and most accurate to control, and its length enables you to work with a large piece of pastry.

ROTARY BEATER

With this and a wire whisk you can do anything a mixer can do. It just takes longer, but in some cases the results are better.

SALAD BASKET

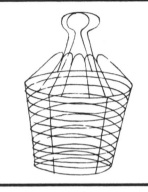

A small wire cage in which to shake dry your freshly washed salad greens.

SCALE

More people should have a kitchen scale. It is the most accurate way of measuring, dry ingredients in particular. If you get a balance scale with gram weights as well as ounces, you will be able to follow foreign cookbooks that give measurements by gram.

SCISSORS

To be used instead of your good knives for cutting string, cheesecloth, paper, etc.

SCRAPERS

Rubber scrapers are to be used only when food is not cooking. Never use them for stirring in a hot pot—unless you like the taste of boiled rubber.

SKEWERS

There are several good dishes to be cooked en brochette.

SOUFFLÉ DISH

Straight-sided ovenware bowl. 1-quart to 3-quart sizes. Best are the white porcelain with fluted sides and a small ridge at the top.

SPATULAS

One small, one large.

SPOONS

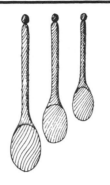

Wooden spoons for tossing salads. Flat wooden spatulas for stirring over the fire.

Large metal serving spoon for coating with sauce.

Demitasse spoon.

Slotted spoon for draining.

Marrow scoop, if you enjoy marrow.

STRAINERS

One small, one large stainless steel.

Chinois or Chinese strainer—a cone-shaped strainer with a very fine mesh for very fine sauces, fats, etc.

STRING

A ball of heavy white string for tying meat and trussing fowl.

TERRINE

For pâtés. Get the covered earthenware 1-quart size.

THERMOMETERS

One for meat, one for candy and fat. Only experts can make expert guesses, and who among us can qualify?

TONGS

To be used instead of a fork for lifting and turning meats and vegetables without piercing.

TRANSPARENT WRAP

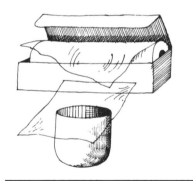

How did we live without it? For an airtight seal on pots or bowls, for airtight wrapping of food for storage or freezing.

WIRE WHISKS

One small, one medium, and one very large one will take care of all beating needs from one egg white to a bowl of whipped cream. A whisk beats more air into your ingredients than either a rotary or electric mixer, which beats too compactly for some purposes.

BASIC SERVING EQUIPMENT

Food that has been carefully prepared deserves to be carefully presented. A beautiful piece of meat, cooked to perfection in a flawless sauce, loses a great deal if it comes to the table half drowned in liquid, with a few sad sprigs of parsley swimming disconsolately at either end of the platter. Even the most tantalizing aroma will not counteract the evidence of our eyes.

A good chef aims to please the sense of taste, of smell, and, not least of all, of sight. This does not mean that dishes are served in an elaborate or fanciful manner. On the contrary, simplicity of presentation is the hallmark of fine French food. But the pieces are arranged meticulously, the sauce is spooned over them with geometric neatness, and any garnish is an intrinsic part of the dish for flavor and balance as well as ornamentation. Furthermore, things look and taste like what they are—camouflage has no place in good cooking.

And though there is an infinite variety of ways to prepare food, the dishes in which it is served have only a few simple and classic shapes. When buying your serving dishes, choose fairly plain ones that will not compete with or detract from the star of the show—the food that will appear on them. Each of the recipes in this book will tell you how to serve up the dish as a most important final step.

BOWLS

Crystal or glass for compotes, berries, or mousses. A shallow bowl is best for mousse.

CAKE KNIFE

For cutting pie and cake.

CAKE PLATE

Round china, glass, or best of all, silver.

CASSEROLES

A 2-quart and a 3-quart, round and oval earthenware or white porcelain and one oval copper casserole.

GRATIN DISHES

Shallow oval oven-glass or enameled cast iron or earthenware which can be placed under the broiler for last-minute browning. A copper au gratin dish for serving in style. Several sizes.

PLATTERS

Oval oven-glass in several sizes.

One flat oval silver platter, with a wooden carving board to fit.

One round silver platter or serving dish.

SAUCE BOAT

China or silver. There is an excellent two-way gravy boat that pours fat from one side and lean juices from the other.

SOUP BOWLS

Oven-proof bowls with lids, for onion soup or any other hot soup that should be served piping.

TUREEN

These are used far too frequently for flowers, while soup comes to the table tepid, in individual plates. For warm-hearted family meals, why not serve your good soup steaming hot out of the tureen? If you don't have one, get one and don't forget a handsome ladle to go with it.

BASIC MATERIALS

The complete kitchen should be thoroughly stocked with ingredients as well as tools. Just as an artist's studio is equipped with a variety of paints, to be used with the brushes and canvas, so the cook's studio—the kitchen—should contain a broad spectrum of the raw materials out of which dishes are created.

For convenience' sake, the ingredients that you use every day ought to be stored where you can get right at them, rather than behind cupboard doors. Flour, sugar, salt, the peppers, spices and herbs that are most common—perhaps eight or ten jars in all—are best kept out on your work counter or on an open shelf above it. In a year's time, think of the hours and energy you'll have saved!

The following list includes the essential herbs, spices, staples, and perishables upon which French cookery depends. Each recipe will have its own marketing list, but if your kitchen contains these basics, you will find you need only shop for one or two main items in order to prepare any of the gourmet recipes in this book.

Staples

BAKING POWDER *Double action type.*

BAKING SODA *A thick paste of baking soda and water applied immediately to a burn is one of my tried-and-true kitchen remedies. I also use a strong solution of baking soda when cleaning the refrigerator. But as for cooking with it, NEVER! Well, almost never. There are a few baking recipes that call for it, but baking soda should not be used in the cooking of vegetables. There are other better ways to keep them green, as you will see.*

BEANS *Flageolets (dwarf kidney beans), kidney beans.*

CHOCOLATE *A good dark sweet chocolate is best. Remember that the flavor of your finished dessert depends upon the quality of the chocolate you use.*

COCOA *Don't get the powdered chocolate drink, but plain cocoa.*

CORN MEAL *White and yellow, to be used for some kinds of gnocchi. Keep in tightly covered jar in refrigerator.*

CREAM OF TARTAR *Used with soda as a substitute for baking powder. Also used to stop crystallization in sugar work.*

DRIED MUSHROOMS *A completely different vegetable from cultivated mushrooms. The two are never interchangeable in a recipe, as their flavors and textures are not at all alike. Dried mushrooms (cèpes or Polish mushrooms) are used to flavor some sauces and soups.*

FARINA *Farina is needed in some starchy dishes, like gnocchi à la Romaine, some desserts.*

FLOUR

A good all-purpose flour that is finely ground.

Cake flour which contains no baking powder.

Potato flour (also called potato starch) is used as a thickening agent when you want a clear shiny sauce. It is also needed in some desserts.

Rice flour, for thickening some soups.

Whole-wheat flour—sometimes called graham flour. This contains the bran and wheat germ usually milled out of white flour.

Arrowroot for thickening desserts.

Cornstarch for some desserts and some soufflés.

GELATIN

The unflavored gelatin is used to stiffen aspics, cold mousses and some chilled desserts.

JAM

Smooth apricot jam to flavor certain sauces, for glazing light colored fruits.

Raspberry and strawberry.

JELLY

Red currant jelly used as a glaze and in some sauces.

Grape, black raspberry, raspberry, and strawberry.

MAPLE SYRUP

For maple cake and on pancakes.

MUSTARD

A favorite flavoring agent in the French kitchen. Dijon mustard, from the city of the same name, has tarragon in it, and is used in many of these recipes. Also, keep a jar of dry mustard on hand.

OLIVE OIL

Spanish olive oil is very aromatic and occasionally you will need a small quantity.

French olive oil is best to use for most purposes (the Italian is too strong).

OLIVES

Green and black; get them with pits for better flavor. We generally use olives alone or for a garnish, but the French enhance sauces and stuffings with them.

Black olives in oil (can be bought at most Italian food stores).

PASTAS

Keep a variety on hand, from the fine spaghetti to the coarse lasagne. Noodles and vermicelli.

PRALINE POWDER

Recipe on page 351. Keep in covered refrigerator jar and use as flavoring for a number of desserts.

RICE

Carolina and Patna, both long-grained rices, to be used for all savories. Carolina rice, to be used only for rice creams because it is starchier.

SALT

Table salt and kosher salt, a pure rock salt which is excellent for rubbing into raw meats and poultry. Please never, never use garlic salt, onion salt or any similar saline abominations.

SUGAR

Granulated—unless otherwise specified, this is the sugar to use.

Superfine—also known as caster sugar, this is called for in some dessert recipes.

Confectioners'—sometimes called powdered sugar, this is used in icings or to flavor whipped cream.

Brown—if you want to store this without having it get lumpy or hard, keep it in an airtight glass jar with a whole orange to lend it moisture and flavor.

Lump—you need lump sugar to rub off the oil of lemon and orange peel for some desserts—crêpes Suzette, for example.

TOMATO PASTE Keep a few small cans on your shelf for thickening and flavoring a number of sauces.

VANILLA EXTRACT Used in some desserts instead of the fresh bean. Be sure to get an expensive brand, the cheap ones are ghastly!

VEGETABLE OIL A good liquid corn oil for deep-fat frying.

VEGETABLE SHORTENING Vegetable fat, sometimes used as shortening in baking, and for deep-fat frying.

VINEGAR Cider vinegars are the best, and you can make your own herb vinegar by adding fresh tarragon (see recipe, page 352).

YEAST Envelopes of dry yeast are less perishable than the fresh cake yeast, which must be refrigerated. Store in a cool dry place, and add water as indicated in the recipe.

The cake yeast is very much better, if you can get it.

Herbs and Spices

These are the aromatic ingredients, used in small quantities, that intensify and dramatize the flavor of each dish. They have been called "the hidden soul of cooking."

Fresh Herbs in Season: You can freeze herbs in small quantities, wrapped in transparent wrap, and have them to use all year round.

CHERVIL

Used for fines herbes and in soups, sauces, salads.

CHIVES

You can grow these all year round in your kitchen. Used as garnish for clear soups, in Vichyssoise, eggs.

DILL

Used in Beef Stroganoff, some sauces, fish dishes, with cucumbers, tomatoes, zucchini, new potatoes.

PARSLEY (BOTH REGULAR AND ITALIAN)

Important ingredient of fines herbes, many sauces, soups and garnishes.

TARRAGON

One of the most popular herbs in French cuisine.

DRIED HERBS: Buy these in jars, and keep them tightly closed. Buy the smallest quantity possible. It is well to have the herbs listed as "fresh" in dried form too. Remember that dried herbs are several times as strong as the fresh, so use with care. You can soak them in a little water before using (1 tablespoon of water to 1 teaspoon of herb) to release their full flavor and aroma.

BASIL Can be used with tomatoes, soup, salad.

BAY LEAF

In soups, stews, one of the ingredients of bouquet garni, and delicious also for flavoring some milk desserts.

MARJORAM Good with pork, lamb, ragoûts, tomatoes, stuffings, stews.

OREGANO For some tomato sauces.

ROSEMARY   *Sprinkled on sautéed potatoes, used sparingly with veal, fish.*

SAGE   *Used in some poultry stuffings, especially for goose and pâté, but use sparingly.*

THYME   *Sometimes used in stews, with fish, on eggs, in bouquet garni.*

Spices:

CARDAMOM   *Powder and seeds. An oriental and Indian spice used in many desserts, rice pilaf, curry and fish mousses. A tiny quantity gives a lift to many sauces.*

CINNAMON      *Keep both powder and sticks on hand.*

CLOVES

An onion stuck with cloves seasons soups and some stews.

CURRY POWDER

A dash of this spice is sometimes used in recipes other than curry.

GINGER

Used in some desserts, some meat dishes. Root ginger, powdered, and crystallized are all good.

MUSTARD SEED

Excellent to have on hand as well as the prepared varieties; can be ground for very hot sauces.

NUTMEG

A few grains of ground nutmeg can do wonders for some sauces, fruits, and vegetables — notably spinach. It's good to have whole nutmegs and a little grater. Nutmeg added to scorched potatoes or any starchy vegetable will take the burned taste and smell away.

PAPRIKA   *A powder made from dried sweet red peppers, much used in Hungarian cookery. The Spanish paprika is best.*

PEPPER

Whole black peppercorns are the entire berry. They are used for dark meats, more robust sauces, salads and the general run of dishes.

Whole white pepper is the inner kernel, and is usually called for with fish, poultry, veal, cream sauces and cream soups.

Both black and white pepper are always to be freshly ground. Coarsely cracked pepper (called poivre mignonnette) is done with a mortar and pestle.

Cayenne is very strong red pepper, and a few grains of it are often used to give zest to a dish. It is most important as a flavoring for all velouté sauces.

SAFFRON   *This bright yellow spicy powder comes from the crocus, and is used to color and flavor a number of Mediterranean dishes, chiefly bouillabaisse and some rices. Also one of the many ingredients of curry powder.*

VANILLA BEAN   *The husk of the bean is good to keep in a canister of sugar for vanilla sugar.*

The fresh vanilla bean, wrapped in foil and stored in the refrigerator, is split and scraped and its little black seeds impart the true rich vanilla flavor to creams and desserts.

Refrigerated Staples

BUTTER

Sweet and salt. Keep sweet butter always in the freezer or it will go rancid. Always store butter tightly covered, as nothing is so quick to pick up every refrigerator aroma as butter. Salt butter is always used for sautéeing, as it browns better. Sweet butter is used in sauces and pastries.

CHEESE

Parmesan, Swiss, Emmenthal and Gruyère cheeses are the ones most called for in recipes. You can keep a small plastic bag filled with a piece of the cheese and grate it as needed.

CREAM

Have both light and heavy sweet cream, heavy sour cream and plain yoghurt.

EGGS

Get the freshest eggs you can, in the large rather than extra-large size. Brown ones are as good as white ones, provided they were laid on the same recent day. Always refrigerate eggs.

MARGARINE

For people who are not supposed to eat butter, corn-oil margarine has become a fairly pleasant substitute. There are some recipes, however, in which there is no substitute for the very best butter. My recommendation is to use neither butter nor margarine on the table. Cook with butter when you must (browning meats, some desserts and sauces) and enjoy these superlative dishes on occasion and perhaps in smaller quantities. But don't spoil a great sauce because of two tablespoons of butter that will be divided among six or eight portions.

MEAT GLAZE

A concentrated meat extract made by reducing brown stock to a thick consistency. Although you can make your own, it is a long process. I find commercial beef extracts highly satisfactory for strengthening, coloring and flavoring a sauce. The quantity you use will depend upon how well you have browned your meat and therefore how much natural glaze you have.

Perishables

Store your vegetables, unwashed (unless they are very dirty) in plastic bags in the refrigerator. They will stay much fresher than if you store them unwrapped and washed, even in a vegetable crisper.

The fresh herbs listed under that heading are, of course, perishable and must be carefully stored in the refrigerator. Stored in screw-top jars, dry and unwashed, herbs will stay fresh a week or more.

CARROTS

Frequently used as a flavoring in soups and sauces. Beware of using too much, as the distinctive sweet flavor can overpower your dish.

CELERY

Stalk and leaves, never used together, are used separately as basic flavoring ingredients of stocks, soups and many sauces, in combination with carrot, onion and leek. Pascal celery is the best.

ENDIVE

Belgian endive for salad or braised as a hot vegetable.

GARLIC

This pungent relative of the onion is an essential in many recipes. But it is often misused. Here are five fundamental rules of good garlic cookery:

1. Garlic must be extremely fresh.
2. Never use a garlic press.
3. Always chop your garlic in a little salt.
4. Cook garlic gently, never brown it.
5. Always cook garlic with some other ingredient—mushrooms, tomatoes or whatever is in the recipe.

LEEKS

"Ay, leeks is good," says Fluellen, the Welshman, in Shakespeare's King Henry V, and French chefs agree. The white part of the leek is a prime flavoring ingredient of soup, and no French kitchen is without this vegetable that looks like an oversized scallion.

LETTUCE

Boston lettuce, romaine, chicory, escarole, field salad, Bibb lettuce, whatever salad greens you use must be thoroughly washed, shaken dry in a basket, and torn by hand, never cut with a knife.

MUSHROOMS

Cultivated mushrooms are used, washed but generally not skinned, in a variety of sauces, as a garnish, and stems and peelings flavor the stock pot. Be sure they are white, firm and very hard.

ONIONS

Yellow onions are most commonly used, chopped fine, as a basic seasoning. The milder red onions should also be on hand. Bermuda onions, for stuffed onions, or in onion soup.
Baby white onions, used whole as a vegetable and garnish.
Scallions.

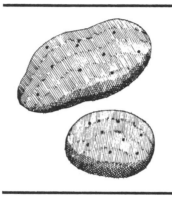

POTATOES

Idaho potatoes, though a bit more expensive, are much the best. New potatoes should also be in your kitchen, as they are best for boiling. Always cook new potatoes, unpeeled, in boiling water. Old potatoes are put, peeled, in cold water and brought to the boil.

SHALLOTS

A cross between onion and garlic, the shallot is a great favorite in French cookery. It blends into sauces smoothly and is easily digestible.

TOMATOES

Another important ingredient of sauces, ragoûts and soups. Try to get the ripe garden tomatoes. Hothouse tomatoes have no flavor.

Wines and Spirits

The French cook with wine in order to enhance the flavor and aroma of their dishes. The alcohol cooks out, so there is no question of the food being intoxicating—except to your sense of smell and taste. There are more practical reasons, too, for using wine or liquor in the kitchen. Wine in a slowly cooked dish tenderizes the meat, and wine or liquor poured in a hot pan will lift the glaze and consolidate the juices into a rich sauce.

Since the flavor is all that remains after cooking, it stands to reason that you will want the best flavor, and *that* you get only from the best wines and spirits. It is a fallacy to use an inferior wine for cooking, although it isn't necessary to go to the other extreme and cook with a great vintage Burgundy either. It is a good idea to use some of the wine you will be drinking with your meal—recipes call for very little anyhow—and that way your palate will receive double pleasure from the same bottle.

BRANDY

Used in very nearly every meat and poultry recipe for blazing and in some desserts.

CALVADOS

The apple brandy of Normandy, sometimes specified in place of regular brandy.

FRAMBOISE

Treat yourself to one bottle of this essence of raspberries once every five years—it is terribly expensive. But it does marvelous things to certain fruit desserts.

KIRSCH

In fruit desserts.

MADEIRA   *Excellent in clear soups, aspic, and some chicken dishes.*

MARSALA

Sabayon sauce.

RUM

The light rum is the nicest for cooking. Very good as flavoring or flamed on some desserts.

SHERRY   *A dry sherry brings out the best in many sauces, chicken and fish dishes.*

VERMOUTH   *This aromatic fortified wine is especially good with fish and veal, though its star role is, as you know, the indispensable minority in a martini.*

**WINES—
WHITE AND RED**   *For marinades, basting liquid, and in many sauces. White wines for the table should be served well chilled, red wines at room temperature and with the cork removed several hours in advance. This gives the red wine a chance to breathe.*

With your kitchen thus equipped and stocked you are now ready to turn out anything from Aspic to Zabaglione.

Chapter 3

BEFORE
YOU
START

Once your kitchen is equipped with the basic tools and stocked with the staple ingredients, you are ready to start to cook. That's when the fun begins. The recipes that follow are designed to give you pleasure, not only at the table but in the kitchen as well. For cooking is a joyous art, and it is a pity that so many housewives lump it with the drudgery of sweeping, dusting and bedmaking.

You will find that you can enjoy your cooking to the utmost if you make a distinct line between the preparation of your ingredients and the actual creative art of cooking. When I cook on television I am able to demonstrate one or two fairly elaborate dishes within the time limits of a half-hour show because much of the preparation—cleaning and chopping of vegetables, measuring of ingredients, stock—has been done in advance.

In my Gourmet Cooking School, the students follow this method and find they can turn out a Cordon Bleu meal in two hours. Along with their recipes, they have also followed the Boy Scouts' maxim, "Be Prepared!"

So if you want to simplify your cooking without compromising its quality, prepare as much as you can in advance. Then the actual making of the dish—even the most splendid gourmet masterpiece—will be a lark. The prepackaged short cuts promise to make cooking easy for you, but since they can never taste as good as your own advance preparations, you are better off doing it yourself.

Perhaps some of you will wonder how I can say that by doing the basic preparations ahead of time you are simplifying your cooking. Since it all has to be done anyhow, isn't the amount of work just the same? Well, that's the strange fact. If you separate preparation very decidedly from actual cooking you can follow your recipe a good deal more quickly and easily. Cleaning and chopping the proper quantities of vegetables, grating cheese, trimming and tying meat or poultry are effortless little tasks when they are performed by themselves and not in conjunction with the step-by-step procedures of the recipe.

Maybe it's psychological, maybe the lack of pressure has something to do with it. But the fact remains that grating a quarter of a cup of Parmesan cheese—no difficult chore in itself—can be a terrible nuisance if you must stop to do it just when you need to add it to a Mornay sauce. Its flavor will not be impaired if you grate the cheese that morning, or even the day before, and keep it in an airtight container. Yet it tastes indescribably better than the cheese you buy already grated, and is just as easy to use *if you have planned ahead*. Try being a two-stage cook, and see if that stage-one preparation doesn't act as a booster to your stage-two creative cookery.

And now to begin: First off, decide several days beforehand what you want to make. Read the recipe carefully so you will know what kind of cooking is involved, what utensils and what ingredients will be needed. Then copy the marketing list given with each recipe. Check off those items that you must order.

At the beginning of each recipe I have also listed what

you might have, all ready to use, on your "preparation tray." This is the technique borrowed from my television experience and school procedure that is such a convenient time-saver. It is based on doing as much as you can the day before. Make the stock if one is called for; blanch nuts, grate cheese, chop parsley and store them in separate airtight containers. Some recipes indicate that they can be made, up to a certain point, the day before. These things will all be listed for you to assemble on your "preparation tray." Do so whenever possible, if you find installment cooking more convenient. Certainly if your meal has several complicated dishes it helps to have a running start. (It might be better at the beginning to tackle only one recipe instead of an entire menu. When you have made several of these dishes successfully you can then go on to a whole victorious meal.)

Another thing that contributes to the pleasure of cooking is your own personal comfort. No one can long be happy in tight shoes, and that goes for the kitchen as well as for the ballroom. So I tell you what I tell my students: "Wear low heels in the kitchen." There is a safety factor involved, too. You will be carrying hot and sometimes heavy pots, and if something has spilled on the floor you don't need the added hazard of high heels. Besides, no one looks at the cook's legs! A comfortable dress and an apron complete the cooking costume.

Make it a habit to do two things as soon as you step into your kitchen for a bout of cooking. First, fill your sink with hot sudsy water. Then, as soon as you've finished with them, your dirty utensils will have a place to soak. Whenever possible, rinse them out and put them away, so you don't accumulate too large a collection. Second, set and light your oven and adjust the racks according to the instructions in your recipe.

Always have one damp cloth and one clean dry one at hand so you can clean up after yourself as you go. That way your kitchen will be neat and orderly at all times. Just because you are cooking up a storm, it doesn't necessarily follow that your kitchen has to look as though a tornado struck it. The Paris chef who was my first teacher used to insist that a kitchen should be as immaculate and orderly as an operating room at all times. And everything was to be kept in a definite place so we would always know where to find things. He was fanatically strict, but his training has stood me in good stead.

Reread your recipe carefully, rehearsing it in your mind. In my cooking classes I always begin by dictating the day's recipes while the students write them down. If I handed the recipes out already typed, each step might not be so carefully noted in advance, and the advantage of a dry run or walk-through would be lost. (I know because we tried it one year, and it did not work as well.)·

Then get out any large utensils called for—mixer, food mill, bowls, pots. Next assemble all your ingredients. Now you are ready to go.

Just remember that even the most complex dish is still prepared only one step at a time. And each step in itself is simple, if you follow the directions *exactly*. There is no special magic in being a good cook. One of the greatest chefs, Escoffier, has boiled his art down to one essential ingredient. "In cooking," says Escoffier, "*care is half the battle*." Surely in every recipe the vital element, though it is never listed, is tender loving care.

So choose your recipe, tie on your apron, proceed with care, and have fun!

MENU 1

Filets de Sole Joinville

Braised Celery or
Endive or Leek

Mousse au Chocolat à la
Normande

Suggested Wine: Montrachet

9 whole fillets of
   gray sole
   (bones and skin too)
1½ pounds of fresh
   salmon
½ pound of cooked
   shrimps shelled
   (net weight)
butter
eggs
heavy cream
1 pint of light cream
salt
Cayenne pepper
ground cardamon seed
dry white wine
onion
carrot
celery
fresh dill
fish stock
bay leaf
peppercorns
Kosher salt
flour
Sherry
½ pound of firm white mushrooms
lemon
parsley
truffles

Filets de Sole Joinville

(Fillets of Sole with Joinville Sauce)

Serves six

This is a superb dish that pleases the eye as well as the palate. Handsome in appearance, rich yet light, Filets de Sole Joinville is the kind of preparation you would expect to find only in a fine French restaurant. The surprise is that it can be made at home quite simply, and can appear at your table looking and tasting like the handiwork of a master chef. The fun of cooking lies in the creative pleasure you can enjoy trying recipes such as this one. When you discover you can do them, cooking will seem as artistically satisfying as painting or writing or making music. And it will nourish the body as well as the soul.

PREPARATION TRAY

ring mold lined with sole fillets

salmon, ground

fish stock (see recipe on page 52)

½ pound of mushrooms, halved or quartered

parsley, chopped

shrimp, cleaned and cooked

lemon juice

truffles, sliced

Take an 8-inch ring mold and brush the interior well with **cool melted butter.**

1   Take **9 medium-sized fillets of gray sole**
2   Using a scissors, cut them in half lengthwise.
3   Wash them in water and **lemon juice** and dry them well on cloth.
4   Line the ring mold in the following way:
    Lay each fillet in the mold with the pale side down, the skin side (darker side) facing up.
    The narrow end of each fillet should be in the center hole, the broader end will hang over the outer edge of the mold.
    The fillets should overlap slightly, fanning out from the center.

When the mold is lined, fill it with the following salmon mousse:

1   Skin and bone: **1½ pounds of salmon** (Keep the skin and bones to use with the sole skin and bones in making fish stock for Joinville sauce.)
2   Put the salmon through a fine meat grinder twice. (This can be done in the morning, and the ground fish refrigerated until you need it. I would also recommend making the fish stock in the morning or the day before. With these two procedures out of the way, the rest of the recipe goes quickly.)
3   Put into a mixer bowl: **the ground salmon**
4   Add: **2 large egg whites, unbeaten**
    (Reserve the yolks for sauce.)
5   When egg whites and salmon are well mixed, beat in very slowly: **1¼ cups of light cream** (As with other forcemeats, the cream must be added almost drop by drop, while the mixer beats vigorously between each addition to incorporate the cream into the mixture.)
6   When all the cream has been added, you can then season with: **2 level teaspoons of salt** (the salt has a chemical reaction on the mixture, and stiffens it properly only if added *after* the cream) .
    a good shake of cayenne pepper
    ½ teaspoon of ground cardamom seed

51

7 Fill the lined ring mold with the salmon mousse.

8 Fold over the ends of the sole—the narrow inner ends first, the broad outer ends on top.

9 Cover with a piece of buttered wax paper. (At this point, if you want to prepare the mold in advance, you can refrigerate it until you are ready to cook it.)

10 Stand the mold in a shallow pan half-filled with hot water, in a preheated 350° oven. Poach for 25 minutes, or until sole mold is just firm to the touch. It is a common error to overcook fish. You will see how firm, moist and flavorful this sole is.

11 Remove the mold from the oven, and carefully pour off the whitish liquid that the sole will have formed.

12 Allow it to stand for at least 5 minutes before turning it out on a warm flat serving dish. (This applies to any food that comes out of the oven.)

13 To unmold, just bring the center of the round platter over the center of the mold, and turn them over. The mold will lift right off, leaving a beautiful circle of white sole, its overlapping slices making a banded, ropelike design. If there is any more liquid from the fish, blot it up with paper towels, as it would otherwise dilute your sauce.

While the sole is poaching (or earlier in the day) you make the following sauce, starting with this fish stock or fumet.

1 In a deep saucepan put:
the bones and skin from the sole
the bones and skin from the salmon
1½ cups of water
¾ cups of dry white wine
a little sliced onion, carrot and celery stalk
1 sprig of celery leaf
1 sprig of fresh dill
1 small bay leaf
a few peppercorns
a little kosher salt

2 Bring slowly to a boil and simmer gently for ¾ hour.

52

3 Strain the stock and store in a screw-top jar to use for sauce. (This can be done well ahead of time.)

Now for the actual Joinville sauce.

1 Melt in a heavy saucepan: **4 good tablespoons of butter (a generous 2 ounces—½ stick)**

2 Stir in, off the fire:
4 level tablespoons of flour
salt to taste
a pinch of cayenne pepper

3 Slowly mix in, still off the fire:
1 good cup of strained fish stock
Use a small wire whisk or a flat wooden spoon, and stir, being sure to reach every part of the bottom of the pan, until mixture is smooth.

4 Continue stirring over the fire until the sauce just comes to a boil and has thickened.

5 Add: **⅓ cup of light cream**

6 Simmer for 10 minutes.

7 Because Joinville is an enriched sauce, you must now mix in a small bowl:
2 egg yolks
2 tablespoons of dry sherry
2 tablespoons of heavy cream

8 The trick to making a velvet-smooth enriched sauce is in how you add the egg yolks and cream. Egg yolk will curdle if you add it suddenly to hot sauce. Therefore you introduce the hot sauce to the enrichment gradually.

9 Beat into the egg yolk mixture:
about 2 tablespoons of the hot sauce

10 Then add a little more of the hot sauce and mix well.

11 Now you can safely pour the egg mixture into the saucepan, and stir the completed sauce over the fire until it reheats without boiling.

12 Set aside, covered tightly with transparent wrap, and keep warm.

To fill the center of the ring mold prepare the following mushroom and shrimps:

1 In a sauté pan heat:
   2 tablespoons (1 ounce—¼ stick) of salt butter

2 When it is foaming, add:
   ½ pound of firm white mushrooms cut in halves or fourths

3 When the mushrooms are thoroughly coated, add:
   2 teaspoons of lemon juice
   a little salt
   freshly ground white pepper

4 Shake over a slow fire for 2 minutes.

5 Add: **½ pound of cooked and cleaned shrimp**
   2 teaspoons of chopped fresh parsley
   2 tablespoons of dry sherry

6 Shake well over a hot fire.

7 Coat the unmolded sole with the Joinville sauce, and coat the serving platter around the mold. There should be a 2- or 3-inch margin from the edge of the mold to the rim of the dish, and this will be covered with the sauce.

8 Fill the center with the shrimps and mushrooms.

9 Decorate the top of the mold with a **slice of black truffle** that will mark each serving (6 or 7 slices).

To serve: This elegant fare should be served on a simple round platter, preferably of silver. The golden sauce, black velvet truffles, pink shrimps and beige mushrooms are colors to delight an artist's eye. When you slice into this delectable mold, each slice is a rim of creamy white sole with a center of light-pink salmon mousse. Most marvelous of all—it tastes even better than it looks!

Braised Celery or Endive or Leek

Serves six

Vegetables that we generally use for salads or seasoning—celery, lettuce, endive, leeks—play a completely different and interesting role when they are served braised. Lettuce, celery and endive achieve a new character as a result of this long and careful cooking process, and we can scarcely recognize them when they are not in their customary crisp raw state. In braising, the vegetable slowly takes on the flavor of the carrots, onion, celery, bacon and brown stock in which it has simmered in the oven. The taste is rich and full-bodied, yet the vegetable itself is bland and light. Braised celery or endive is a welcome departure from the usual, garden-variety old favorites that are served with most meals.

MARKETING LIST

3 large roots of white
   celery or leeks
6 Belgian endives
onion
carrot
celery
parsley
bacon
beef or chicken stock,
   strong
meat glaze
tomato paste
potato flour

PREPARATION TRAY

celery or endive or leeks, blanched

mold, lined with bacon

½ cup all together of sliced onion, carrot
(and celery if you are braising endive)

1 cup of strong stock (see recipe on page 276)

parsley, chopped

55

Remove the leafy tops from: **3 large roots of white celery,** well washed. (Store the tops to use in stock.) This should leave three roots, about 6 inches in length, with their stalks joined together.

1 Cut the celery *lengthwise,* in quarters if it is thick, in half if it is thin.
2 Put the pieces in a pan and cover with cold water.
3 Bring slowly to a boil, then remove the vegetable and drain it.

If you are using endive or leek, the method of blanching it is the same, except that you add **1 tablespoon of tarragon vinegar** to the water. (And, of course, there is no leafy part to trim off of the endive. Just quarter each lengthwise. Keep the leek whole and cut off the top green leaf.)

Vegetables prepared by blanching them first and then cooking them according to recipe have the advantage of firmness, color, flavor and texture that is lost when this step is omitted. In French cooking most vegetables are blanched first.

Line an oven-glass bread mold with: **1 or 2 slices of bacon**

1 Scatter on top: **¼ cup all together of sliced onion, carrot (and celery if you are braising endive or leek).**
2 Place on top of the sliced vegetables: the celery or endive or leek
   1 small bay leaf
   a sprinkle of salt
3 Scatter on top: **¼ cup all together of sliced onion, carrot and celery**
4 Cover with: **2 strips of raw bacon**
5 To **1 cup of strong stock** add:
   ½ teaspoon of tomato paste
   ½ teaspoon of meat glaze
6 Mix well, and pour this liquid over the vegetables.
7 Cover the oven-glass dish with a piece of buttered wax paper.

8 Braise in a preheated 375° oven for 1 or 1½ hours (until the vegetable is tender).

9 With a slotted spoon, carefully remove the celery or endive or leek.

10 Arrange the pieces on the bias on a flat *au gratin* dish.

Strain the liquid from the oven-glass dish into a saucepan.

1 Mix together:
a good ½ teaspoon of potato flour
1 tablespoon of cold water

2 When it is smooth add it to the cooking liquid in the saucepan.

3 Stir over the fire until it comes to a boil.

4 Carefully pour this brown sauce over the vegetables.

5 Sprinkle with a little **finely chopped fresh parsley** and serve.

Note: A delicious variation of this recipe is braised Boston lettuce. Cut the heads of lettuce in half, and bring the outer leaf over the cut portion so it forms a small fist. The procedure is exactly the same as for the celery, except that you braise the lettuce for 30 to 45 minutes only.

Mousse au Chocolat à la Normande
(Normandy Chocolate Mousse)

Serves six

There is nothing more festive at the end of a meal than a beautifully molded dessert. This Normandy Chocolate Mousse is really that old favorite—chocolate icebox cake—with a French accent. Made in a charlotte mold—a deep tin or copper form with smooth sloping sides—the dessert has a simple classic elegance of appearance, as well as a delicious flavor.

MARKETING LIST

3/4 pound of dark
    sweet chocolate
24 Cats tongues or
    lady fingers
light rum
sweet butter
Confectioners' sugar
eggs
Vanilla bean
salted almonds
2 Cups of heavy cream
1½ yards of Satin
    Ribbon (1" wide)

PREPARATION TRAY

¾ pound of chocolate, broken in pieces

charlotte mold, lined

24 cats' tongues or ladyfingers

½ cup of salted almonds, pulverized

2 cups of heavy cream, whipped and flavored

Take a 1-quart charlotte mold.

1   Cut a circle of heavy white writing paper exactly to fit the bottom of the mold.

2   Line the sides of the mold with:
24 cats' tongues (Allemagne Buiscotti, sold in packages) or **24 ladyfingers** if they are good and firm.

3   Put **a speck of butter** on the flat side of the cats' tongues or ladyfingers, and stick them to the walls of the charlotte mold, standing upright. Be most careful not to leave gaps or spaces between them.

Fill the lined mold with the following mousse:

1   Cut into small pieces: **¾ pound of dark sweet chocolate**

2   Put into a medium-size heavy pan with:
5 tablespoons of light rum
2 tablespoons of water

3   Stir with a wooden spoon over a very slow fire until the chocolate dissolves.

4   Remove from the fire to cool, but do not allow the chocolate to set.

In a mixer bowl, cream:

1   **12 tablespoons (6 ounces—1½ sticks) of sweet butter** (It is always preferable to have butter at room temperature for creaming, or else cut it into small pieces.)

2   When it is light and creamy add: **½ cup of confectioners' sugar**

3   Beat very well. Then, one at a time, add:
3 egg yolks (The whites are to be beaten separately.)
½ cup of finely ground salted almonds (The almonds can be pulverized in an electric blender.)
the cool chocolate

In a metal bowl, over another bowl of ice, whip with a large metal whisk: **2 cups of heavy cream**

59

1 Beat until cream begins to thicken, then add:
  ¼ cup of confectioners' sugar
  2 inches of vanilla bean, slit open lengthwise, and
  its little seeds thoroughly scraped into the cream.
  (The scraped pod can then be put in a canister or
  jar of granulated sugar to make vanilla sugar.)

2 Continue beating until the cream is stiff enough to
  hold its shape.

3 Add to the chocolate mixture:
  ½ of the whipped cream
  3 egg whites beaten to soft peaks

4 Blend carefully with a rubber scraper.

5 Fill mixture into the lined mold.

6 Cover top with transparent wrap and freeze for
  2 hours.

7 Run a knife carefully between mold and cats'
  tongues or ladyfingers, and turn out on a flat serving dish. Remove the circle of white paper from
  the top.

8 Decorate with the rest of the whipped cream which
  has been filled into a pastry bag with a rose tube.

9 Pipe rosettes of cream around the top.

10 Tie the satin ribbon around the sides. It will
   cover the spots of butter on the outside of the cats'
   tongues. Besides, many French cakes are tradition-
   ally brought to the table decorated with a satin
   ribbon and bow, and it is a charming Gallic touch.

This dessert, when it comes to the table, has a certain
distinction that ordinary icebox cake often lacks. It is
the subtle difference, perhaps, that exists between a chic
Paris original and a little dressmaker's pretty frock. It
isn't fussy, and the quality is superb.

Quiche Lorraine

Ragoût de Veau en Daube

**MENU
2**

Tossed Salad

Hot Strawberry Soufflé

Suggested Wine: Chablis

Quiche Lorraine
(Cheese and Bacon Tart)

Serves six

From the province of Lorraine comes this famous old regional dish that is France's more sophisticated version of Italy's pizza. Where pizza is made with bread dough and a hearty, spicy filling, quiche is a flaky pastry shell filled with creamy custard, bacon and cheese.

An excellent luncheon dish or hot hors d'oeuvre, quiche Lorraine acquired a sudden popularity and snob appeal here a few years ago as a result of Cary Grant's serving it in a movie in which he played a fashionable Riviera jewel thief. Since that time the simple peasant pie of Lorraine has become a cliché of cocktail party one-upmanship. This should not detract from the fact that it is a good honest dish in its proper place—which, as far as I'm concerned, is not balanced on one's lap in a crowded living room.

MARKETING LIST

flour
butter
bread crumbs
Parmesan cheese
bacon
eggs
Dijon mustard
Dry Mustard
Salt
Cayenne pepper
2½ cups Light Cream
parsley

PREPARATION TRAY

baked pastry shell

1 pound of bacon, cooked in small pieces

⅓ cup of bacon fat, strained

½ cup of Parmesan cheese, freshly grated

parsley, chopped

Make the following pastry shell first:

1 Measure out: **a scant 2 cups of all-purpose flour**

2 Add: **½ teaspoon of salt**

3 Cut into flour: **12 tablespoons of soft salt butter (6 ounces—1½ sticks)**

4 Rub butter into the flour until it resembles coarse corn meal. Work up quickly to a firm dough with: **⅓ cup of ice water and a little lemon juice**

5 Roll out the dough on a lightly floured board.

6 Line a 10-inch flan ring, placed on a cookie sheet, with the dough.

7 Trim off neatly around the edge with a pastry pincer.

8 Prick all over the bottom with a fork.

9 Line pastry shell with a piece of buttered wax paper over which you sprinkle a good quantity of raw rice to hold it flat.

10 Bake in a preheated 375° oven for ½ hour.

11 Remove flan ring, paper and rice.

12 Put pastry shell back in oven for 10 minutes more, then remove it.

13 Cook: **1 pound of bacon,** cut across in thin pieces, in a heavy frying pan until crisp. Set aside bacon, and strain the fat.

Now, sprinkle the bottom of the pastry shell with:

2 tablespoons of bread crumbs
2 tablespoons of grated Parmesan cheese
half of the crisp bacon pieces

1 Put in a bowl:
2 whole eggs plus 2 yolks
mix in: **1 level teaspoon of Dijon mustard**
½ teaspoon of dry mustard
½ teaspoon of salt
75 grains (roughly!) of cayenne pepper
⅓ cup of strained bacon fat
⅓ cup of freshly grated Parmesan cheese

2   Pour onto this mixture: **2¼ cups of scalded light cream.** (The cream should be heated *just to the boiling point,* but not permitted to boil.)

3   Stir well.

4   Fill shell to top with the custard mixture.

5   Bake in a preheated 350° oven for 25 minutes.

6   When the custard is set, let it cool a little so it will be firm. Then scatter the rest of the **bacon** on top, sprinkle with **freshly grated Parmesan** and some **chopped parsley.** Now call Cary Grant. (The *quiche* may be eaten at once, or you may reheat it before serving it later.)

Ragoût de Veau en Daube
(Casserole of Veal with Wine)

Serves six

A daubière is the covered casserole or braising pan used for the winy robust stews that are a mainstay of French provincial cookery. Each region has its own way with beef or veal daubes, though the special southern flair of Provence makes its recipes the most famous. The olives and garlic in this daube are a Provençal touch.

In a French country kitchen the daube might simmer away for hours, filling the house with its tantalizing aroma. But since we are using a tender cut of veal to begin with, such long cooking is unnecessary. Even so, you will get an extra dividend of savory fragrance when you cook this dish.

Note: You can turn this into a ragout of boeuf en daube by simply substituting 2 pounds of top sirloin of beef for the veal rump, and then proceeding in the same fashion. You will also need ¾ pound of finely ground veal for the quenelles, and red wine instead of white wine for the sauce.

MARKETING LIST

2½ pounds of Veal rump
salt butter
Calvados
tomato paste
meat glaze
potato flour
Chicken stock
white wine
red currant jelly
white pepper
eggs
light cream
salt
garlic
shallots
chives
½ pound white
    button mushrooms
lemon
black and green olives
white bread
Vegetable oil
parsley

PREPARATION TRAY

meat, trimmed and cubed

½ pound of veal, finely ground

½ teaspoon of garlic, chopped

2 teaspoons of shallots, chopped

2 teaspoons of chives, chopped

½ pound of mushrooms, washed
(and cut in half, if large)

2 teaspoons of lemon juice

24 black and green olives, pitted

chicken stock

parsley, chopped

bread, sliced and trimmed

65

Carefully remove all skin, sinew and fat from the veal. Cut the meat into neat 1½ inch squares, setting aside about ½ pound of scraps with a bit of the discarded fat.

In a deep heavy Dutch oven heat:

1 **4 tablespoons (2 ounces—½ stick) of salt butter**
Stir with a wooden spoon until the butter begins to color.

2 Put in a few pieces of **veal** and allow them to brown very quickly on all sides. The pieces must not touch each other as they brown. Remove them and set them aside as they brown, replacing them with a new lot, until all the meat has been well browned.

3 Replace all the browned pieces in the pan.

4 Heat in a tiny pot: **⅓ cup of Calvados**

5 Tilt the pot until the flame ignites the brandy, then pour it over the veal. When the Calvados has burned out, remove the veal with a slotted spoon.

Stir into the pan juices with a wooden spoon:

1 **2 tablespoons (1 ounce—¼ stick) of butter**

2 Stir in, off the fire:
1 level teaspoon of tomato paste
1 level teaspoon of meat glaze
3 level teaspoons of potato flour

3 When smooth, mix in, still off the fire:
1¾ cups of good chicken stock
½ cup of dry white wine
1 teaspoon of red currant jelly
1 teaspoon of freshly ground white pepper
(You don't need salt because the meat glaze is salty, but you can taste for seasoning just to be sure.)

4 Stir sauce over the fire until it comes to a boil.

5 Put back the veal pieces and place the pan on the middle shelf of a preheated 375° oven for 1½ hours, basting a few times.

While the *daube* is cooking, put the ½ **pound of veal scraps and fat** through a fine meat grinder twice.

1 Put the **ground meat** into a mixer bowl and add:
    2 egg whites, unbeaten

2 Beat until well mixed.

3 Every recipe has its tricky spot, the thin ice so to speak, where you must tread most carefully. Here, and in the preparation of any kind of forcemeat where you add cream to the mixture, the trick is to do it very slowly, drop by drop, and to beat it in vigorously.

4 So, slow down the beater, add a **few drops of light cream,** then speed the beater up until the cream is well-incorporated into the meat mixture. Continue this procedure of adding slowly and beating quickly until you have beaten in: **1 cup of light cream** (Beware of using heavy cream here. It must be light cream or you will wind up with a messy mixture of butter and lumps of veal.)

5 And last of all you add your seasonings. It may seem more efficient to put them in with your forcemeat at the very beginning, but there is a good reason for adding them last. If you have added your cream too quickly and as a result your mixture is too liquid, salt has a chemical reaction on these ingredients and will stiffen the mixture. The forcemeat should be quite thick.

6 Add, beating at high speed:
    1 teaspoon of salt
    (Taste mixture, and add more salt if necessary.)
    ½ teaspoon of freshly ground white pepper
    ½ teaspoon finely chopped garlic
    2 teaspoons finely chopped shallots
    2 teaspoons finely chopped chives

7 Mix well.

About 15 minutes before the veal *daube* is cooked, remove it from the oven.

1 Heat two teaspoons in the gravy. Fill one warm spoon with veal forcemeat, and cup it with the other to form a small egg shape. Drop this into the veal gravy. Repeat until all the forcemeat has been used.

2 Replace pan in oven for 10 minutes.

Meanwhile, heat in a sauté or frying pan:

3 tablespoons (1½ ounces) of butter

1 When it foams add: **½ pound of small white button mushrooms** (Or if slightly larger, cut them in half.)

2 Coat mushrooms with **butter,** then

3 Add:

2 teaspoons of lemon juice

a little salt and freshly ground white pepper

4 Shake over a moderate fire for 2 or 3 minutes.

5 Add: **24 black and green pitted olives**

6 Mix well, and add mushrooms and olives to the veal *daube.* Cook in oven for another 5 minutes.

7 Cut in half on the bias: **3 slices of good white bread** with crusts removed.

8 Fry until golden brown in:

¼ cup of vegetable oil

Serve the veal *daube* in a casserole with the fried bread triangles placed around the edge. Sprinkle the top with **freshly chopped parsley.**

This is a dish that can be prepared well in advance, needing the last-minute addition of only the fried bread and parsley. It is a delicious way to serve an economical cut of meat, for the flavorful *daube* overcomes the sometimes tasteless and insipid veal we get here.

1 pint screw top jar
2 teaspoons Kosher salt
1 teaspoon freshly
    cracked white
    pepper,
½ teaspoon freshly
    cracked
    black pepper
¼ teaspoon granulated
    sugar
½ teaspoon dry mustard
1 teaspoon Dijon Mustard
1 teaspoon lemon juice
2 teaspoons finely
    chopped fresh garlic
5 tablespoons good
    tarragon vinegar
2 tablespoons french
    olive oil
10 tablespoons
    Vegetable oil
1 raw egg (beaten)
½ cup light cream

French Salad Dressing
(For Tossed Green Salad)

One pint

One of the delights of a good French meal is the simple green salad. Intended to "refresh the palate," the crisp clean taste of the greens, coated with a smooth yet slightly tart dressing, is the perfect finale to a savory main course.

No matter how delicious your dressing, however, it can be utterly ruined if your greens aren't right. Only use the freshest, crispest lettuce. Boston lettuce, romaine, chicory, endive, field or Bibb lettuce are all excellent. They should be thoroughly washed in cold water, dried first in a salad basket to rid them of excess moisture, and then leaf by leaf gently blotted in a clean towel until absolutely dry. Only then can they be refrigerated. Wet salad greens don't get coated and shiny with dressing. They only dilute it and it sinks to the bottom of the bowl in a watery puddle.

When you are ready to serve your salad, take the chilled crisp greens, and break them up by hand into bite-sized pieces. Never cut lettuces with a knife. Put them in a salad bowl, sprinkle with freshly chopped parsley or the whole leaves of fresh chervil, and then pour your dressing.

The best way to mix the salad is with your hands. Turn and toss the lettuce until each leaf is shiny and well coated, and be sure no pool of dressing remains at the bottom of the bowl. This is the classic salade simple and I for one shall be very glad to see it replace most others.

Put ingredients in jar in the order on your marketing list. Replace screw top tightly and shake well; chill before using.

With the addition of:

> 1 finely chopped hard-boiled egg
> 1 tablespoon finely chopped chives
> 1 tablespoon finely chopped parsley
> 2 teaspoons finely chopped green olives
> 1 tablespoon small well-drained capers

this dressing is turned into a Sauce Vinaigrette which can be served with cold asparagus, globe artichokes, broccoli, etc.

Hot Strawberry Soufflé

Serves six

Sweet soufflés, or soufflés d'entremets, are made either with a cream base or a fruit base. The hot lemon soufflé (recipe on page 126) is a cream base flavored with lemon juice and lemon peel. But this strawberry soufflé is a different type since the cream is mixed with a thick strawberry purée, and has sliced strawberries added to it. The procedure is slightly different for each, though the end result is a gossamer puff. The beauty of a soufflé is short-lived—one must catch it at the moment of its full-blown perfection or it is forever lost. Perhaps it is for this reason that soufflés hold a special place in our affections. Their fugitive and evanescent charm make us value them far above the more solid, lasting foods. Somehow guests always take it as a special tribute when you serve them a soufflé—it is a moment of perfection shared, and it happens all too rarely.

MARKETING LIST

fresh strawberries
granulated sugar
sweet butter
framboise
all-purpose flour
heavy cream
eggs
confectioners' sugar

PREPARATION TRAY

soufflé dish, prepared (see instructions on page 352)

2 cups of strawberries, puréed, framboise added

1 cup of strawberries, sliced, framboise added

Prepare a 6-cup soufflé dish according to directions on page 352.

1   Wash and hull: **3 cups of fresh strawberries**
2   Purée in a blender: **2 cups of the strawberries**
3   Slice: **1 cup of strawberries**
4   To the puréed strawberries add: **4 tablespoons of framboise liqueur**
5   Pour over the sliced strawberries: **2 tablespoons of framboise liqueur**
6   Set aside the sliced strawberries in the freezer for 30 minutes.

In a heavy saucepan melt: **2 tablespoons (1 ounce—¼ stick) of sweet butter**

1   Stir in, off the fire: **4 slightly rounded tablespoons of flour.** (When making a soufflé you never want to cook the flour out of the oven.)
2   Mix in:
    1 cup of heavy cream
    2 cups of puréed strawberries
3   Stir over the fire until it just thickens. Do not really cook it for any length of time.
4   Beat in, one at a time:
    6 egg yolks
    6 rounded tablespoons of granulated sugar
5   In a large metal bowl put **8 egg whites**
6   Beat them with a large wire whisk until you can turn the bowl upside down and the whites will adhere to it. (They must be quite stiff but not dry or they will not hold up your soufflé. Hand beating in a metal bowl is hard work, but it gives you the best results for soufflés.)
7   Remove the sliced strawberries from the freezer and fold them gently into the warm sauce.
8   Pour this mixture on top of the beaten egg whites.
9   Fold it in most carefully with a rubber scraper.
10 Fill into the prepared soufflé dish.
11 Sprinkle the top with **granulated sugar**

12 Bake on the bottom shelf of a preheated 375° oven for about 45 minutes or until a cake tester or straw can pierce the soufflé and come out clean.

13 When the strawberry soufflé comes out of the oven, carefully remove the cuff of wax paper.

14 Sprinkle the top generously with **confectioners' sugar.**

15 Heat a skewer on the stove until it is red hot.

16 Lay it on the sugar twice to make an X.

Serve this luscious beauty plain or with the sabayon sauce on page 128. Only in place of the lemon and lemon rind in that recipe, substitute 2 tablespoons of framboise for flavoring.

Wrap the soufflé dish in a starched white napkin and serve it at once. (This dessert can be assembled and allowed to stand, uncooked, for about 30 minutes before being put into the oven for 45 minutes. If you start to bake it just as you begin your main course, that should be about right. It is much better to time it so that you have to wait for your dessert for a few minutes rather than the soufflé wait for you. I have yet to meet anyone who would not gladly twiddle his thumbs for a while in happy anticipation of a dessert soufflé.)

MENU
3

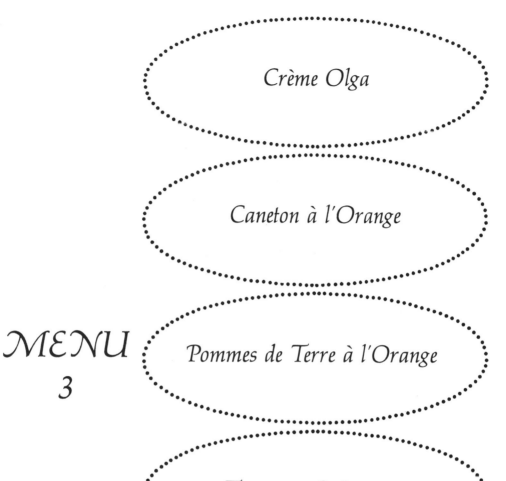

Crème Olga

Caneton à l'Orange

Pommes de Terre à l'Orange

Tarte aux Marrons

Suggested Wine:
Nuits-Saint-Georges

Crème Olga
(Scallion and Raw Mushroom Soup)

Serves six

French soups in particular seem to be named after people —mistresses of kings, actresses, and occasional nonentities like Elisa, Miss Betsy and—in this case—Olga. Whoever Olga was, we can guess that she must have been boldly individualistic to have inspired a soup made of scallions and raw mushrooms. But she must also have been a gentle-woman of exquisite taste, for the soup turns out to be a subtle concoction daintily topped with a dollop of whipped cream sprinkled with cayenne.

There are many attractive covered soup bowls on the market these days, and a table set with them for the first course would start any dinner party off handsomely. You can win a reputation as a hostess with imagination if you serve an unusual and delectable soup in equally unusual and striking bowls. And nothing could be simpler as a first course.

MARKETING LIST

5 bunches of Scallions
(green onions)
3/4 pound of firm but
not hard white
mushrooms
sweet butter
5 cups of light
chicken stock
light cream
heavy cream
lemon
salt
white peppercorns
cayenne
flour

PREPARATION TRAY

5 bunches of scallions, chopped fine

5 cups of chicken stock (see recipe on page 353)

½ pound of mushrooms, sliced fine

¼ pound of mushrooms, sliced *very* fine

¾ cup of heavy cream, whipped

74

Put in a mixing bowl:

8 tablespoons (4 ounces—1 stick) of sweet butter

1 Beat with a wooden spatula until it is very light and fluffy.

2 Add: **5 bunches of scallions,** carefully washed, dried and very finely chopped. (Use the green stalks as well as the white tips.)

3 Mix thoroughly and put into a heavy pan.

4 Add: **1 teaspoon of salt**
½ teaspoon of freshly ground white pepper
(Taste for seasoning, and correct if necessary.)

5 Cover the pan and cook very slowly for 10 minutes, being careful not to let the scallions brown. You just want to stew them in the butter.

6 Take the pan off the fire and stir in: **2 tablespoons of flour**

7 When the mixture is smooth add, still off the fire: **5 cups of light chicken stock**

8 Stir over the fire until the soup boils.

9 Let it simmer for 10 minutes, uncovered.

10 Wash and dry well: **½ pound of firm (but not hard) white mushrooms**

11 Slice them finely, stems and all, and add them to the soup, off the fire.

12 Rub the soup through a strainer at once or put it through a food mill. (You don't want the mushrooms to cook at all.)

13 Add to the strained soup: **1¼ cups of light cream**

14 Reheat the soup, and when it is hot add: **¼ pound of very, very finely sliced raw mushrooms**

15 Serve at once in individual cups or bowls topped with:
1 tablespoon of plain whipped cream seasoned with **a bit of salt**
a sprinkle of cayenne

Caneton à l'Orange
(Roast Duckling with Orange)

Serves six

The rich, slightly gamy flavor of duck fairly cries out for a sauce that is both sweet and tart. That is why ducks and oranges seem to be meant for each other, and have long been served together by French chefs.

However, French ducks differ in breed from their American cousins, and French custom in their preparation also differs from ours. There, duck is served "somewhat underdone," with the breast meat still pink, and the juices quite rosy. Try it that way for a change, as the orange sauce in this recipe takes care of what you might at first consider "slightly raw" duck. But if you don't dare chance it, roast your duck to a fare-thee-well. The sauce remains delicious even on crisp duckling, though M. Escoffier would shudder at the thought.

MARKETING LIST

2 4-or 5-pound
  ducklings
4 chicken livers
6 oranges
garlic
peppercorns
butter
salt
dry sherry
dry white wine
red wine
brandy
orange marmalade
bitter orange
  marmalade
tomato paste
meat glaze
potato flour
chicken stock
red currant jelly

PREPARATION TRAY

orange sauce (can be made the day before and refrigerated)

2 oranges, quartered

2 ducklings, washed and dried

4 cloves of garlic, peeled and bruised

Remove the innards, wash and dry thoroughly: **2 ducklings**

1   In the cavity of each put:
    1 large orange cut in quarters
    a little salt
    2 bruised cloves of garlic (Crush them slightly with
    a fork to release their juices.)
    a few peppercorns
    a small lump of butter
2   Truss the ducklings carefully (see page 356).
3   Place them on a rack in a large shallow roasting pan
    with: **½ cup of good dry white wine**
4   Roast them uncovered in a preheated 375° oven for 1
    hour and 50 minutes. (This is for duck in the
    French manner, with the juices running a pale pink.
    You might prefer to cook yours 30 minutes longer.)
5   Baste the ducks every 20 minutes. Tip the pan back
    and forth to slosh the juices around, then baste.
    Each time, add a little wine and water to the pan to
    keep at the same level (about ¼ inch of liquid).
6   Brush the ducks with **a little melted butter** after
    each basting.
7   After 40 minutes, turn the ducks over on their
    breasts. (Lift them with wooden spoons. Do not
    pierce their skin!) After 20 minutes turn the ducks
    on their backs again.
8   10 minutes before the ducks are ready to come out
    of the oven, spread the breasts lightly with **orange
    marmalade.** This will give them a beautiful glaze.
9   Remove the ducks to a warm platter and let them
    stand about 5 minutes before carving.
10 Carve them carefully (see page 357) and arrange
    the pieces neatly on a hot flat serving dish.

Pour over the ducks the following orange sauce:

1   In a sauté pan heat: **4 teaspoons of salt butter**
2   Add: **the duck livers** and **4 chicken livers**
3   When they are brown on both sides, heat in a small
    pan: **6 tablespoons of brandy**
4   Ignite the brandy and pour it over the livers.

5   Remove the livers and stir the pan juices well.

6   Add to the pan:

4 tablespoons of butter (2 ounces—½ stick)

the finely shredded rind of 3-4 oranges (Peel the bright orange rind with a swivel-bladed potato peeler, being careful not to get any of the bitter white skin. Cut the strips of peel lengthwise into thin shreds, using a sharp chef's knife. Save the oranges to use for the final addition to the sauce.)

4 teaspoons finely chopped fresh garlic

7   Cook very slowly without browning for 2 or 3 minutes.

8   Stir in, off the fire: **2 level teaspoons of tomato paste**

2 level teaspoons of meat glaze

4 good teaspoons of potato flour

9   When this is smooth, mix in, still off the fire:

2 cups of good chicken stock

½ cup of dry sherry

½ cup of good red wine

⅔ cup of orange juice

⅔ cup of orange marmalade

4 tablespoons of bitter marmalade

2 teaspoons of red currant jelly

1 teaspoon of freshly cracked black pepper

10   Stir over the fire until the sauce comes to a boil.

11   Put back the livers and allow the sauce to simmer for 15 minutes. (If you have made your sauce a few hours in advance, you can remove it from the fire, give it an airtight cover of transparent wrap and let it stand until you are ready to use it.)

12   Just before serving, remove the livers, slice them and return them to sauce.

Add: **skinned sections of 3 or 4 navel oranges** (Use the oranges that you peeled earlier. Be sure you remove every trace of the white skin from the sections.)

13   Carefully pour this sauce over the carved ducks and serve. A hot oval silver serving platter is excellent, and you may garnish it by putting the following orange potatoes around the ducks.

Pommes de Terre à l'Orange

(Orange Potatoes)

Serves six

These potatoes are the ideal accompaniment for duckling with orange, but they are also good with baked ham and roast pork. I think it is important to introduce variations into your garnishes with main courses, and if you must have meat and potatoes, at least play it in as many different keys as possible.

PREPARATION TRAY

potato mixture

melted butter

jelly roll tin, buttered

MARKETING LIST

6 - 8 Idaho potatoes
salt
Clove
Sweet butter
eggs
4 oranges

79

Peel and cut in half across:

1   **6 large Idaho potatoes** (8 if they are small) .

2   Put them in a saucepan, cover them with cold water and bring it to a boil.

3   Add: **2 teaspoons of salt**
2 whole cloves

4   Simmer briskly until the potatoes are soft. (Test them with an icepick, as the fewer holes you stab into food the better it will be.)

5   When the potatoes are soft, drain them and shake the pan over the fire to dry them out thoroughly.

6   In a mixer bowl put: **the cooked potatoes**

7   Beat until smooth and add:
5 tablespoons (2½ ounces) of sweet butter
2 whole eggs (not large)
4 egg yolks
the grated rind of 4 oranges

8   Beat well. (If you beat the potatoes well enough you can just add water, instead of the butter and eggs. The potatoes won't be as rich but they will still be light and fluffy—if you beat them very well indeed.)

9   Fill the mashed orange potatoes into a pastry tube with a large star tip.

10   Pipe in large rosettes on a well buttered jelly roll tin.

11   Sprinkle a little **melted butter** on top and brown under the broiler.

12   Carefully slide a spatula under the rosettes and place them around the duck (or ham or pork) on the hot platter.

Another way of serving orange potatoes which I sometimes like for a change is to fry them in the following manner:

1   When you have made the above potato mixture, spread it out onto a flat platter, cover with transparent wrap and chill well in the refrigerator.

2   When the potatoes are chilled, take the mixture off the platter by the tablespoon.

3   Roll each spoonful lightly in flour and then roll with the flat of your hand to form large cork shapes.

4   Brush the cork shapes with **whole beaten egg**

5   Roll them in **fine bread crumbs**

6   Fry them in deep fat at 350°, a few at a time, until they are golden brown.

7   Drain well on paper towels before serving.

Both the duchess potatoes (with orange) or the croquettes are excellent ways of serving plain potatoes too. Just omit the orange and clove and season with salt and pepper.

Tarte aux Marrons
(Chestnut Cream Tart)

Serves six

Like a good jazz musician, chestnuts can be either sweet or hot. On page 209 you have the recipe for a hot chestnut purée that is a savory accompaniment to meats. Here we have puréed chestnuts in another mood, making a rich and luscious butter cream whose sweetness combines with crunchy meringues.

Meringues, made with beaten egg whites and sugar, are just about the simplest of all pastries. It is said that Marie Antoinette used to get away from it all by going over to the Petit Trianon and cooking up a batch of her favorite meringues. In her day, spoons having been invented before pastry bags, they were simply shaped by spoon. And you can do yours that way, too, if you can't handle a pastry bag, though the shape will not be as perfect.

MARKETING LIST

eggs
superfine sugar
cream of tartar
granulated sugar
salt
1 pound can of
    chestnut purée
light rum
sweet butter
heavy cream

PREPARATION TRAY

1 9-inch pastry shell, baked (see recipe on page 63)

meringues (can be baked in advance and stored in an airtight tin)

butter cream can be made in advance and refrigerated

To make your meringues, allow to stand at room temperature for
1 hour: **6 eggs**

1   Very carefully separate the eggs, being certain not
to get even a speck of the yolk in the egg whites or
they will not beat up foamy and stiff. If any yolk
should fall into the white, remove it with a clean
dry spoon. You will need 3 egg yolks for the cream
filling, so put them in a scparate bowl.

2   Put the egg whites in a mixer bowl and beat slowly
until they form soft peaks.

3   Sift together:
1 cup of superfine sugar
½ teaspoon of cream of tartar

4   Add slowly to the egg whites, beating all the time.

5   Continue beating quickly and add:
a pinch of salt

6   Beat until the egg whites are thick, very stiff and
shiny, and hold their shape.

7   Fill the meringue into a pastry bag with a small
plain tube about the size of a quarter. (Unless you
want to shape the meringues with a spoon à la
Marie Antoinette.)

8   Put a small dab of meringue at each corner of a
jelly roll pan.

9   Cover the pan with wax paper and paste it down at
the corners with the meringue.

10   Pipe the meringue mixture on top in small domes
the size and shape of half eggs.

11   Sprinkle the tops well with **granulated sugar**

12   Put them in a preheated 275° oven for ½ hour.

13   They should just begin to color and be firm and
dry to the touch. (These meringues will be light
and crisp. If you bake them in a warmer oven they
will be chewy, but for decorating the top of the
chestnut tart, or for meringue shells you want them
light and brittle.)

14   Allow the meringues to cool, then remove them by
sliding a small spatula or palette knife underneath
each one.

15   Store them in an airtight tin.

For the chestnut tart, make the following chestnut butter cream:

1   In a mixer bowl put: **3 egg yolks** (Use 3 of the yolks left over from the meringue recipe.)
2   Beat them until they are light and fluffy.
3   In a heavy pan put: **1 cup of granulated sugar**
    ¾ cup of water
    ¼ teaspoon cream of tartar
4   Stir over a slow fire until the sugar dissolves.
5   Cook until the mixture forms a light thread (about 230° on a candy thermometer).
6   Turn the mixer on high. While the yolks are beating fast pour the sugar mixture slowly over them.
7   Continue beating until the mixture is stiff and cold.
8   Add while beating: **¾ pound (3 sticks) of sweet butter in small pieces, bit by bit.** The butter should be at room temperature and slightly soft.
9   Add: **1-pound can of unsweetened chestnut purée** (There is a sweetened purée, but it is too syrupy.)
10 Flavor with: **2 or 3 tablespoons of light rum**
11 Fill this chestnut butter cream into a pastry bag. (The butter cream can be made in advance and refrigerated until you are ready to use it. In that case, beat it a bit to soften it before using.)
12 Fill a 9-inch baked pastry shell (see recipe on page 63) with the cream, using a spoon or pastry tube.
13 Decorate with:
    1 cup of heavy cream, whipped and flavored (see recipe on page 133) and piped in rosettes through a pastry tube.
14 Place meringues around the top.

This chestnut tart will taste delicious no matter how you decorate it, but the whipped cream and meringues give you an opportunity to let your imagination go and make something lovely to look at as well. The small meringue domes can be dusted with cocoa so they resemble toadstools. I confess that no one in his right mind would dream of eating *real* toadstools (except Alice in Wonderland) but these confections make a delightful decoration.

MENU

4

Beignets Soufflés au Fromage

Petits Poussins
à la Hambourg

Epinards à la Hambourg

Fresh Strawberry Mousse

Suggested Wine: Montrachet

Beignets Soufflés au Fromage
(Cheese Fritters)

Serves six as a first course, more as canapés

If you bake the pastry dough called pâte à choux you have cream puffs, if you fry it in deep fat you have beignets soufflés (see recipe on page 230), and if you add cheese to the dough you have a most delicious appetizer. Aside from being one of the simplest of all pastries to make, this is one of the most versatile, and therefore a valuable addition to your repertoire. Since each recipe varies a little, I'm giving you this one for Beignets Soufflés au Fromage right from the beginning. You can make the dough in advance for these delectable puffs and store it in the refrigerator until you are ready to fry it. Incidentally, if you make very small cheese beignets, the size of marbles, they are sensational as a hot canapé to serve with cocktails. And they take only the merest jiffy to fry.

MARKETING LIST

flour
eggs
Parmesan cheese
Dijon mustard
dry mustard
salt
cayenne pepper
Vegetable oil

PREPARATION TRAY

pastry, made in advance

Parmesan cheese, grated

86

1   In a heavy pan put: **1 cup of cold water**
    8 tablespoons (4 ounces—1 stick) of butter, cut into pieces

2   Stir with a wooden spoon until the butter is dissolved and the liquid reaches a rolling boil. Don't let it boil for any time as there will be evaporation.

3   Immediately throw in, all at once:
    1 cup of flour

4   Lower the heat and stir with a wooden spoon until the mixture comes away from the sides of the pan and forms a large ball.

5   Place in a mixer bowl the ball of dough.

6   Beat in, one at a time:
    4 eggs
    (Be sure each egg is well mixed before adding the next one.)

7   Add, still beating:
    ¼ teaspoon of salt
    a dash of cayenne
    ½ teaspoon of dry mustard
    2 level teaspoons of Dijon mustard
    1 scant cup of freshly grated Parmesan cheese

8   At this point, you can store the pastry (*pâte à choux*) in a covered bowl in the refrigerator until you are ready to use it. If you do, let the bowl stand at room temperature for at least an hour before frying the *beignets*.

1   In a deep-fat fryer heat:
    vegetable shortening or vegetable oil to a depth of about 2½ to 3 inches

2   Using a fat thermometer (the same as a candy thermometer) let the fat heat to 350°.

3   Then form the mixture into small balls, using two teaspoons. (If you are making canapés, use a demitasse spoon to get them marble-sized.)

4   Keeping the *beignets* as round as possible, push them off one spoon with the other into the hot fat. Fry just a few at a time.

5   The *beignets* will roll over by themselves when the bottoms get golden brown.

6   Wait until the *beignets* are golden brown all over before removing them with a slotted spoon. If you take them out too soon they will collapse. Otherwise they will puff up to 2 or 3 times their size, and will stay that way.

7   Drain the browned *beignets* well on paper towels.

8   Sprinkle them with **grated Parmesan cheese**

Serve them on a starched napkin and sprinkle with a little more grated cheese. (This absorbs any remaining fat, yet the starched cloth will not become limp and greasy.)

Petits Poussins à la Hambourg

(Stuffed Squab As Done in Hamburg)

Serves six

I learned this recipe when I worked as a chef, before World War II, in one of the large hotels in Hamburg, Germany. I do not mean to spoil your appetite for stuffed squab, but you might be interested to know that it was a great favorite with Mr. Hitler, who dined at the hotel often. Let us not hold that against a fine recipe though.

Petits poussins are actually tiny spring chickens, but it is not always possible to find such small ones here, and squabs make an even more delicious substitute. One of the great nuisances about eating squab is the dozens of tiny bones you must contend with for every morsel of flesh you get. By the time you have finished, your plate looks like a charnel house, you are exhausted, and there is a lingering suspicion that the game was not worth the candle. Squab can be pretty slim pickings.

But in this recipe the squab is boned, and then stuffed with a meaty dressing that supplements as well as complements its own not-too-plentiful flesh. Another advantage is that a great part of the work can be done in advance—the day before, if you wish. I served these once for Thanksgiving when there were only three of us. It was very festive, and we were all doubly thankful not to have to face leftover turkey the next day. There is never a shred of leftover squab!

MARKETING LIST

6 Squabs (have your butcher split the skin down the back of each and remove ribs, breastbone and backbone, leaving thigh and wingbones in)
12 chicken livers
butter
Calvados
garlic
mushrooms
lemon
6 oz. cooked tongue
pistachio nuts
3 green apples
flour
sugar
heavy cream
truffles
fresh tarragon

PREPARATION TRAY

squabs, stuffed and trussed

truffle, chopped

fresh tarragon, chopped (if you use dried tarragon, let it soak in a little warm water)

2 cups of heavy cream, lightly whipped

89

If your butcher cannot bone your squabs for you, you can do it yourself with a little care (and a little luck the first time). Take your boning knife and slit the skin of each squab down the back. Cut skin and flesh carefully away from the spine, ribs and breastbone so that you can free the carcass skeleton, leaving the whole skin with the breast and other meat, lying flat. Leave the wing bones and thigh bones intact. Reserve the carcass bones. (If your butcher does this job for you, be sure to have him send you the bones he removes.)

Season the inside of each squab with **a little salt and freshly ground white pepper**

1 Now, in a sauté pan, brown: **12 chicken livers and the squab livers in 2 tablespoons of very hot butter**
    2 Flame with: **6 tablespoons of Calvados**
    3 Remove the livers and add to the pan:
      6 tablespoons (3 ounces—¾ stick) of butter
    4 When hot add:
      12 sliced mushrooms
      ¼ teaspoon of finely chopped garlic
    5 Cook briskly for 2 minutes with:
      1½ teaspoons of lemon juice
      salt
      pepper
    6 Add: **6 ounces of shredded cooked tongue**
      3 tablespoons of blanched pistachio nuts
      the livers, carefully sliced

1 Skin, core and slice: **3 green apples** (Slices should be small and about ¼ inch thick.)
    2 Dry slices thoroughly on paper towels.
    3 Dust them with **flour**
    4 Sauté the apple in hot butter and **a little sugar**—but don't let the slices get too soft.

1 Mix with the other ingredients, and mound up on each squab for stuffing. (The boned squabs will be lying flat and spread-eagled on your board.)

2   Shape the squabs around the stuffing and sew them up carefully, making sure that the skin is securely closed and there are no openings out of which the stuffing can pop while the birds are cooking.

3   Turn each squab on its back, and tie each with fine string. (see directions for trussing fowl on page 356).

(At this point you can refrigerate the squabs and cook them later, or you can go for broke and finish up the recipe in one fell swoop.)

4   Put in a heavy sauté pan:
8 tablespoons (4 ounces—1 stick) of salt butter
When it is hot, put in the squabs. Brown them slowly with the lid on, turning them so they brown all over.

5   Flame with **¾ cup of Calvados**

6   Place the bony carcasses alongside the birds.

7   Set the pan, uncovered, on the top shelf of a pre-heated 375° oven for 45 to 50 minutes.

8   Baste twice, adding one or more tablespoons of Calvados each time, if necessary.

9   Turn the birds once or twice, using a wooden spoon.

10 When cooked, remove squabs from the pan, remove the string used in trussing, discard bones, and carefully stir into the pan gravy, a tablespoon at a time, beating it in with a wire whisk: **2 cups of lightly whipped heavy cream**

11 Add: **2 tablespoons of finely chopped truffle**
2 tablespoons of finely chopped fresh tarragon
(If you cannot get fresh tarragon, hydrate the dried herb in a little warm water before using.)

To do them full justice, the squabs ought to be served in a little copper casserole with the sauce spooned over them. But earthenware will do nicely. This lily needs no gilding.

Epinards à la Hambourg

(Spinach with Mornay Sauce)

Serves six

This is the classic vegetable accompaniment for the stuffed squab à la Hambourg, and it was always served with it there. In this country, where spinach is hardly one of the best beloved of vegetables, it seems strange to some people to find it paired off with a delicacy like squab.

I can only say, try it this way and see if it too isn't a delicacy. Chances are you will not echo the child in the New Yorker cartoon who tasted broccoli and protested, "I still say it's spinach, and I say the Hell with it!" This is spinach, but with a difference, and viva la différence!

MARKETING LIST

3 packages of
  frozen spinach
  (or 3 pounds of
  raw spinach)
butter
3/4 cup small
  fried croutons
flour
cayenne pepper
dry mustard
Dijon mustard
milk
Parmesan cheese
light cream

PREPARATION TRAY

spinach, cooked, drained and pressed dry

¾ cup of croutons (see recipe on page 163)

⅓ cup of Parmesan cheese, freshly grated

au gratin dish, buttered

1 Put: **3 packages of frozen spinach** in a pan with a sprinkling of **water** and a **little salt**

    2 Cook until spinach is just soft. Do not overcook.

    3 Drain thoroughly in a colander with a plate on top of the spinach and a weight (a brick neatly covered in foil is good) on the plate. Press out all moisture.

    4 Put spinach through meat chopper with fine blade.

    5 Mix in: **2 tablespoons (1 ounce—¼ stick) of melted butter**

    ¾ cup of small fried croutons

    (Do not add the croutons until you are ready to serve up the spinach. They are the "difference," in this dish. Their crisp contrast with the soft vegetable is what turns the trick. But if they are imbedded in the chopped spinach for too long a time, they will become soggy and you will end up with just plain garden-variety you-know-what.)

    6 Form the spinach-and-crouton mixture into large egg shapes by molding it with two tablespoons.

1 Arrange "eggs" in rows on a buttered *au gratin* dish and top each with a tablespoon of the following Mornay sauce:

    2 Melt in a small pan:

    2 good tablespoons (1 ounce—¼ stick) of butter

    3 Stir in, *off the fire*: **3 tablespoons of flour**

    season with salt and cayenne pepper

    ¼ teaspoon of dry mustard

    ½ teaspoon of Dijon mustard

    4 Mix in, still *off the fire*: **1 scant cup of milk**

    5 Stir over the fire until it just comes to a boil.

    6 Then add: **¼ cup freshly grated Parmesan cheese**

    3 tablespoons of light cream

    7 Simmer for a few minutes.

    8 Coat the spinach "eggs" with this sauce.

    9 Sprinkle the top with a little more **cheese** and a little **melted butter**

    10 Brown under the broiler.

Eat it and weep—for all the wasted years when you thought spinach was a horrid dish.

Fresh Strawberry Mousse

Serves six

This is a most delicate light dessert, which can be prepared well in advance and is ready to serve straight out of the refrigerator. You can vary it by substituting raspberry, apricot, peach, or other fruit pulp. Or you can make a delicious coffee mousse by substituting 2 tablespoons of good instant coffee dissolved in 2 tablespoons of boiling water for the fruit pulp. In that case use only 2 packets of gelatine, and use rum instead of framboise.

PREPARATION TRAY

2 boxes of strawberries, puréed in a blender

2½ cups of heavy cream, whipped and flavored

lemon juice

red currant glaze

12 perfect whole strawberries

MARKETING LIST

9 eggs
granulated sugar
Confectioners' sugar
2 boxes of Strawberries
2½ cups of heavy cream
fresh Vanilla bean
plain gelatine
lemon
raspberry liqueur (framboise)
red currant jelly

1   Put into a mixing machine bowl:
>   **5 whole eggs and 4 egg yolks**
>   **9 rounded tablespoons of granulated sugar**

2   Beat until mixture thickens and holds its shape. This is one thing you need not fear overbeating. While the machine works away, you can do the rest.

Purée: **2 boxes of strawberries.** Save 12 of the prettiest to use as decoration later. Hull the rest and put them in blender. This will give you 2 cups of fresh strawberry purée.

1   Put in a metal bowl over another bowl of ice **2½ cups of heavy cream**

2   Beat with large wire whisk until it begins to thicken.

3   Add: **2 inches of scraped fresh vanilla bean**
>   **2 heaping tablespoons of confectioners' sugar**

4   Continue beating until cream holds its shape.

1   Put in a small pan: **2¼ packages of plain gelatine**

2   Add: **2 tablespoons of lemon juice**
>   **6 tablespoons of water**

3   Stir over a very slow fire until the gelatine dissolves. Use a metal spoon, and you can see at once when the gelatine is completely dissolved and there are no more crystals.

1   Then, remove egg mousse from the machine and stir the strawberry purée into it with a rubber scraper. (If you mixed them together by machine you would break down the egg mousse too much.)

2   Carefully fold in ¾ of the whipped cream. Add: **3 or 4 tablespoons of raspberry liqueur (framboise)**

3   Lastly—and this is the really tricky bit, because if you're not very careful, your gelatine will set in layers in the mousse—carefully and thoroughly stir in the gelatine. You want to be sure to wait until the gelatine is about the same temperature as the mousse for best and smoothest results.

Now pour your mousse into a beautiful bowl—a shallow crystal bowl is perfect if you have one—and put it in the refrigerator to set. When it is set, decorate around the edges with the whole strawberries you saved. Brush them with a little **red currant jelly** which has been dissolved over a slow fire with **2 tablespoons of framboise,** strained and cooled. Decorate the center with the rest of the **whipped cream** piped through a pastry tube.

A fitting finale for a beautiful meal.

MENU
5

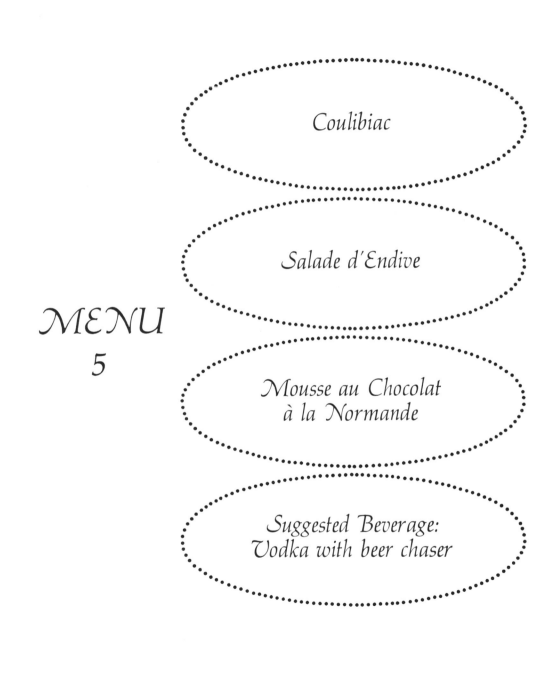

Coulibiac

Salade d'Endive

Mousse au Chocolat
à la Normande

Suggested Beverage:
Vodka with beer chaser

Coulibiac

(Fillet of Beef Baked in Brioche Pastry)

Serves six to eight

For a winter dinner party this unusual dish is both hearty and elegant. It is made with a piece of roasted fillet of beef that is then encased in a shell of brioche dough. When you slice into what looks like a golden loaf of pastry, the center of each slice is a juicy rare circle of fillet. A veritable bull's-eye.

I once made a "poor man's Coulibiac" for friends of mine. Their faces fell when I brought out what was apparently just a hot loaf of white bread—though it was home baked at that. But their spirits rose when I started to slice the bread and each slice had a meaty interior of ground beef. You can do this same recipe substituting your favorite meat loaf for the fillet, and using the white bread dough (see recipe on page 185) in place of the brioche dough.

Originally Coulibiac was a crust of brioche dough wrapped around fish or chicken, but now the beef filling is more popular. Rich man's or poor, Coulibiac is a lovely dish for a cold night. It was invented in wintry Russia in the days when that country still had both rich men and poor.

MARKETING LIST

brioche dough
egg
2 pound piece of
    fillet of beef
    (the thick end)
Kosher salt
black peppercorns
Calvados
white string
¼ pound of sliced
    boiled ham
Dijon mustard
salt butter
1 can of Liver Pâté
    (4 oz. size)
white peppercorns
salt

PREPARATION TRAY

brioche dough

fillet of beef, roasted, seasoned and refrigerated

liver *pâté*, prepared

bread mold, buttered

98

1 On a rack in a shallow roasting pan put: a **2-pound piece of fillet of beef** (from the thick end)

  2 Roast it, absolutely plain, in a preheated 375° oven for 50 minutes.

  3 Remove the partially cooked beef and after it is cool, carefully strip off all fat, skin and sinew.

  4 Rub the meat all over with: **coarse kosher salt** and **freshly cracked black pepper**

  5 Sprinkle the meat thoroughly with: **Calvados** (Place your thumb over the bottle opening and shake liberally.)

  6 Tie white string tightly around the meat near both ends and in the middle.

  7 Wrap it tightly in aluminum foil.

  8 Leave it in the deep freeze for about 30 minutes. (You want the meat well chilled so that it won't overcook when it is baked in the pastry.)

1 On a sheet of wax paper lay out: **4 thin slices of boiled ham**

  2 Lay them side by side so that they form 1 large sheet of ham.

  3 Sprinkle with: **Calvados**

  4 Spread with a **little Dijon mustard**

1 In a mixer, cream: **8 tablespoons (4 ounces—1 stick) of slightly soft salted butter**

  2 Add: **1 can of liver pâté** (4 ounce size) **a little salt a little freshly ground white pepper**

  3 Beat well and add: **2 tablespoons of Calvados**

  4 Spread this mixture on the ham.

  5 Remove the beef from the freezer.

  6 Unwrap and untie it.

  7 Lay it on top of the *pâté* and wrap it well with the ham.

1 Butter the largest size oven-glass bread mold.

  2 Take a full recipe of **brioche dough** from the refrigerator. (See recipe on page 113.)

3 Roll out a little over half the dough on a lightly floured board.

4 Line the buttered mold carefully with the dough.

5 Brush the edges with: **whole beaten egg**

6 Put the ham-wrapped fillet of beef in the center.

7 Cover with another piece of rolled-out brioche dough.

8 Tuck the edges of this top piece in securely with a knife, so that when the dough rises it will be well anchored.

9 Cover with a clean cloth, place it on a jelly roll pan, and allow it to rise (or prove), out of drafts and in a warm room for 25 minutes.

10 Brush the top of the dough with: **beaten egg**

11 Bake in a preheated 400° oven for 30 minutes, then at 375° for 30 minutes.

12 If the crust should get too brown before the time is up, reduce the oven heat and cover the top with a brown paper bag.

13 Remove the *Coulibiac* from the oven and allow it to settle in the mold for 5 minutes.

14 Then slide the blade of a knife around the edges. Turn out and serve on a warmed oval silver platter fitted with a wooden carving board.

The *Coulibiac* should be sliced and eaten piping hot so that the juices from the rare meat soak into the brioche pastry. It makes dunking quite unnecessary, and indeed the only other things you do need are a nice crisp salad and a fire on the hearth.

Salade d'Endive
(Belgian Endive Salad)

Serves six to eight

In the United States we sometimes call chicory "curly endive." The Belgian endive which is cultivated in the dark, somewhat like mushrooms, is a vegetable of quite a different color. And by itself it makes a distinguished salad.

Belgian endive comes in short, tapered stalks, its smooth leaves tightly furled, its color a creamy white, shading to pale yellow at the tip. Crisp and not quite bitter, all it needs is a coating of French dressing and a sprinkle of freshly chopped parsley.

PREPARATION TRAY

endive, washed and chilled

parsley, chopped

dressing made

MARKETING LIST

8 endives
French Dressing
parsley

Salade d'Endive

1 Wash the **endive** well in cold salted water, then in clear cold water.
2 Shake well in a salad basket, and dry thoroughly on paper towels.
3 Discard any outer leaves that are discolored.
4 Cut endive stalks in half lengthwise and separate all the leaves.
5 Place them in a small wooden salad bowl and pour over them **a little French dressing** (see recipe on page 69).
6 Sprinkle well with **freshly chopped parsley**

Since Belgian endive actually comes from Belgium, it is not easily available all over the country. There is nothing else quite like it, in spite of the mix-up of names. So if you cannot find it in your city (most of the Eastern seaboard cities have it), serve a plain green salad instead.

Mousse au Chocolat à la Normande

(Normandy Chocolate Mousse)

(See recipe on page 58.)

Quenelles de Brochet

Boeuf en Gelée

MENU
6

Hot Brioche

Baba au Rhum

Suggested Wine:
Red Burgundy

Quenelles de Brochet
(Dumplings of Ground Pike)

Serves six

When properly prepared, quenelles are like airy little fish soufflés served in a creamy and delectable sauce. The entire dish is a miracle of lightness and subtle flavor—typical of the ambrosia that a French chef can distill out of little more than a bit of ground pike. It is one of the dishes that originated in Lyons, and Lyonnaise cooking is justly famous. Unfortunately, even in France there are only a few top restaurants that serve quenelles at their fabulous best. In this country they are even more of a rarity, and when quenelles appear on a menu at all, they are all too likely to turn out to be soggy first cousins of New England codfish cakes. So, if you want to taste the real thing, the surest way is to do it yourself, using the following recipe.

MARKETING LIST

2½ pounds of Pike
ground raw
(1 pound net)
(Have fishmonger
send you head,
skin and bones)

eggs
butter
light cream
heavy cream
cloves
nutmeg
Dijon mustard
dry white wine
onion
carrot
celery
parsley
bay leaf
flour
Parmesan cheese
Sherry or Brandy

PREPARATION TRAY

quenelle mixture, which has been refrigerated

fish stock (see recipe on page 52)

½ cup of freshly grated Parmesan cheese

au gratin dish, buttered

1   Make a paste first, by putting in a pan: **1 cup of cold water**
          4 tablespoons (2 ounces—½ stick) of salt butter, cut up in pieces
          a good pinch of salt

2   Bring slowly to a boil.

3   When bubbling, throw in **1 cup of all-purpose flour.** Stir with a wooden spoon until smooth. (This paste—for those of you who have browsed through French cookbooks and been awed by the intricacies of some of their preparations—is nothing more nor less than a *panade.* Used to bind various kinds of forcemeat, a *panade* sounds far more tricky and esoteric than it really is. You have just made one quite easily.)

4   Turn the *panade* into a mixer bowl and beat in, one at a time: **2 eggs**
          2 egg whites

5   Then beat in, teaspoon by teaspoon, **the ground raw pike**

6   Remove mixture from bowl.
    Put in bowl: **12 tablespoons (6 ounces—1½ sticks) of butter cut into pieces.** (It is best if this has stood at room temperature for a while.)

7   Beat until light and creamy.

8   Add fish mixture slowly to butter, while beater is on.

9   Beat in slowly: **⅓ cup heavy cream** (Add this a few drops at a time with mixer on low, then speed it up until cream is absorbed. Continue doing this until you have used all the cream.)
    a good ½ teaspoon of ground nutmeg
    3 good teaspoons of salt
    2 good shakes of cayenne
    1 level teaspoon of Dijon mustard

10   Rub mixture through strainer, or better yet, put it through a food mill.

11   Chill in a covered shallow bowl for at least half an hour. (Actually the *quenelle* mixture can be made up to this point and refrigerated even a day ahead of time.)

1 When you are ready to make the *quenelles*, form them into 3-inch long sausage shapes on a lightly floured board.

2 Put them in a deep pan of very *hot* water—but it must not be boiling. Cover the surface of the water with 2 or 3 paper towels. This will keep the *quenelles*, which swell and rise to the surface, from forming a nasty skin if they are exposed to the air.

3 Poach for 15-20 minutes. (Can be longer if you wish.)

4 When poached, arrange the *quenelles* on a buttered *au gratin* dish.

Spoon over them the following sauce:

1 Make a fish stock with the **skin, bone and head of the pike in a saucepan**

2 Add: **¾ cup of dry white wine**
3 cups of water

3 Bring slowly to a boil.

4 When bubbling, reduce to a simmer. Carefully skim off scum.

5 Add: **¾ cup, in all, of sliced onion, carrot and celery**
2 teaspoons of salt
8 black and white peppercorns
1 small white onion stuck with 2 cloves
1 sprig of parsley tied to 1 bay leaf

6 Simmer gently for 1½ hours. (At this point the liquid should be reduced to 2½ cups. Any fish stock that is not used in this recipe can be stored in a covered plastic container and frozen for future use.)

7 Strain.

1 Melt in a pan: **6 tablespoons (3 ounces—¾ stick) of butter**

2 Stir in, off the fire: **4 tablespoons of flour**

3 Season with **a little salt, a few grains of cayenne**

4 Carefully and slowly add and stir in:
1½ cups of fish stock

106

5 Stir over the fire till it boils.
Add: ⅓ **cup of light cream**
bit by bit, add : **3 teaspoons of butter** and
¼ cup of freshly grated Parmesan cheese

6 Simmer 5 or 6 minutes. (Sauce should be rather thick and shiny.)

7 Mix in a small bowl:
2 egg yolks
2 tablespoons of dry sherry (Once, when I had no sherry, I substituted brandy. Didn't hurt it a bit.)
2 tablespoons of heavy cream

8 Pour a little warm sauce on the egg yolks, beating all the time.

9 Now add egg yolks to sauce in pan, and reheat *without boiling*.

1 Carefully coat *quenelles* with this sauce. Spoon it, rather than pour it over them.

2 Sprinkle top with **freshly grated Parmesan cheese, and cool melted butter**

3 Brown under broiler for a few minutes.

If this recipe seems arduous, you can simplify the preparation by making the fish stock and *quenelle* mixture the day before. You can also poach an extra quantity of *quenelles* and wrap them individually in transparent wrap and pop them in the freezer. When you wish to use the *quenelles*, simply put them in hot—but not boiling—water, wrapping and all. When they are heated through, unroll them from the wrapping, place them in an *au gratin* dish, cover them with sauce, and *voilà*—instant, home-made *quenelles*. Delicious!

Boeuf en Gelée
(Beef in Aspic)

Serves six

This is one of the deceptively simple but elegant dishes of classic French cookery. When we were doing this recipe in class one day I commented that it was a truly haute cuisine dish. "Haute cuisine, what's that?" asked one of the students. "High class, dearie," I explained, "and rather difficult." It stems from the great culinary traditions of the eighteenth and nineteenth centuries when chefs like Carême created dazzling architectural displays with pastries and aspics, and cooking was considered a branch of the fine arts.

For boeuf en gelée the meat is roasted very simply—but it must be cooked and sliced to perfection. The aspic, too, must be perfect—clear, well-flavored, firm but not rubbery. The vegetables are boiled plainly, but just the proper amount to leave them brightly colored and of good texture. Arranging them and the meat in the aspic takes an artist's touch. The result is a beautiful dish in which everything has been so well prepared that each food has its own clear, pure flavor, and you eat a creation that looks elaborate but tastes simple.

MARKETING LIST

2½ pounds of fillet of beef in one piece, the thick end
Kosher salt
white peppercorns
brandy
Strong chicken and beef stock
tomato paste
Dry Sherry
plain gelatine
eggs
truffles (optional)
baby carrots
baby white turnips
green peas
(or any vegetables in season)

PREPARATION TRAY

beef, cooked, seasoned, tied and wrapped
and refrigerated

chicken and beef stock, cold and fat-free
(see recipe on page 276)

vegetables, cut and cooked

(this dish must be assembled in the morning and
refrigerated for at least 4 hours)

1 Place on a roasting rack in a roasting pan:

a 2½-pound piece of fillet of beef (the thick cut)

2 Don't do anything to it beyond wiping it off with a damp cloth—no trimming, tying or seasoning yet.

3 Roast the fillet for ¾ of an hour in a preheated 375° oven for very rare meat. Use a meat thermometer for exact degree of rareness that suits you best.

4 Remove the beef and allow it to get cold.

5 Trim off all fat, membrane and sinew.

6 Rub the meat well with:

a little kosher salt

a little freshly ground white pepper

7 Massage into the meat so that it really penetrates **some good brandy**

8 Tie the meat at 1-inch intervals with fine white string. This will hold the juices in and give the meat a firm texture and good shape when you want to slice it later.

9 Wrap it tightly in foil.

10 Put it in the freezer for ½ hour to get all the flavor of the seasonings into the meat as it chills rapidly.

1 For the aspic, put into a large heavy saucepan:

6 cups of strong chicken and beef stock, cold and fat free (See the *pot-au-feu* recipe on page 276.)

1 tablespoon of tomato paste (to clarify the stock, not to flavor it) .

¼ cup of sherry

2 tablespoons of plain gelatine

3 beaten egg whites

2 Beat with a wire whisk over a moderate fire until the stock reaches a rolling boil. (It might be a good idea to taste for seasoning at this point and add salt if necessary.)

3 Draw it aside and let it stand for 10 minutes while the egg whites rise to the surface.

4 Line a colander with a cloth rung out in cold water, and place it over a large bowl.

5 Pour the aspic slowly through the cloth. The frothy egg whites will have collected any particles that

clouded the stock. They will remain above in the damp cloth, while a perfectly clear aspic strains through into the bowl.

6   Set the bowl of aspic aside to cool.
7   Put an oval silver (or other metal) platter into the deep freeze to get very cold.
8   Remove the chilled platter.
9   Stir a **small amount of the aspic** in a pan over a bowl of ice.
10   When the aspic is on the point of setting (syrupy) pour a layer of it on the bottom of the platter.
11   Put it in the refrigerator to set firmly.

1   Remove the beef from the freezer.
2   Unwrap it, untie it, and cut it very evenly and carefully into thin slices.
3   When the layer of aspic has set on the platter, remove the platter from the refrigerator.
4   Arrange the beef in overlapping slices down the length of the platter on top of the set aspic.
5   Chill another small amount of aspic over ice until it is on the point of setting.
6   Pour this smoothly over the sliced beef, using a large basting spoon.
7   Put the platter back in the refrigerator to set the aspic for another 10 minutes. (As you can see, there is nothing really difficult about working with aspic, but it is fussy work and takes time. Its saving grace is that you can do it in advance and then produce a glamorous dish right out of your refrigerator.)

Now you want to decorate the platter with this vegetable garnish:

1   Plainly boil, each in its own pan of lightly salted water:
1½ dozen tiny carrots (You can cut larger carrots into baby carrot shapes.)
1½ dozen baby white turnips (You can cut them down to size, too.)
1 cup of green peas
1½ dozen short spears of asparagus

(Use any assortment of vegetables that are in season, and are small, firm and of varied colors. Cook until *just* done—not too soft, please.)

2 Allow the vegetables to get cold. Drain and dry them most carefully.

3 Arrange them in alternating little bundles around the jellied beef. Here your own sense of color and design will come into play.

4 Coat each bundle with cool, on-the-point-of-setting aspic.

5 If you want to be very grand you can decorate the beef with **slices of truffle** and give it another coat of aspic.

6 Put the platter back in the refrigerator to set.

7 Take the rest of the aspic and pour it into a plate or jelly roll pan in a ½-inch layer. Let it set.

8 Turn the layer of set aspic out on a piece of wax paper on the chopping board.

9 With a large chef's knife, chop it into neat little cubes. (The wax paper will keep it from sticking to your knife or the board.)

10 Decorate between the vegetable bundles and around the beef with little mounds of **chopped aspic**

This is a beautiful buffet or summer supper dish, and can also be done with leftover roast beef or *boeuf à la mode*, as long as you can slice it attractively. I must say, any leftover beef served in this fashion becomes more elegant than the original, more royalist than the king!

Hot Brioche

Makes from twelve to eighteen, depending on size

Why bake your own brioches when you can buy perfectly good ones at most French pastry shops? Well, for one thing, you can buy the brioches all right, but no one has yet figured out how to sell the heavenly aroma of baking bread. For perfuming a house, it is better than the finest incense in the world. Secondly, there is a certain elemental satisfaction in baking breadstuffs, as you will discover the first time you knead dough, take a fragrant crusty loaf from the oven, and serve and taste this most fundamental food of all created, by your own hands. And finally, home-baked products taste better because you put into them the very best ingredients, including that one beyond price—love.

Incidentally, this recipe is a classic one that has not altered since 1682. I took it out of an old French cookbook of that era, and though "love" was not one of the ingredients listed, I suspect that good cooks through all the ages have used it judiciously.

MARKETING LIST

yeast
all purpose flour
salt butter
granulated sugar
salt
eggs

PREPARATION TRAY

bowl of brioche dough, well chilled

buttered brioche molds

You may as well make a big batch of brioches while you are at it, as the dough freezes well, and you can have freshly baked brioches several times for the same initial effort.

1 In a measuring cup put: **½ cup of lukewarm water** (be sure it is tepid and not hot).
  2 Dissolve in it: **2 packages of yeast or 2 yeast cakes**
  3 In a small bowl, measure: **1 cup of all-purpose flour**
  4 Add: the dissolved yeast and water.
  5 Stir with a wooden spoon until you get a thick mass.
  6 Turn this dough out onto a lightly floured board and knead it. (Press it out flat with your hands; pick up the far edge and fold it over toward you; push the dough away from you with the heels of your hands lightly; turn the dough, fold it over toward you again, and again push it away from you.)
  7 Continue kneading until you get a smooth surface on the bottom of the dough.
  8 Take the ball of dough and with a sharp knife cut a cross on the top of it like a hot cross bun.
  9 Open up the four points to make it look like a flower.
  10 Drop this dough "flower" into a pitcher of luke-warm water. (Take great care not to get the water too hot or it will kill your yeast.)
  11 Leave it until the expanding dough "flower" rises to the top (about 10 or 15 minutes) .

1 In a mixer bowl, beat: **10 ounces (2½ sticks) of salt butter** (This is easier to do if the butter is not too hard and cold.)
  2 When it is light and creamy, remove the butter to another bowl but—good news!—don't wash the mixer bowl or beater.
  3 Put into the mixer bowl:
3 cups of all-purpose flour
1 teaspoon of salt
1 tablespoon of sugar
7 eggs

113

4   Stir these ingredients with a wooden spoon to mix them roughly, then beat by machine until the mixture is shiny.

5   Add the creamed butter.

6   Mix well.

7   Carefully lift the yeast "flower" from the pitcher of warm water. (Be sure you remove it as soon as it has risen to the surface.)

8   Cradle it in your hands to let all the liquid drain off. The ball of dough will feel warm and alive (as indeed it is).

9   Add it to the mixture and beat until all is well blended.

10   Wipe out a large china bowl with a damp cloth and dust it lightly with flour.

11   Put the brioche dough in, and cover the bowl tightly with transparent wrap.

12   Cover it with a cloth and leave it at room temperature, protected from drafts, until the dough rises to double its bulk. (About 1 hour, but watch it, as the time varies and you don't want the dough to rise too much.)

13   When the dough has risen, break the rise by stirring it a few times until it has sunk to its original level. (This permits some of the gas to escape, and lets in fresh oxygen.)

14   Cover the bowl of dough with transparent wrap and place it in the freezer to set and get firm. This should take at least an hour, but ideally you could leave it overnight in the refrigerator until you were ready to use it. Brioche dough is very sticky, and you can best handle it when it is chilled.

1   Turn the dough out on a lightly floured board.

2   Flour your hands and, using them, roll the dough out into a long sausage a little smaller than a salami.

3   Well butter some brioche molds.

4   With a floured knife blade, cut the roll of dough into pieces that will fit your brioche molds, and with your cupped hands, narrow the bottoms so they fit

into the molds about ⅔ full. (These pieces must be very smooth.)

5 With your floured index finger make an indentation in the center of each.

6 Then mold small pear-shaped pieces of the dough and place them, narrow point down, in the indentations. These will be the little hats on top of the baked brioches.

7 Cover the filled molds with a towel and allow the dough to rise at room temperature until it is double in bulk (about half an hour). This process is called "proving." Any dough that has yeast in it has to do about 80% of its rising outside the oven. If you put it straight in the oven before it has "proved" it will not rise at all, as the heat kills the yeast.

8 Brush the surface of the raw brioches with either **whole beaten egg** or **beaten egg yolk and milk,** depending upon how high a gloss you want. With beaten egg yolk and milk you get brioches so shiny you can almost see your face on their surface!

9 Bake in a preheated 375° oven for about 30 minutes.

10 Turn out of the molds at once and wrap the brioches in a napkin. (When rolls or breads cool covered with a cloth, the crust is soft. A crisp crust results from allowing them to cool uncovered. Brioches are supposed to have soft crusts.)

11 For freezing extra dough, cut the sausage of dough while it is still cool and firm into pieces the size you will need. Wrap each piece individually in lightly floured squares of transparent wrap. When you want to use them, remove them from the freezer, let them come to room temperature, unwrap and put them in the molds, and follow the procedure as above.

Brioches are wonderful served warm with butter and jam for breakfast. But home-baked brioches served as a hot bread for dinner lift the meal out of the ordinary and set you apart as a very special hostess.

Baba au Rhum

(Rum Baba)

Serves eight

Of all the French pastry desserts, Baba au Rhum *is probably the most famous. "Baba" is the Polish word for old grandmother, and the shape of the mold looks a bit like a dumpy granny in long skirts. The fact that "granny" is also deliciously rum-soaked—sometimes even ablaze with liquor need not concern us here. Some long-ago chef was probably having his little joke. And as a result we have a justly celebrated dessert.*

Babas freeze well, and it is possible in this case to have your cake and freeze it too. Before being soaked in the rum syrup, some of the babas can be wrapped and put in the freezer "dry." Just remember to warm them ever so slightly after defrosting them, as both cake and rum syrup should be warm for the soaking process to be most effective.

MARKETING LIST

Yeast
Currants
all-purpose flour
light rum
eggs
granulated sugar
salt
Sweet butter

PREPARATION TRAY

babas already baked

syrup made and ready to reheat

(soak warm *babas*
for 30 minutes before serving)

1   Put into a warm china bowl: **4½ ounces of all-purpose flour** (1 scant cup. You see what I mean about the inaccuracy of this kind of measurement? Much better to have a scale and measure by weight.)

2   Make a well or depression in the center of the flour.

3   Into a small bowl put: **¼ cup of lukewarm milk or water**

4   Add: **1 package of dry or fresh yeast**

5   Stir with a small spoon until the yeast has completely dissolved.

6   Pour this lukewarm liquid into the well in the middle of the flour.

7   Add: **3 beaten eggs**

8   Beat all the ingredients together lightly with your hand, using it like a whisk to get as much air as possible into your dough. This makes the *babas* light. Beat until the batter is beautifully smooth and shiny. Then cover the bowl with a towel, keep in a warm place out of drafts until the mixture has risen to double its bulk (about ¾ of an hour in a warm room) .

9   While the yeast mixture is rising, place in another bowl: **2 tablespoons (1 ounce—¼ stick) of sweet butter**

10   Beat it to a light cream.

11   Mix in: **1 tablespoon of granulated sugar** and **a pinch of salt**

12   Add this to the yeast dough when it has risen to double in bulk.

13   Add: **2 tablespoons of currants,** well cleaned

14   Mix lightly with a spoon.

15   Brush well with **creamed butter** or **shortening** smeared on with a paper towel: 18 *baba* molds

16   Fill each ¼ full of the dough.

17   Place them on a jelly roll pan, cover with a cloth, and allow the dough to rise just to the top of the molds. This should take about ½ hour. (If the dough is permitted to rise for too long a time, or if it rises too much because the kitchen is too warm, the *babas* will have an unpleasantly yeasty flavor.)

18 As soon as the dough has risen sufficiently, put the *babas* to bake in a preheated 375° oven for 20 to 25 minutes. They are ready when they have shrunk away a little from the sides of the molds and are a lovely even brown.
19 Remove the molds from the oven.
20 Slide a thin-bladed knife around the inner edge of the molds and turn out the *babas*.

When the *babas* are lukewarm, soak them in this rum syrup:

1 Into a saucepan put:
2½ cups of granulated sugar
½ teaspoon of cream of tartar
1½ cups of water
½ cup of light rum
2 Simmer for 5 minutes after the sugar has melted. Take care not to let the syrup get too thick.
3 Stand the slightly warm *babas* on a cake rack over a bowl, and pour the syrup slowly over them while it is still hot.
4 Let them soak in the syrup for about half an hour, spooning it over them frequently. You don't want the *babas* to get too soggy, yet they should be well moistened throughout with the rum syrup.
5 Just before serving, you sprinkle the *babas* with more rum.
Or, if you want to be spectacular, heat the rum, ignite it, and pour it over the *babas* which will then come to the table flaming.

Note: You can use this recipe in an 8-inch ring mold instead of the individual *baba* molds. In that case the baking time should be increased to 35 or 40 minutes. The ring-shaped *baba* (properly called a Savarin) is soaked in rum syrup too. It is brushed all over with strained melted down apricot jam and the top of the Savarin is decorated with glacéed cherries and angelica leaves. Its center can be filled with fresh berries, whipped cream or more correctly with pastry cream. (See recipe on page 261.)

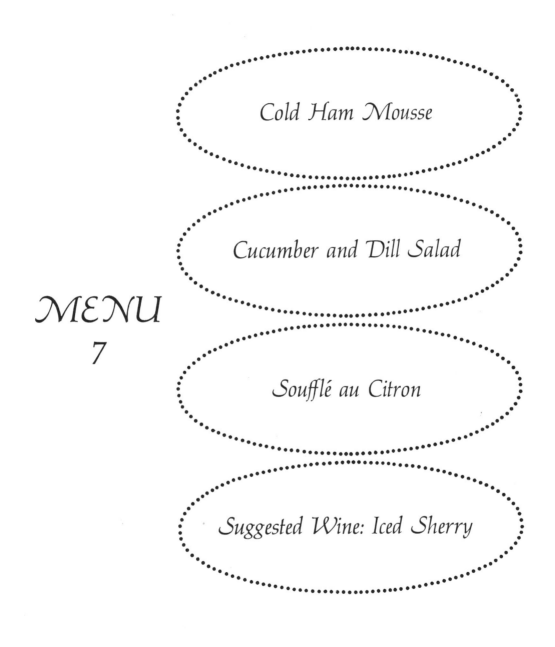

Cold Ham Mousse

Cucumber and Dill Salad

MENU
7

Soufflé au Citron

Suggested Wine: Iced Sherry

Cold Ham Mousse

Serves six

These cold dishes are a delightful way to present food in summer. (You can make this same mousse with salmon, chicken or veal, by the way.) Because they are so attractive, they tempt appetites jaded by the heat. And for the cook, a cold mousse decorated with aspic allows the widest scope for artistic experimentation. In this recipe I have suggested two choices of garnish, but the possibilities are infinite. Decorating with aspic is a cool job, and can be done in stages to suit your convenience. Hard-boiled eggs, truffles, olives, cold vegetables, all lend themselves to aspic-coated designs of your own invention. If you have any artistic talent at all, this is where you can give it free rein. For the fun of cooking is to use as much of yourself, as many of your abilities, as possible. That way cooking becomes a rewarding occupation rather than a dreary chore.

3 cups of ground lean ham
4 thin slices of ham
flour
milk
vegetable oil
gelatine (unflavored)
eggs
heavy cream
tomato paste
Aspic (strong chicken
    or veal stock)
sweet butter
salt
Cayenne
Madeira
    (alternate decoration)
1 pound of fresh young asparagus
pimiento strips

PREPARATION TRAY

ham mousse refrigerated
in prepared soufflé dish

8 ham cornucopias, set

stock for aspic

120

1   Into a tin-lined copper saucepan put: **8 tablespoons of water**
    2 tablespoons of vegetable oil

2   Mix together in a bowl:
    4 tablespoons of flour (not too level)
    1 tablespoon of plain gelatine
    a little salt
    a dash of cayenne

3   Add this to the oil and water in the saucepan.

4   Stir in: **a good 1¼ cups of milk**

5   Stir over the fire until it just boils. (You now have a fairly thick *panade* with which to bind your other ingredients together.)

6   Remove the *panade* from the saucepan to a platter, cover it with transparent wrap and chill it thoroughly. (This part of the recipe and the grinding of 3 cups of ham can be done in advance.)

1   In a mixer bowl, cream: **½ pound (2 sticks) of sweet butter**

2   Add, bit by bit, with the mixer on:
    the chilled *panade*
    3 cups of finely ground lean ham

3   Rub mixture through a strainer or food mill over a large bowl.

4   Fold into the strained mixture:
    1 teaspoon of tomato paste combined with
    2 tablespoons of Madeira
    2 egg whites beaten stiff but not dry, folded into
    1 cup of whipped heavy cream

5   Taste the mousse and correct the seasoning.

6   Fill the mixture into a soufflé dish.

7   If you want a very impressive looking mousse, use a soufflé dish a little too small to hold the entire quantity—a 6-inch dish in this case. Tie a cuff of wax paper around it (see directions on page 352), and oil, do not butter, the wax paper. (You use butter for hot dishes, oil for cold. Butter stiffens and sticks when chilled, defeating your purpose.)

8   Fill the mousse above the edge of the soufflé dish, reserving a little for stuffing ham cornucopias.

9   Put the mousse in the refrigerator to set.

While it is setting, make the following garnish:

1 Line 8 small cornucopia molds with: **8 half slices of ham** that have been cut into triangles. (Fold each triangle of ham around your thumb so it is the shape of a cornucopia, and then place it inside the mold.)

2 Using a pastry bag and plain tube, pipe the remaining ham mousse into each of the cornucopias. Smooth the tops off.

3 Place **a slice of truffle** at the open end and chill thoroughly.

When the cornucopias have chilled and set, coat the open end of each one with the following aspic on the point of setting.

(I must break in here to say that at this point in the recipe, when I am dictating it in the cooking classes, some of my students groan. Yet they were the very ones who ooohed and ahhed at the beautiful finished product. And they found, when they came to the actual making of the mousse and its decoration, that it was fun to be able to create such a professional looking work of culinary art. And not really so difficult after all.)

2 So, for the aspic, put into a saucepan (tin-lined copper or stainless steel) :
4 cups of strong chicken stock, cold and completely fat free. (You scrape off the layer of congealed fat that will have formed on top of the cold stock; see recipe on page 353.)
1 tablespoon of tomato paste
4 tablespoons of plain gelatine
¼ cup of Madeira
3 beaten egg whites

3 Bring this mixture to a rolling boil, beating it slowly but thoroughly with a wire whisk *at all times.* The egg whites will turn white as they cook, and they will rise to the surface, carrying with them all the tiny particles that clouded the stock.

4 Turn off the fire, and allow the pan to stand undisturbed for 15 minutes.

5 Then pour the clarified stock and egg whites through

a colander lined with a damp towel. The stock will strain through into a bowl, clear and transparent, while the egg white and the impurities it collected will remain on the cloth.

6   Pour into a shallow mold:
   about 3 cups of aspic

7   Put it to set in the refrigerator. This will be chopped for garnish later.

Put into a small saucepan, resting in a bowl of chopped ice:
   1 cup of aspic

2   Stir with a spoon until it is on the point of setting (it will become thick and syrupy). Coat the open end of each of the 8 cornucopias with the aspic. Put them, still in their molds, slanting upwards on a rack until the aspic sets.

3   Remove the cornucopias from their molds and arrange them on top of the ham mousse (from which the paper cuff has been removed) like a cartwheel, with the pointed ends at the center and the open ends near the edge.

4   Turn the set aspic out on a piece of wax paper and chop it fine. (The wax paper keeps it from sticking to the board and knife.)

5   Fill the spaces between the cornucopias with this chopped aspic which sparkles like hundreds of little topazes.

You can make any number of decorations with aspic.

If you prefer to make your ham mousse without using a paper cuff, fill a larger soufflé bowl up to 1 inch from the top.

2   When it is chilled and firm, cover the surface with a ¼-inch layer of aspic on the point of setting.

3   Allow that to set, and arrange on top of it:
   8 small bundles of cooked asparagus tips, each trimmed with a band of **pimiento.**

4   Coat the decoration with **aspic**

5   Decorate around the edge of the mousse with **chopped set aspic**

Cucumber and Dill Salad

Serves six

"Cool as a cucumber" is deliciously descriptive of the delicate flavor, the crispness and the pale green color of this ideal hot-weather salad. But it is necessary to improve on nature a bit when serving raw cucumbers. They benefit from a little special handling—being sliced paper thin, standing for a while with salt sprinkled on them, and having their flavor heightened with a little sugar and vinegar. And raw cucumber ought always to be served really well chilled. This is quite a different tasting vegetable when served this way rather than in the fairly thick, unpeeled slices one so often encounters in salads. Try it and see if you don't like this method best.

MARKETING LIST

6 long thin cucumbers
Salt
fresh dill
granulated sugar
white peppercorns
tarragon vinegar
Vegetable oil

PREPARATION TRAY

cucumbers, sliced, salted

fresh dill, chopped

tarragon vinegar

124

Take: **4 long thin cucumbers**

1   First cut off tips, then the stalk ends (it is important to trim them in this order or they will have a bitter taste).

2   Peel them with a potato parer.

3   Cut them into very thin slices. (A *mandoline*, the French slicing gadget on page 13, is ideal for this.)

4   Arrange the slices in a shallow dish.

5   Sprinkle them with:
    a little salt

6   Mix them together and let them stand in a cool place for 1 or 2 hours.
    (The salt will draw out the excess liquid, soften the slices a little, and bring out the taste.)

7   Drain off the liquid and thoroughly dry the cucumber slices on paper towels.

8   In a bowl put the:
    cucumber slices
    1½ heaping tablespoons of finely chopped fresh dill
    1½ teaspoons of granulated sugar
    scant ¾ teaspoon of freshly ground white pepper
    1 tablespoon of tarragon vinegar
    3 tablespoons of vegetable oil

9   Mix well and refrigerate the bowl of salad, covered tightly with transparent wrap.

Be sure to serve this very well chilled.

Soufflé au Citron
(Hot Lemon Soufflé with Sabayon Sauce)

Serves four to six

There is no dessert more pleasing to the palate, sumptuous yet simple, than a hot soufflé. This one carries the tart flavor and fragrance of lemon beneath its puffy golden crust. Served with a frothy sabayon sauce, it is as light as a cloud and a graceful climax to a well-planned dinner. Serving a dessert soufflé takes a bit of careful planning too. But you can have everything prepared in advance except the beating of the egg whites and the blending of them with the lemon mixture. The ingredients for the sabayon sauce can be waiting in their bowl until ten minutes before serving time. Pop your soufflé in the oven an hour before you will be ready for dessert, excuse yourself in time to whip up the sauce, and reappear as the hostess with the mostest concern to give her guests a very special treat.

MARKETING LIST

Lemons
Sweet butter
flour
Salt
light Cream
Granulated sugar
Confectioners' Sugar

PREPARATION TRAY

6-cup soufflé dish, buttered and cuffed

3 lemons, rind grated, and lemons juiced

Prepare a 6-cup soufflé dish according to directions on page 352. Set it aside until needed.

1   In a small heavy pan (preferably tin-lined copper) melt: **3 tablespoons (1½ ounces) of sweet butter**

2   With a wire whisk, stir in, off the fire:
3 slightly rounded tablespoons of flour
a pinch of salt

3   When the *roux* (warm mixture of flour and butter) is smooth, mix in:
1 cup of light cream

4   Turn up the fire, and stir over the fire until it only just comes to a boil. When this white sauce has thickened, add, off the fire:
the finely grated yellow rind of 2 lemons
⅓ cup of strained lemon juice
3 heaping tablespoons of granulated sugar

5   Off the fire, beat in, *one at a time*:
4 egg yolks

6   Put into a large metal bowl:
6 egg whites

7   Beat with a large wire whisk until bowl can be reversed and the stiff egg whites will adhere to it. (Beating egg whites this way instead of with an automatic mixer is harder work, but it is worth it. You get more air, and therefore more volume, in your eggs, and you do not overbeat them and get them too dry. For a really airy soufflé this is the best.)

8   Pour all the lemon sauce *evenly* all over the egg whites.

9   Fold it in very carefully and lightly with a rubber scraper. The consistency of your egg whites and this folding process are the keys to a successful soufflé.

10   Pour the soufflé mixture into the prepared dish.

11   Sprinkle the top with **granulated sugar**

12   Stand the dish in a pan of hot water and bake it in a preheated 375° oven for exactly 1 hour. It should

be lightly browned and well puffed, and a cake tester should come out clean.

13 Remove the soufflé from the oven, and dust the top with **confectioners' sugar.** Remove the paper cuff from the dish.

You may serve the lemon soufflé just as it is, which is pretty delicious. Or you can give it the super de luxe addition of the following hot sabayon (also known as zabaglione) sauce:

1 In a small china bowl put:

2 whole eggs

4 egg yolks

2 tablespoons of lemon juice

4 teaspoons of grated lemon rind

6 heaping tablespoons of granulated sugar

2 Stand the bowl in a small frying pan of hot (but *not* boiling) water over a slow fire.

3 Beat with a rotary beater until the sabayon sauce holds its shape.

Start to prepare this sauce about 10 minutes before the soufflé is done, as a frothy sabayon cannot wait long before being served.

Incidentally this sabayon served as is or with sherry substituted for the lemon flavoring is a lovely dessert on its own. Spoon it into champagne glasses and serve it with Palets de Dames (see recipe on page 215) or some other *petits fours secs.* I'm always delighted when one recipe will serve several purposes!

Smoked Salmon with Capers
and Lemon

Chicken Paprika

Gnocchi Parisienne

MENU
8

Tossed Salad

Maple Cake

Suggested Wine: Chablis

Smoked Salmon with Capers and Lemon

Serves four

If you are fortunate enough to live in a city where you can get really good smoked salmon, count your blessings! There is no more delicious first course, and there is no preparation necessary. But everything depends upon the quality of your salmon.

The Nova Scotia salmon or the smoked salmon imported from Scotland are the best. They are neither too salty nor too oily—the two things you want most to avoid with this fish.

Once you have your lovely salmon, the rest is simplicity itself. Your plates should be chilled, and the salmon will go directly on them with no lettuce leaves or any other distractions. I even go so far as to think the pale pink slices look best on very simple china, preferably white. One need not improve upon perfection!

MARKETING LIST

½ pound of smoked
   salmon, sliced thin
lemons
capers
sweet butter
pumpernickel bread

PREPARATION TRAY

pumpernickel bread,
sliced thin and buttered

lemons, cut in wedges

1   On chilled individual plates (salad size) put:
    2 or 3 thin slices of smoked salmon

2   Sprinkle over them:
    a few capers (These are the pickled berries of a plant that is related to the mustard, and they are pleasantly tangy.)

3   Put on the plate:
    1 or two wedges of lemon (At the Four Seasons Restaurant in New York, they wrap their lemon wedges tightly in a layer of fine cheesecloth or gauze. That way when you squeeze the lemon the juice is less likely to squirt in someone's eye, and no seeds can drop into your food. A nice touch.)

4   Serve separately:
    thinly sliced fingers of **pumpernickel bread** that have been lightly spread with **sweet butter**

Smoked salmon is excellent served as an hors d'oeuvre in the living room, with drinks. In that case, arrange it on a large platter with the capers and lemon, serve with the buttered pumpernickel, and give your guests hors d'oeuvres plates, forks, knives and napkins. This is one hors d'oeuvre that lives up to the meaning of the word—it is literally "outside of work," since so little work is involved.

Chicken Paprika

Serves four

Anything with paprika is apt to be a Hungarian specialty—
it is the Hungarian name for the sweet pepper that colors
and flavors goulash, the national dish. And in this recipe
the combination of paprika and sour cream does something
marvelous to chicken. French cooks, who know a good
thing when they see it, have borrowed paprika dishes from
the Hungarians. But they are more inclined to use the
Spanish paprika, which is sweeter than the Hungarian. This
recipe calls for Spanish paprika, but don't worry if you
can't get it. Use the other if you must, and you will have
a more pungent, less subtle sauce.

MARKETING LIST

3½ pound chicken for
roasting
(not a big one)
Salt butter
brandy
onion
Celery
Carrot
Spanish paprika
flour
tomato paste
meat glaze
Chicken stock
heavy Sour Cream
green pepper
red pepper
(if this is not
available, use
canned
pimiento)

PREPARATION TRAY

chicken, washed, trussed and seasoned

onion, carrot and celery, sliced

chicken stock (see recipe on page 353)

green pepper, blanched and diced

red pepper, blanched and diced

132

1   Take a **3½ pound roasting chicken,** truss it and brown it according to the recipe for *Poulet Majorca* on page 326.

    2   Flame the chicken with:
    3 tablespoons of brandy

    3   Remove the chicken from the *cocotte* or casserole and add to the pan:
    2 tablespoons (1 ounce—¼ stick) of butter
    a little sliced onion
    1 stalk of celery, sliced
    1 small carrot, sliced (Don't use too much carrot as its sweetness will spoil your sauce.)

    4   Cover, and cook the vegetables very slowly until they are soft.

    5   Then stir in, off the fire:
    1 good tablespoon of Spanish paprika

    6   Cook slowly for 5 minutes, stirring occasionally. If the paprika scorches it will taste unpleasantly bitter, so watch it.

    7   Add: **3 level tablespoons of flour**
    Cook slowly.

    8   Stir in:
    1 tablespoon of tomato paste
    1 teaspoon of meat glaze

    9   Stir in, off the fire:
    1¾ cups of chicken stock (See recipe on page 353.)

   10   Stir over the fire until the sauce comes to a boil.

   11   Let it simmer a few minutes.

   12   Rub it through a strainer.

   13   Return the strained sauce to the *cocotte*.

   14   Carefully carve the chicken (see directions on page 356) and add to the sauce.

   15   Place the *cocotte* on the top shelf of a preheated 375° oven.

   16   Cook for 45 minutes, basting occasionally.

1   When done, arrange the chicken pieces in a casserole.

    2   Bring the sauce again to a boil.

    3   Beat in slowly, with a wire whisk:
    1½ cups of heavy sour cream
    (Take a dab of the sour cream on a rubber scraper,

scrape it off with the whisk, and quickly and lightly beat it into the sauce. The sauce must be kept *below* the boiling point from now on or the sour cream will curdle. Continue beating the cream in, dab by dab until you have used it all.)

4   Add at the last:

1 finely diced green pepper that has been blanched and drained. (Put the whole pepper in a pan, cover with cold water, bring to a boil, then drain pepper. Cut it in half, discard the seeds, and with a sharp knife, chop into fine dice.)

1 finely diced red pepper that has been blanched and drained.

(If you cannot get a red pepper, just dice a canned pimiento, which does not have to be blanched first.)

5   Pour this sauce carefully over the chicken.

6   Put a good spoonful of **plain sour cream** on top.

A true Hungarian rhapsody!

Gnocchi Parisienne

(Parisian Gnocchi)

Serves four

Nearly every European country has its favorite way of preparing gnocchi, little dumplings or flat cakes made of some kind of starch. The Italians make theirs of a semolina porridge (see recipe on page 191), the Germans use a potato dough, Austrian and Hungarian cooks poach a cream puff paste (pâte à choux) to which cheese has been added. Parisian gnocchi are an adaptation of this last, frequently served with a Mornay sauce and browned under the broiler.

These are all very good, very light ways to serve a starch with your meals, and something of a novelty on American menus.

PREPARATION TRAY

gnocchi can be poached in advance

au gratin **dish, buttered**

Mornay sauce made and kept covered
(see recipe on page 93)

or Parmesan cheese, grated

butter, melted

MARKETING LIST

butter
flour
eggs
Dyon mustard
Dry mustard
Salt
Cayenne pepper
Parmesan cheese
Mornay sauce

For *gnocchi Parisienne* you start as though you were going to make cream puffs.

1   In a small heavy pan put:
      1½ cups of cold water, measured carefully
      3 tablespoons (1½ ounces) of butter (If the butter is cold, cut it into small pieces to facilitate melting. If the water boils before the butter is completely melted, some of the water will evaporate, and that will throw off the balance of your recipe.)

2   The moment the water reaches a rolling boil, throw in all at once:
      1½ cups of flour

3   Off the fire, mix with a wooden spoon until you have a smooth dough that comes away from the sides of the pan and forms a large ball.

4   Put it into a mixer bowl.

5   Add, one at a time:
      3 large or 4 small eggs

6   Beat until each egg is incorporated into the dough before adding the next one.

7   Beat the last one until the dough is shiny.

8   Beat in:
      1 level teaspoon of Dijon mustard
      ½ teaspoon of dry mustard
      1 level teaspoon of salt
      a good shake of cayenne
      ⅓ cup of freshly grated Parmesan cheese

9   Mix well.

10   Fill this dough into a pastry bag with a large plain tube.

Have ready a large pan: **¾ full of boiling salted water**

1   Reduce the heat so the water just simmers. It should scarcely move.

2   Pipe out 1-inch long pieces of *gnocchi* dough, cut them off with a knife, and let them drop right into the hot water.

They will sink to the bottom, but as they poach they puff up to the size of walnuts and will float to the top.

3   Cover the surface of the hot water with a double layer of paper towels. (This will keep the *gnocchi* moist when they float. Otherwise their top sides will be exposed to the air and will dry out.)

4   In about 15 or 20 minutes the *gnocchi* will be set. Be sure the water remains at the gentlest simmer throughout, because if it boils, the *gnocchi* will disintegrate and you will be left with a lovely pan full of mush.

   You can test for doneness by cutting one *gnocchi* in half to make sure it is set.

5   When you serve this with chicken paprika you won't want a sauce on the *gnocchi*. Simply sprinkle them with a little **melted butter** and **grated cheese,** and brown under the broiler in an *au gratin* dish if you wish.

To serve with a Mornay sauce, butter an *au gratin* dish. Remove the *gnocchi* with a slotted spoon and drain them on paper towels. Arrange them in the dish and cover them with Mornay sauce (see recipe on page 93) . Brown under a hot broiler for a few minutes.

One great advantage to serving *gnocchi*—aside from the fact that they are so light and delicious—is that they can be poached in advance and then refrigerated. When you need them you can let them come to room temperature, cover them with the hot sauce, put them under the broiler, and there you are!

Tossed Salad

(See recipe on page 69.)

Maple Cake

Serves eight

Every home cook should know how to make one simple layer cake with a fabulous frosting. This one is a beauty, and you must use a good maple syrup so it will taste as good as it looks. The beaten egg whites in the cake and in the frosting make it high, white and handsome, a very light morsel in spite of looking so rich.

MARKETING LIST

vegetable shortening
Granulated sugar
eggs
Cake Flour
milk
salt
baking powder
butter
Maple syrup

PREPARATION TRAY

2 8-inch layer pans, buttered and
lined with paper

cake racks, oiled

frosting made

1   In a mixer bowl, cream: **1 cup of vegetable shortening**
        1 cup of granulated sugar
   2   When it is light and fluffy, add: **1 whole egg**
     and, one at a time: **3 egg yolks**
   3   Sift: **1½ cups of cake flour** (*Not* self-rising.)
   4   Add it to the mixture at moderate speed, 2 or 3 tablespoons at a time.
   5   Alternating with: **a little milk** until you have used **½ cup of milk**
     Begin and end with the flour.
   6   Remove the bowl from the mixer, and stir in carefully with a rubber scraper:
     2 level teaspoons of baking powder
     3 egg whites, stiffly beaten

1   Butter: 2 8-inch layer pans
   2   Line the bottoms with circles of wax paper.
   3   Butter again.
   4   Divide the batter evenly between the two tins.
   5   Bake in a preheated 350° oven, with the rack in the middle slot, for ½ hour.
   6   Test for doneness with a cake wire. If it comes out clean, the cake is baked.
   7   Remove the pans from the oven, and after a few minutes turn the layers out to cool on oiled racks.

Sandwich and cover the layers with the following maple frosting:
   1   Put in a small saucepan: **3 cups of maple syrup**
   2   Let it boil for 5 minutes.
   3   In a mixer bowl put: **¾ cup of egg whites** (about 5 egg whites depending upon size) .
   4   Beat until the egg whites form peaks.
   5   Slowly pour on the boiled syrup in a thin trickle, beating hard the entire time.
   6   Continue beating until the frosting holds its shape.
   7   Sandwich the layers, putting the flat side down on the lower layer, and the flat side up on the top layer.
   8   Cover the cake with frosting, and with a wide spatula make a cartwheel of raised domes on the top.

"Scrumptious" is the word for this.

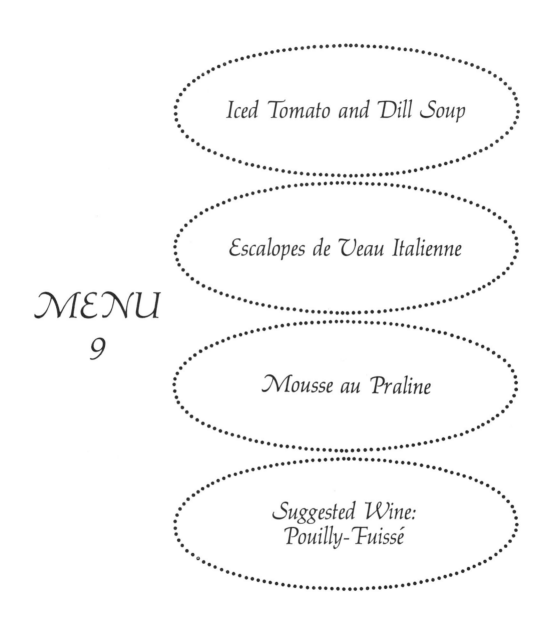

MENU
9

Iced Tomato and Dill Soup

Escalopes de Veau Italienne

Mousse au Praline

Suggested Wine:
Pouilly-Fuissé

Iced Tomato and Dill Soup

Serves six

This is a delightful chilled soup to serve in warm weather. The fresh tomatoes give it a flavor that is incomparable— far more subtle and delicate than the all-too-familiar canned tomato soups. And the chopped fresh dill adds just the right fillip. I believe it was the Duchess of Windsor who once complained, "Soup is so boring." But with a soup like this, one might take an answer out of Porgy and Bess, and reply, "It Ain't Necessarily So."

PREPARATION TRAY

tomatoes, sliced

onions, sliced

garlic, peeled

rice flour and water mixture, prepared

fresh dill, chopped

½ tomato, skinned and shredded

MARKETING LIST

ripe tomatoes
yellow onions
garlic
salt
white peppercorns
Italian tomato paste
rice flour
light cream
heavy cream
fresh dill

1   Cut into fine slices:

      2 pounds of very ripe tomatoes, washed
      2 yellow onions, peeled
      2 large cloves of garlic, peeled

2   Put into a large heavy pan with:

      1½ cups of water
      1 teaspoon of salt
      ¼ teaspoon of freshly ground white pepper

3   Cover the pan.

4   Cook slowly until the tomatoes are soft and mushy (about 20 minutes).

5   Taste for seasoning, remembering that chilled foods lose a bit of their flavor and therefore need a little more.

6   Remove from the fire and stir in:

      2 tablespoons of Italian tomato paste

1   In a quart measuring pitcher put:

      4 tablespoons of rice flour
      ½ cup of cold water

2   Stir until you have a smooth paste.

3   Then add:

      2½ cups of cold water, mixing until smooth.

4   Stir this mixture into the tomato soup.

5   Bring it to a boil.

6   Put the soup through a strainer or food mill.

7   Chill it thoroughly (for several hours).

8   When you are ready to serve, add:

      1½ cups of light cream
      ½ cup of heavy cream
      2 generous tablespoons of freshly chopped dill

Serve this soup icy cold and in chilled cups. Or better yet, serve it in bowls surrounded by chopped ice. The chill seems to accentuate the tang of the ingredients.

Escalopes de Veau Italienne
(Veal Scallops Italian Style)

Serves six

Veal can be rather pallid and bland unless it is prepared with ingredients that lend it zest. That is why Italian recipes for veal are particularly popular—they are nothing if not zesty.

This is a delicious and relatively simple way to prepare veal scallops which are at their best in the company of tomatoes, zucchini, garlic and cheese. I particularly like this dish because it is such a good-tasting and good-looking way of serving meat and vegetables together. So often vegetables are forced into a meal for dietetic reasons alone, but here they are a necessary and excellent part of the whole, giving you vitamins and pleasure at one and the same time.

MARKETING LIST

6 Veal scallops ¼" thick
Salt
fresh black peppercorns
flour
Salt butter
brandy
meat glaze
tomato paste
potato flour
Chicken stock
Dry white wine
dry sherry
red currant jelly
2 zucchini
6 tomatoes
garlic
imported Swiss gruyère cheese
Parmesan cheese

PREPARATION TRAY

veal slices, flattened

zucchini and tomato, cooked but not mixed

Gruyère cheese, sliced and wrapped

chicken stock

garlic, chopped

butter, melted

Parmesan cheese, grated

144

1   Put between 2 sheets of wax paper:

> **6 slices of veal scallops cut less than ¼ inch thick**
> Pound them with the heel of your hand to break down the membrane.

2   Dust the slices lightly with **salt, pepper and flour** (Clap each one between your palms to give it a light, even dusting of flour.)

3   In a heavy sauté pan heat:

> **2 scant tablespoons (1 scant ounce) of salt butter**

4   When the butter is very hot put in:

> 2 slices of veal, lying flat and not touching. (This is important or they will not brown, they will stew.)

5   Place a flat lid on the meat, with a weight on top of it, so it presses the slices flat as they brown.

6   When the slices have browned on one side, turn them over and brown them on the other side without the lid. Remove veal and keep it warm.

7   Continue cooking the veal, 2 pieces at a time until they have all been browned.

8   Now put all 6 slices back in the pan. In a tiny pot heat: **¼ cup of brandy**

> Ignite it and pour it over the veal.

When it has been flamed, remove the veal from the pan.

1   Stir the juices well, and add:

> **1 good tablespoon of butter**

2   Stir in, off the fire:

> **1 teaspoon of meat glaze.** (If the veal browned very well, you will have a good deal of natural glaze in your pan. Use 1 teaspoon, more or less, depending upon how much veal glaze you have.)
> **1 teaspoon tomato paste**
> **2 teaspoons potato flour**

3   Mix in, still off the fire:

> **1¼ cups of good chicken stock**
> **¼ cup of dry white wine**
> **2 tablespoons of dry sherry**
> **1 teaspoon of red currant jelly**
> **a little freshly ground black pepper**

4   Stir the sauce over the fire until it boils.

145

5 Reduce it to a simmer and put back the veal.
6 Cover the veal well with the sauce.
7 Cover the pan with wax paper and the lid. (This cuts down condensation and prevents moisture from diluting your sauce.)
8 Simmer gently for 10 minutes only. The veal is cooked. It only wants to absorb the sauce.

While the veal is simmering:
1 Take: **2 zucchini** and cut them in half lengthwise, then in slices ¼ inch thick.
2 Place the slices in a pan, cover them with cold water, and bring to a boil.
3 Drain, and return the zucchini to the pan with:
1½ tablespoons of butter
½ teaspoon of salt
a little freshly ground black pepper
4 Cover with buttered wax paper.
5 Cover with tightly fitting lid and cook for 5 minutes only.

1 In a frying pan put:
4 tablespoons (2 ounces—½ stick) of butter
6 skinned and thickly sliced tomatoes
2 good teaspoons of chopped garlic
a bit of freshly cracked black pepper
2 Cook briskly for 2 minutes only.
3 Mix the zucchini and tomatoes gently but well.
4 Arrange on the bottom of an oval oven-proof serving dish.
5 Put the veal slices on top, overlapping one another.
6 On top of each veal slice place: **a thin slice of imported Swiss Gruyère cheese**
7 Pour over the sauce. Sprinkle generously with **freshly grated Parmesan cheese** and a little **melted butter**
8 Place under the broiler until the cheese browns.

This is a delicious and convenient dish because it can be assembled in advance and kept warm. Incidentally the tomatoes and zucchini prepared in this manner are a fine vegetable dish on their own.

146

Mousse au Praline

(Praline Mousse)

Serves six

If you want a beautiful dessert for a buffet, this is it. We put it out on the sweet table in my restaurant, The Egg Basket, in a handsome crystal bowl, and even chocolate addicts have been known to bypass the mousse au chocolat or the chocolate roll in favor of this creamy delicacy. The praline flavoring is not as much used in this country as it is in France, so it still has a certain novelty. I'll wager that this is a dessert you won't meet at every other dinner party in the neighborhood.

MARKETING LIST

eggs
granulated sugar
salt
light rum
gelatin
lemon
heavy cream
Confectioners' sugar
fresh Vanilla bean
whole filberts
Praline powder

PREPARATION TRAY

praline powder (see recipe on page 351)

lemon juice

1 cup of heavy cream, whipped

¾ cup of heavy cream,
whipped and flavored

1 Place in a mixer bowl: **2 whole eggs and 2 egg yolks**
         6 tablespoons of granulated sugar
         a pinch of salt
  2 Beat in a mixer at full speed until the mixture is thick enough to hold its shape.
  3 Remove the bowl from the mixer and stir in:
         3 tablespoons of light rum

1 In a small pan over a slow fire put: **1 packet of gelatine**
         1 tablespoon of lemon juice
         4 tablespoons of water
  2 Stir with a metal spoon until the gelatine is completely dissolved and no longer granular.
  3 Let it cool for a few minutes.
  4 Carefully stir the dissolved gelatine into the mousse, gradually, with a rubber scraper.
  5 Then fold in, a little at a time, still with scraper:
         1 cup of heavy cream, whipped stiff
         3 tablespoons of praline powder (see page 351)
  6 Fill the mousse into an 8-inch shallow crystal bowl.
  7 Put it in the refrigerator for several hours.

When the mousse has set, decorate the top with whipped cream:
  1 In a large metal bowl, over another bowl of ice, place: **¾ cup of heavy cream**
  2 Beat with large wire whisk until it begins to thicken.
  3 Then add: **1 tablespoon of confectioners' sugar**
         1 inch of fresh vanilla bean, slit up one side. Scrape the tiny black seeds from pod into the cream.
  4 Continue beating until the cream is stiff. Fill into a pastry bag with a large star tube. Pipe designs around the top of the mousse. Decorate it with **whole filbert nuts,** and serve the praline mousse well chilled.

The secret of a creamy smooth mousse lies in having your gelatine thoroughly dissolved, and then stirring it into the egg and sugar mixture evenly. The whipped cream, too, must be just stiff enough, and must be gradually and completely blended with the other ingredients. If these two steps are performed with care, you will have a perfect result every time.

148

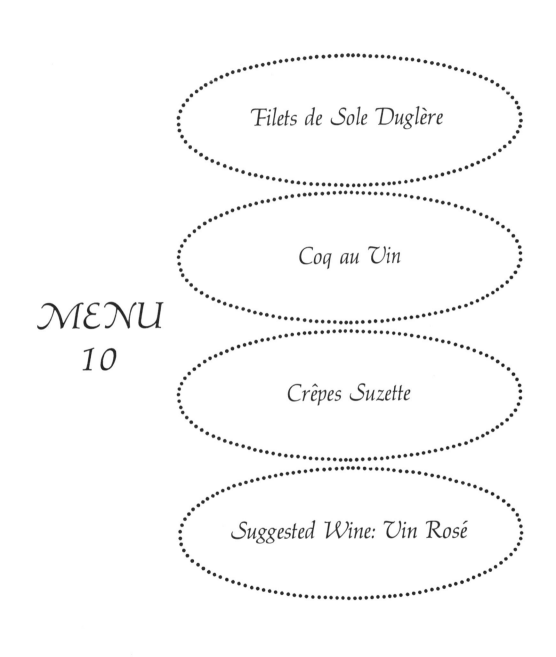

**MENU
10**

Filets de Sole Duglère

Coq au Vin

Crêpes Suzette

Suggested Wine: Vin Rosé

Filets de Sole Duglère
(Fillets of Sole with Fresh Tomatoes)

Serves six

Poaching fish in wine and serving it with a sauce based on its cooking liquor is the classic method in French cuisine. There are a remarkable number of variations on that theme, but this one, Duglère, which uses tomatoes, I like especially. It was named for the famous chef of the Café Anglais which flourished in Paris many years ago. Duglère had the happy thought of flavoring a cream sauce with morsels of fresh tomato, and thus immortalized his name.

Tomatoes are easily obtainable all year round, and they combine superlatively with delicate fish. If your family has grown bored with the same old cycle of fried, broiled and baked fish, give them a change with this. I would bet that as a result, inexpensive and nutritious fish will take its place with the most favored gourmet delicacies in your repertoire.

When you serve Filets de Sole Duglère with a border of duchess potatoes piped around the serving platter (see recipe on page 75) it is an excellent luncheon dish.

MARKETING LIST

6 whole fillets of gray sole
lemon
mushrooms
tomatoes
dry white wine
butter
light cream
Parmesan cheese
flour
parsley
bread crumbs
salt
cayenne pepper
white pepper

PREPARATION TRAY

fish, washed, dried, seasoned, placed on buttered baking dish

poaching liquid ready

tomatoes, skinned, quartered and pipped

tomato pulp, strained

Parmesan cheese, grated

parsley, chopped

butter, melted

150

1   Wash the **sole fillets** in a little **lemon juice** and **water.** (This is always a good thing to do with fish unless it has been freshly caught. It makes the flesh whiter and does away with the fishy smell of any but the most recent catch.) Dry well on paper towels.
2   Melt a **little butter** and brush an oblong oven-glass baking dish with it.
3   Season the outer (dark) sides of the fillets with:
a little salt
a dash of cayenne
4   Fold the fillets over lengthwise, and arrange them on the bias on the buttered baking dish.

Pour over them the following sauce:
1   In a small pan melt:
3 tablespoons (1½ ounces) of salt butter
2   Add: **3 small firm mushrooms, sliced**
3   Shake the pan until the mushrooms are well coated with butter.
4   Then add: **1 tablespoon of lemon juice**
a dash of salt
a sprinkle of freshly ground white pepper
5   Cook briskly for 2 minutes only.
6   Add: **1 generous cup of dry white wine**
⅜ cup of water
7   Bring this slowly to a boil.
8   Carefully spoon all of this sauce over the fillets.
9   Cover the baking dish with a double piece of buttered wax paper.
10   Poach in a preheated 350° oven for 15 minutes.
11   Remove the baking dish from the oven and carefully arrange the poached fillets on a hot, oven-proof serving dish. Cover them with the wax paper to keep them warm.

They will be served with the following sauce:
1   Strain the liquid in which the sole poached, and set it aside.
2   Pour boiling water over:
4 medium-sized firm tomatoes

151

3   Count to 10, pour off the water, and plunge the tomatoes into cold water.

4   Peel the skin off; cut the tomatoes into quarters..

5   Remove the pith and rub it through a fine strainer. This should give you about ¾ cup of fresh tomato pulp.

6   Cut the remaining tomato quarters into fine shreds. (All of this can be done while the fish is poaching.)

1   In a small tin-lined copper pan melt:
    6 tablespoons (3 ounces—¾ stick) of sweet butter

2   Stir in, off the fire:
    4½ slightly rounded tablespoons of flour
    ½ teaspoon of salt
    a dash of cayenne

3   When this is a smooth paste add, still off the fire:
    the strained fish stock
    the fresh tomato pulp

4   Stir over the fire until it thickens and just boils.

5   Then add: **¾ cup of light cream**
    ⅜ cup of freshly grated Parmesan cheese

6   Stir in, bit by bit:
    1 tablespoon of sweet butter cut in small pieces

7   Let the sauce simmer for about 5 minutes.

8   Then add: **1 tablespoon of chopped fresh parsley**
    the shredded tomato

9   Before you cover the fillets of sole with this sauce, be sure that any excess liquid from the fish has been poured or wiped from the serving dish. It would dilute the sauce.

10   Carefully spoon the sauce over the fillets.

11   Sprinkle with: **1½ tablespoons of dry bread crumbs**
    1½ tablespoons of grated Parmesan cheese
    3 tablespoons (1½ ounces) of melted butter (dot the surface lightly) .

12   Brown the dish quickly under a hot broiler just before serving.

Coq au Vin

(Young Rooster Cooked in Wine)

Serves six

2 2½ pound Chickens
(whole)
6 Chicken livers
baby white onions
button mushrooms
Chablis
Burgundy
brandy
Dry Sherry
Calvados
tomato paste
meat glaze
potato flour
Chicken stock
lean salt pork
or ham
parsley
Salt butter
Sugar
salt
white pepper
red currant jelly
white bread

We do not have anything in our poultry markets to compare with the young cockerels that are used for this classic dish in Burgundy, where it originated. I think you come closest to the original if you use young chickens rather than capon, as is sometimes suggested, for the latter is too fat and rich for this particular preparation, even though at one time in its life it was indeed a cockerel. Which proves that one can be too literal in translating—even recipes—from the French, and thereby miss the whole point. I prefer Coq au Vin cooked in a mixture of red wine, white wine, brandy and sherry because I find this orchestration of spirits produces a more interesting result than the Burgundy wine alone. If the purists are shocked by this heresy they may use red wine exclusively, but not, I hope, until they have tried the dish once this way. Our scientifically raised poultry, lacking the strength and flavor of the French barnyard variety, need all the help they can get from the rest of the stewpot. This recipe aims to give it to them.

PREPARATION TRAY

chickens, washed and trussed

24 baby onions, blanched

¼ pound of salt pork, blanched

½ pound of mushrooms, halved or quartered

lemon juice

6 slices of bread, trimmed and cut in half diagonally

parsley, chopped

wines and brandy, measured out in separate cups

chicken stock

153

Tie up the chickens carefully. (See directions on page 356.)

1 In a heavy 3-quart Dutch oven heat slowly:
    5 tablespoons (2½ ounces) of salt butter

    2 When it foams put in, breast side down:
    2 trussed chickens

    3 Cover the pan and brown very slowly all over—each side of the breast, each leg, the wishbone (known in England as "the merry thought"), the back. Turn chickens by means of a wooden spoon inserted in the cavity.

The slower the chickens brown, the better. A good slow browning keeps the flesh moist and creates a good glaze. This should take about 30 minutes, and the chickens should be a little under half-cooked.

1 In a small pot heat: **⅓ cup of Calvados**

    2 Ignite it, and pour it blazing over the chickens.

    3 Remove the chickens from the pan and set them aside.

    4 Stir the pan juices to lift up any glaze.

    5 Stir into them, off the fire:
    3 teaspoons of potato flour
    1 teaspoon of tomato paste
    1 teaspoon of meat glaze. (If your chickens browned very well, you may find you will need less of this.)

    6 When the mixture is smooth, stir in, still off the fire: **1¼ cups of chicken stock**
    ¼ cup of Burgundy
    ¼ cup of dry white wine
    ¼ cup of brandy
    ¼ cup of sherry
    1 teaspoon of red currant jelly
    a little cracked white pepper
    (No salt, because the meat glaze is salty, but it is always wise to taste for seasoning.)

    7 Stir this sauce over the fire until it boils. Then reduce it to a simmer.

8 Carefully carve the chickens for casserole. (See directions on page 356.)

9 Add the pieces to the sauce and baste well.

10 Place pan, without the lid, on the top shelf of a preheated 375° oven.

11 Cook for 35 or 40 minutes, uncovered, basting once or twice.

1 While the chicken is cooking, put into a pan:

2 dozen baby white onions, skinned

2 Cover them with **cold water**

3 Bring it to a boil, and then remove and drain the blanched onions.

1 In a sauté pan heat until foaming:

3 tablespoons (1½ ounces) of butter

2 Add the drained, blanched onions.

3 Shake over a brisk flame until the onions begin to brown.

4 Sprinkle them with:
½ teaspoon of salt
a little freshly ground white pepper
2 tablespoons of granulated sugar
(This will give the onions a marvelous flavor and a rich caramel-like glaze.)

5 Continue shaking the pan over the fire until the onions have acquired a deep brown glaze.

6 Remove from the heat.

1 Next, cut into dice:

¼ pound of lean salt pork (or ham if you cannot get the salt pork)

2 Blanch it. (Put into a pan of cold water, bring to a boil, and drain.) *Omit this step when using ham.*

3 Add the salt pork or ham to the onion pan, turn up the heat, and when the diced pork gets crisp season it with salt, pepper, a little sugar, and shake in the pan until it is golden brown.

1 Last of all, in a small sauté pan heat until foaming:

> **2 tablespoons (1 ounce—¼ stick) of butter**

2 Add: **½ pound of button mushrooms.** (If the mushrooms are large, half or quarter them, if small leave them whole.)

3 Coat the mushrooms well in the foaming butter.

4 Add: **½ teaspoon of lemon juice**
a little salt
a little freshly ground white pepper

5 Shake over a brisk fire for only 3 or 4 minutes.

6 Add the onions, salt pork and mushrooms to the *coq au vin* 10 minutes before serving.
(Incidentally, this is a dish that can be prepared up to this point the day before. It is delicious reheated.)

1 Trim the crusts from: **6 slices of white bread**

2 Cut them in half diagonally.

3 In a sauté pan heat until foaming:
4 tablespoons (2 ounces—½ stick) of butter

4 Place the bread triangles in the foaming butter and keep them flat by resting a small cake tin on top of them. This weight will give your bread snippets (I love that word!) a nice even tan. Turn them and brown the other side. Keep a close watch or the bread might burn!)

To serve: Arrange the *coq au vin* in an oval casserole with the two pairs of drumsticks crossed upright at either end. The other pieces of chicken and the sides of the casserole will support them. The drumsticks should be wearing little paper frills.

Sprinkle with **freshly chopped parsley,** and surround the casserole with snippets (I do love that word!) of bread fried to a golden brown.

Crêpes Suzette
(Flaming Pancakes with Orange Butter)

Serves six

This is a dessert designed to build up the host's ego. It is a pyromaniac's delight, accomplished with what seems to be a small indoor bonfire and great showmanship. With a little practice, the man of the house can learn to heat the orange butter and the folded pancakes and blaze them in a chafing dish with some flaming brandy. The really tricky part will all have been done in the kitchen hours before, but the hand that shakes the chafing dish for that final flaming display will rock the world. And it will be a man's world at that. For Crêpes Suzette is a man's dessert, created to dramatize the flamboyant male whether he be host, maitre d'hotel or just the guy who is ordering them to woo his lady love. On top of all this, they happen to taste marvelous too.

MARKETING LIST

flour
egg
salt
milk
sweet butter
superfine granulated
  sugar
Navel oranges
Curaçao, Cognac
  or Grand Marnier
lump sugar
granulated sugar

PREPARATION TRAY

pancakes, made

orange butter, made and refrigerated

orange rind, slivered

6 lumps of sugar, rubbed over orange skin

fresh orange juice

liqueur or cognac

navel oranges, skinned and sectioned

note: if the *crêpes* are to be warmed and blazed at the table use one of your handsomest trays for the preparation tray.

157

The pancakes, or *crêpes,* can be made several hours ahead of time, and if you stack them on a cake rack and cover them with an inverted bowl they will not dry out before you are ready to use them. This recipe will give you 9 large (omelet-pan sized) or 12 smaller (6 inch) *crêpes.* Remember that this is a very, very thin pancake, and needs only enough batter to coat the bottom of the pan.

1   In a mixing bowl put:
> **4 rounded tablespoons of flour**
> **1 egg**
> **1 egg yolk**
> **a pinch of salt**
> **4 tablespoons of milk**
> **2 tablespoons (1 ounce—¼ stick) of melted sweet butter**

2   Beat the mixture with a small wire whisk until it is smooth and velvety.

3   Then add:
about ¾ cup of milk (Add this gradually, and continue beating. When the mixture reaches the consistency of light cream, you have used enough milk and need not use it all.)

4   Pour the *crêpe* batter into a covered container and refrigerate it for at least half an hour. (This is an excellent batter to keep on hand in your refrigerator at all times, as you can make *crêpes* with any number of fillings for a last-minute entrée or dessert.)

1   Heat well a heavy *crêpe* or omelet pan.

2   Rub the bottom out with very little **salt butter,** using a wad of wax paper. The pan must be hot enough for the butter to almost smoke.

3   If the batter has become too thick after standing, thin it out with a few drops of milk.

4   Cover the bottom of the pan with a thin coat of batter. A ladle that holds about 4 tablespoons should be just about right for pouring the batter.

Lift the pan and tilt it around the moment the batter is put in, to spread it evenly and thinly.

5 Brown the *crêpe* on one side. (This should only take a minute or so.)

6 When it is evenly browned, turn it carefully, using a spatula (it is as delicate as a bridal handkerchief). Let the other side cook for about another ½ minute. It will not be as beautifully browned as the first side, but that doesn't matter since *crêpes* are like people on first acquaintance—they show only their best side.

7 Use up all the batter in this fashion.

When you are ready to serve the *crêpes*, lay them wrong side up, and spread the less attractive side with the following beautiful orange butter:

1 In a mixer bowl put:
6 tablespoons (3 ounces—¾ stick) of sweet butter

2 Beat it until it is very light and fluffy.

3 Then add slowly:
**3 heaping tablespoons of superfine granulated sugar
the grated rind of 1 orange
2 tablespoons of curaçao, cognac or Grand Marnier**
(This orange butter can be made up in advance and refrigerated until you are ready to use it. Just let it stand at room temperature until it is soft enough to spread easily.)

4 When you have spread the wrong side of the *crêpes* with the orange butter, fold them each in half and then in half again, forming small wedge-shaped triangles.

Have ready to go into a suzette pan or chafing dish the following:

the rind of 1 brightly colored orange, cut into thin slivers across
6 large lumps of sugar that have been well rubbed over the skin of an orange until they have absorbed its oil
¾ cup of granulated sugar

159

6 tablespoons (3 ounces—¾ stick) of sweet butter
½ cup of strained fresh orange juice
½ cup of curaçao, cognac or Grand Marnier

1 Cook these ingredients in the chafing dish slowly and gently, stirring them from time to time until they are syrupy.

2 Then add: the **skinned sections of 2 or 3 navel oranges** (depending upon their size).
Place the stuffed pancakes in the hot sauce, spooning it over them evenly.

3 Have ready: ⅓ **cup of Grand Marnier, warmed**

4 Ignite it and pour it over the *crêpes*.

5 Shake the chafing dish a little to get the flaming sauce distributed over the *crêpes*.

6 When the pyrotechnics die down, serve the *crêpes* and their sauce on warm dessert plates.

If the host is going to man the chafing dish, all ingredients should be set out for him on a tray so that all he has to do is put them into the warm pan, stir, and set it on fire. It is a very good idea to have one practice session in the bosom of the family before putting this show on the road, however. After the first time, it gets easier and easier, and it is far more impressive than playing with fire over an outdoor barbecue.

MENU
11

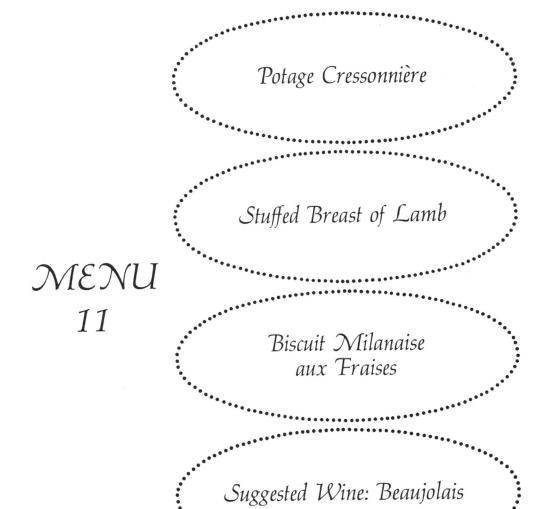

Potage Cressonnière

Stuffed Breast of Lamb

Biscuit Milanaise
aux Fraises

Suggested Wine: Beaujolais

Potage Cressonnière
(Water Cress and Potato Soup)

Serves six

The household kitchens of the French provinces are famous for the excellence of their simple vegetable soups. Many of them are based on those two most commonplace and inexpensive vegetables—leeks and potatoes, to which some other vegetable in season is often added. But always the soup tastes honestly of its ingredients, prepared with the most scrupulous care, and enhanced only with fresh cream and butter. It is important, therefore, to use the best potatoes—Idahos—and the freshest water cress for this soup. Prepared in this fashion their true flavors will come through, and you will have a smooth creamy soup with a fresh country taste.

MARKETING LIST

Idaho potatoes
Yellow onions
White Celery
Water Cress
butter
salt
White peppercorns
milk
Light cream
Very small Croutons

PREPARATION TRAY

potatoes, peeled and sliced

onions, sliced

celery, sliced

butter, frozen

water cress, washed and dried, and large leaves
picked and set aside

milk and cream, scalded

croutons, made

162

1   Peel, cut in half lengthwise, cut in ¼-inch slices:
    6 large Idaho potatoes
2   Slice: **3 yellow onions**
    3 large pieces of white celery without leaves
3   Put sliced potatoes and vegetables in a large pan
    with: **1 level tablespoon of salt**
    1 teaspoon of freshly ground white pepper
    Only enough water so that you just see it between
    the vegetable slices.
4   Place on top of the vegetables: **12 tablespoons (6
    ounces—1½ sticks) of frozen butter**
5   Cover the pan tightly and cook very, very slowly until
    the potatoes are soft. Do not stir at the beginning,
    as you want the butter to melt and drip slowly over
    the vegetables. After it is all melted you may stir
    occasionally. The secret of this soup is to stew the
    vegetables in the butter first.
6   While the potatoes are cooking, wash and dry:
    1½ bunches of water cress
7   Remove all the large leaves and set them aside.
8   When the potatoes are soft, add to them:
    the stalks and small water cress leaves. Let them
    stand, off the fire, until the cress wilts.
9   Put mixture through a strainer or a food mill.
10 Return the strained mixture to the pan and add:
    1½ cups of scalded light cream
    ¾ cup of scalded milk
11 Reheat, but be very careful not to let the soup boil.
12 Just before serving, add:
    the **large water cress leaves** that were set aside.

Serve with the following croutons:
1   Take a **small loaf of honest white bread,** 1 day old.
2   Remove the crusts.
3   Cut into tiny cubes.
4   In a sauté pan melt:
    a little butter, bacon fat or chicken fat
5   When the fat foams add: a few croutons at a time.
6   Let them get golden brown, drain them on paper
    towels, and serve them with the soup separately.

2 small breasts
    of lamb, boned
3 ounces of
    ground Veal
3 ounces of
    ground Pork
Kosher salt
black peppercorns
brandy
Yellow onions
salt butter
garlic
Dry bread crumbs
mushrooms
Dried thyme
eggs
light cream
bacon
red wine
1 chicken liver
tomato paste
meat glaze
potato flour

chicken stock
Dry sherry
red currant jelly
2 marrow bones
bay leaf
Celery
Dijon mustard

Stuffed Breast of Lamb

Serves six

There are very few inexpensive cuts of meat to be had these days, and most of them don't lend themselves to very exciting dishes. Breast of lamb, however, is one economical meat that can be transformed with a stuffing and a sauce into something as "loverly" as Eliza Doolittle in My Fair Lady.

It's no great trick to make a kingly repast from a fillet of beef, but how much more challenging to do it with a less desirable cut of meat! I don't doubt but that an imaginative chef will, one of these days, cook up a masterpiece with sows' ears.

PREPARATION TRAY

meat, seasoned, rolled up and chilled

onion, chopped

garlic, chopped

mushroom, chopped

forcemeat, made

sauce can be prepared in advance and kept in a pan tightly covered with transparent wrap

164

Have your butcher bone: **2 small breasts of lamb**

1 Spread them out on your chopping board and sprinkle them with:
   a little kosher salt
   freshly ground black pepper
   a liberal moistening of brandy

2 Roll the meat up tightly and wrap it in foil.

3 Refrigerate it for at least 10 minutes to let the seasoning and brandy soak in.

1 Chop fine: **1 yellow onion** (The best way to chop an onion is to cut it in half, place the flat surfaces on your cutting board, and with a large chef's knife, cut in thin slices across. Turn the slices around, holding them together, and chop the strips into fine pieces. You will find that this method keeps the juices in the onion because it is cut sharply and cleanly rather than pounded at.)

2 Heat in a pan: **2 tablespoons (1 ounce—¼ stick) of salt butter**

3 Add: **the chopped onion**
   a little salt
   a little freshly ground black pepper

4 Cook slowly until the onion becomes translucent and soft, but not brown.

5 Then add: **1 large finely chopped clove of garlic** (Chop it in a little salt and the pieces won't stick to your knife or board.)
   2 tablespoons of dry bread crumbs
   2 tablespoons (1 ounce—¼ stick) of butter
   1 finely chopped mushroom

6 Cook for a few minutes and add:
   ½ teaspoon of dried thyme (Rub the herb between your palms to bring out its full fragrance.)

7 Set aside to cool.

1 Into a mixer bowl put: **3 ounces of ground veal**
   3 ounces of ground pork

2 Mix in: **1 large raw egg white,** unbeaten

3 Add slowly: **½ cup of light cream** (Whenever you add cream to a forcemeat, do it almost drop by drop.

165

Slow up the mixer and add a few drops, then speed up until the cream has been absorbed. Repeat until all the cream is used.)

4 Add to the forcemeat, mixing well:
the cooked onion, mushroom, bread crumb mixture.

1 Remove the breasts of lamb from the refrigerator and spread them out flat.

2 Spread the forcemeat mixture on top of each breast.
3 Roll up each breast tightly.
4 Cover with: **thin slices of bacon,** overlapping.
5 Tie down with string each slice of bacon.
6 Place the rolls on the roasting rack of a shallow roasting pan.
7 Pour on the bottom of the pan:
about 3 tablespoons of red wine
8 Roast in a preheated 375° oven for 1 hour and 20 minutes.
9 Baste every 20 minutes adding:
a little wine or water each time (When you baste, always add a bit of liquid first, tilt the pan around so the new liquid mixes with the old and picks up any of the meat drippings. Never baste with cold liquid.)

To serve: Remove the strings from the lamb rolls. Slice as much as you will need. On a hot *au gratin* dish, arrange the slices so they overlap. Place the uncut piece at one end of the dish. Spoon over everything the following sauce (which is a sort of bar-sinister Bordelaise) :

1 In a heavy pan heat: **½ teaspoon of salt butter**
2 When it is very hot and brown add:
1 chicken liver
3 Brown it quickly on all sides.
4 Flame it with:
2 tablespoons of brandy
5 Remove the liver and add to the pan:
1 tablespoon (½ ounce) of butter
6 Stir in, off the fire: **1 teaspoon of tomato paste**

166

    1 teaspoon of meat glaze
    2 teaspoons of potato flour
    1¼ cups of chicken stock (see recipe on page 353)
    ¼ cup of red wine
    2 tablespoons of sherry
    2 teaspoons of red currant jelly

7 Stir over the fire until it boils, then set aside, covered with transparent wrap, until you make the second half of the sauce.

1 In a heavy pan heat: **1 teaspoon of butter**

    2 Brown quickly in it: **2 marrow bones**

    3 Cover with:
       1 cup of red wine
       1 bay leaf
       a few black peppercorns
       a sprinkle of salt
       a little sliced celery stalk
       1 bruised clove of garlic (crush it a little with the back of a spoon)

    4 Bring this slowly to a boil, then add:
       the first sauce
       the chicken liver, which you had removed, remember?

    5 Simmer (*do not boil*) very gently for 1 hour.

    6 Strain the sauce and remove and set aside the liver.

    7 Remove the marrow from the bones and crush it with:
       ½ teaspoon of Dijon mustard

    8 Add it slowly to the strained sauce, beating it in with a whisk.

    9 Add the liver cut in thin slices lengthwise.

    10 Pour a little of this sauce over the lamb and serve the rest separately.

This is a delicious sauce with any grilled meat, even hamburgers. It is also one of the best-known sauces to serve with sautéed kidneys, improving them enormously. Certainly if "manners maketh the man," the manner of serving it maketh the meat. Breast of lamb served in this fashion is economy transformed into elegance.

Biscuit Milanaise aux Fraises

(Sponge Cake with Strawberries)

Serves six to eight

This is a simple, delicious and good-looking way to use a
Biscuit Milanaise. It is as pretty as an elaborately frosted
cake, but with fewer calories and much less trouble. Try it,
too, with peaches or apricots as suggested at the end of the
recipe.

MARKETING LIST

3½ cups of fresh
    Strawberries
raspberry or
    red currant jelly
Dry sherry or Madeira
blanched almonds
lemon

PREPARATION TRAY

Biscuit Milanese

1½ cups of strawberries, washed, hulled and sliced

2 cups of strawberries, washed and hulled

⅓ cup of raspberry or red currant jelly, strained

lemon juice

grated rind of 1 lemon

fruit glaze

1 cup of almonds, blanched, chopped and browned

Make the following Biscuit Milanaise in advance:

1 In a mixer bowl put:
   2 eggs (2 ounces each)
   2 egg yolks (reserve the whites)
   ½ pound of superfine granulated sugar
   2 ounces (⅜ of a cup) of all-purpose flour
   2 ounces (⅜ of a cup) of potato flour
   a pinch of salt

2 Mix together with a wooden spoon. Then turn your mixer on to medium speed and beat for at least 15 minutes. You want a very light, fluffy mixture.

3 Beat to soft peaks: **2 egg whites**

4 Fold them carefully into the mixture.

5 Add: **the grated rind of 1 lemon**

6 Brush a 7-inch spring-form cake pan with melted salt butter.

7 Dust it out thoroughly with flour. Knock the tin once or twice to remove all surplus flour.

8 Pour in the batter. Stand tin on a cookie sheet.

9 Bake in a preheated 350° oven for 40-50 minutes. The cake is done when its top springs back lightly to the touch. It should rise about 3 or 4 times its original bulk.

10 Remove the cake from the oven and slide a thin-bladed knife around the edge of the pan.

11 Turn it out onto a cake rack to cool.

When it has cooled, carefully cut the cake in half so that it makes 2 layers. Use a thin knife.

1 In a small bowl put:
   1½ cups of sliced strawberries
   (Keep 2 cups of the strawberries whole.)
   1 teaspoon of lemon juice
   ⅓ cup of strained raspberry or red currant jelly
   the grated rind of 1 lemon

2 Mix carefully together.

3 Spread this mixture on the cut side of the bottom half of the cake.

4 Replace the top half of the cake.

Biscuit Milanaise aux Fraises

1 In a saucepan place:

> **1 large jar (12 ounces) of raspberry or red currant jelly** (Depending upon which you used above.)
> **1 tablespoon of dry sherry or Madeira**

2 Warm a little and strain this mixture.

3 When it is cool, carefully brush all over the sand-wiched cake with this glaze.

4 Measure out: **1 cup of blanched almonds**

5 Chop them finely and brown the nuts in a pan in a moderate oven. Stir them often so that they brown evenly. When they are a golden color, remove them.

6 When the chopped browned almonds are cool, stick them around the sides of the cake. The glaze will hold them.

7 Cover the top of the cake with:
2 cups of perfect whole strawberries
(Stand them on their broad base, points up, so close together that they touch on all sides.)

8 Carefully glaze the tops of the strawberries with more of the jelly glaze, using your pastry brush.

You can garnish this Biscuit Milanaise with sliced or halved peaches or apricots if you prefer. In that case, use apricot jam instead of the red jam for the glaze.

Braised Endive

Hot Chicken Mousse
with Hollandaise Sauce

Hot Dilled Cucumbers

MENU
12

Home Baked White Bread

Glace-Crème au Praline
or Tartelettes aux Fraises

Suggested Wine: Chablis

Braised Endive

(See recipe on page 55.)

Hot Chicken Mousse
with Hollandaise Sauce

Serves four

This is another of those light, melt-in-your-mouth delicacies that one so rarely encounters brought off to perfection. It is the kind of dish that might well become the specialty of your house, and what a blessing for you! For most of the preparation can be done in advance, and if you heed each step with care the results will be excellent and easy to achieve. You can vary the hot chicken mousse by serving it with hollandaise sauce as suggested in this menu, or with a velouté sauce (recipe follows). You can also vary the vegetable garnish in the center of the mold. However you serve this it is wonderful, and open to many interpretations.

MARKETING LIST

3 small or 4 large
  half breasts
  of chicken
eggs
light cream
sweet butter
salt
flour

PREPARATION TRAY

chicken mixture, strained and chilled

8-inch ring mold, buttered

172

Have your butcher bone **3 or 4 half breasts of chicken**, depending on size.

1 Remove the skin and all membranes from:
3 or 4 half chicken breasts.

2 Put them through the meat chopper with fine blade *twice*.

3 Put the ground chicken in a mixer bowl and add:
½ cup of unbeaten egg white (Separate eggs, reserving yolks for later use. 3 to 4 egg whites, depending upon size, equals ½ cup.)

4 Mix well, then add, drop by drop:
1½ cups of light cream (Add a drop of cream with the mixer on low, then turn up the speed until the cream has been absorbed. Continue doing this until all the cream has been beaten into the chicken.)
2 level teaspoons of salt
1 teaspoon of freshly ground white pepper

5 Remove the chicken mixture from the bowl.

6 Cream in the bowl: **8 tablespoons (4 ounces—1 stick) of slightly soft sweet butter**

7 Remove butter from the bowl and set it aside.

1 In a heavy saucepan put:
½ cup of water
2 tablespoons (1 ounce—¼ stick) of butter
a pinch of salt

2 Bring slowly to a boil and when it is bubbling, throw in: **½ cup of flour**

3 Stir with a wooden spoon until it forms a large ball and comes away clean from the pan.

4 Put this *panade* into the mixer bowl.

5 Beat until it is quite smooth.

6 Add, one at a time:
1 large egg
1 egg white

7 Mix in: the creamed butter

8 Then mix in: the chicken

9 Rub the completed mixture through a strainer or put it through a food mill.

10 Fill the strained mixture into a well-buttered 8-inch ring mold.

11 Cover it with buttered wax paper.

You can do all of this well in advance and refrigerate the filled and covered ring mold until you are ready to poach the mousse. This preparation can be done in the morning.

When you are ready to poach the mousse, stand the covered ring mold in a shallow pan of hot water.

2 Put it to poach in a preheated 350° oven for 25 minutes. (It may take a little longer if the mold has been refrigerated.) The mousse is done when it is just firm to the touch. If it is overdone it will be too dry. If it is undercooked it will be too soft to hold its shape, so be very careful to test it properly.

3 Remove the mold from the oven and let it stand for about 5 minutes before unmolding.

4 Then remove the wax paper and run a small sharp knife carefully around the edges.

5 Place a hot round serving dish over the mold. Reverse them and carefully lift off the mold.

This is a most delicate mousse, and its flavor comes from the chicken, good sweet butter, cream and eggs. That is why it is excellent served with a hollandaise sauce which follows or with the rich, velvety *velouté* sauce whose recipe follows the hollandaise.

To serve: present the ring of chicken mousse on a hot round serving dish—a silver platter or large china one. Coat the mousse carefully with the sauce, using a large basting spoon. Fill the center of the ring with the dilled cucumbers.

Hollandaise Sauce

This sunny yellow sauce has an undeserved reputation for bringing gloom to the kitchen. It is really quite simple to make, and there need be no disasters, no curdling or separating or frantic last-minute difficulties, because hollandaise is not that temperamental. For the ten or fifteen minutes that it takes to prepare, you do have to be in constant attendance. But that is a small price to pay for the golden smoothness, sparked with a little tartness, that is such an excellent accompaniment to delicate fish, chicken, vegetable and egg dishes.

With this foolproof recipe you can even make your hollandaise an hour or two before serving it, and it will wait patiently without spoiling, in a pan of very warm water, covered tightly with transparent wrap. The whole trick is in the temperature. Like Goldilocks' porridge it must be not too hot, not too cold, but JUST RIGHT. Using the following procedure, as you will see, you can turn out a perfect hollandaise every time.

MARKETING LIST

Eggs
Tarragon Vinegar
Heavy Cream
butter
lemon

PREPARATION TRAY

2 egg yolks

4 ounces of frozen butter, cut in little pieces

a few drops of fresh lemon juice

1 Put into a small oven-proof bowl (preferably earthenware or oven-glass because it doesn't get too hot) :

2 egg yolks (Save the whites in a cup and store, covered, in the refrigerator to use another day.)

2 With a small wire whisk beat in:

1 tablespoon of tarragon vinegar (See recipe on page 352.)

¼ teaspoon of salt (scant)

a few grains of cayenne pepper

2 tablespoons of heavy cream

3 Stand the bowl in a shallow frying pan of hot water over a slow fire. *This is where many a good hollandaise goes wrong.* The water must be hot but not ever boiling. By setting the bowl into a shallow pan of hot water you are improvising what the French call a *bain-Marie.* Your sauce is surrounded by an even heat instead of cooking above the heat, as it would do in a double boiler. (As you know, you can scramble eggs very nicely in a double boiler, and that is just what you *don't* want to do when making a hollandaise. Hollandaise curdles because the egg yolks have coagulated from too much heat. Then you are well on the road to scrambled eggs instead of a smooth sauce.)

4 Beat with your whisk until the sauce thickens—hollandaise should be light textured.

5 When the mixture is thick enough to coat a spoon, you can start adding butter. (If you add your butter before the mixture has reached the desired thickness, your sauce will be too thin, as the butter is not a thickening agent, it merely extends the sauce. Nor do you want to let your sauce get too thick before adding the butter, as it may curdle then. It's a good idea to have a little cold milk or cream nearby with which to thin the sauce a bit, if necessary.)

6 The trick to adding the butter is to have it very, very cold and cut up into small pieces which you will add one at a time.

7   Have 4 ounces of **frozen butter** cut in little pats, and as you continue beating your sauce, drop a piece of butter in, and when it dissolves, drop another in, beating constantly, until you have incorporated it all. The slower the butter melts in the egg yolk, the better it is.

8   Finally, beat in:
    2 or 3 drops of lemon juice—no more—for added flavor.

9   Remove your whisk, and cover the bowl with transparent wrap to get it absolutely airtight. Leave it in the pan of warm water until you are ready to use it. If you want to reheat it a little, be sure you keep the flame low under the pan of water, don't let it boil, and keep stirring your sauce.

Sauce Velouté
(Velvet Sauce)

The attitude of the French toward their cooking shows nowhere more clearly than in their names for food. Catch a French chef saying plain "white sauce"—or thinking of it in those terms, either, which is probably the secret of his success. A "white sauce" is either Béchamel, named for the seventeenth-century financier who invented it—and just as rich—or velouté, liquid velvet. Béchamel is made with butter, flour and milk or cream; velouté with butter, flour and chicken, veal or fish stock. Those are the basic ingredients. A wide variety of seasonings and enrichments come into play depending upon what the sauce will be served with. Another nice touch in nomenclature is that these two, and a handful of other leading sauces, are known as "mother sauces." From which all blessings flow.

Follow the directions carefully, and don't skimp on your attention or your ingredients and you, too, can make a smooth, subtly flavored sauce. If the ingredients are put together properly, if your stock is strong and flavorful to begin with, your butter, eggs and cream fresh and sweet, your sauce will need very little in the way of seasoning.

In this recipe we are making a velouté sauce enriched by the addition of egg yolks, cream and sherry. The addition also serves to bind the sauce. This might be considered a tricky operation, but I promise you if you do each step carefully as directed you will have a smooth velvety sauce. And having done it once you will be able to do it forever after.

| MARKETING LIST |

Sweet butter
all-purpose flour
Cayenne pepper
Salt
Strong chicken stock
light cream
eggs
dry sherry
heavy cream

PREPARATION TRAY

chicken stock

line up other ingredients in the order used (this will save time when you must beat in each quickly in order to have a smooth sauce)

You will be greatly helped in your saucemaking if you have a good heavy saucepan, preferably tin-lined copper. The more evenly heat is conducted the less chance there is of scorching your sauce on the bottom of the pan. Stainless steel has a tendency to burn, aluminum discolors a white sauce when a wire whisk is used, so that leaves only oven-glass or enamel as compromise choices if you have no copper.

1   In a heavy 1½ quart saucepan melt:
4 tablespoons (2 ounces—½ stick) of sweet butter
(Melt the butter over low heat and *watch it.* You don't want it to foam or color.)

2   Stir in, off the fire: **4 tablespoons of flour**
(This mixture of melted butter and flour is a *roux*, and in one form or another it is the basis of nearly all French sauces, dark as well as light. Many recipes instruct you to cook the flour and butter together. I find that the hot butter mixed with the flour *off the fire*, and in a saucepan capable of holding the heat, gives a better result. There is no danger then of overcooking your *roux*, in which case it will not absorb the liquid later and you will have a curdled, lumpy sauce with a disagreeable taste. The flour will cook sufficiently later when you simmer the *velouté* sauce prior to adding its enrichments.)

3   Stir in your flour with a small wire whisk until you have a smooth, thick paste. (It is better to have it too thick than too thin, as it is easier to thin the sauce out later than to make it thicker.)

4   Season the *roux* with: **a pinch of salt**
a dash of cayenne
(Your chicken stock should have about 90% of the flavor needed in the sauce. Be sure the stock is strong and well seasoned.)

5   Mix in with a wire whisk:
1 good cup of strong chicken stock (See recipe on page 353.)

179

6   Stir over a moderate fire until the sauce begins to thicken a little. (One secret of a good sauce is gentle heat. Never use high heat—medium to low will ease the raw ingredients into a state of cooked perfection.)

7   Add: **½ cup of light cream**

8   Stir over moderate heat until the sauce comes to a boil.

9   Add, bit by bit: **3 teaspoons of sweet butter** (Beat the sauce with the whisk until each bit of butter has been completely absorbed before you add the next bit.)

Up to this point you have an ordinary *velouté* sauce, which this final addition of butter has made smooth and well-blended. But for a thicker, richer, more delicious sauce we make the following additions:

1   In a small china bowl mix: **2 egg yolks**
2 tablespoons of dry sherry
3 tablespoons of heavy cream

2   Beat in, very gradually, with a wire whisk:
½ cup of the hot sauce
(By mixing the egg yolks with the cream and sherry first, and then very delicately with a little of the hot sauce, you get the eggs used to the heat gradually. This keeps them from curdling or scrambling.)

3   Pour the yolk mixture back in the saucepan, beating all the time.

4   Reheat without boiling. (A sauce that contains egg yolks and fat might curdle if its temperature approaches the boiling point.)

5   While you reheat the sauce, stir with a wooden spatula. Use it with vigor, not to agitate the top part of the sauce, but to scrape the entire bottom of the pan, including the edges, so the sauce cannot possibly scorch.

If you use this *velouté* on the chicken mousse, carefully coat the unmolded ring by using a large basting spoon and ladling the sauce neatly over it.

This is a delicious sauce for chicken, turkey, eggs, and some vegetable dishes. It can be used for fish if you substitute fish stock (see recipe on page 52) for the chicken stock.

First Aid for Sauces

If, in spite of your best care, your sauce should separate, don't you come apart too! Play it cool. A tablespoon or so of cold water beaten into the sauce will pull it back together.

If your sauce is too thick, heat it till it simmers, then beat in, a spoonful at a time, a little cream or stock until the sauce is the right consistency.

If the sauce is too thin, the problem is a bit more complicated. You can boil it down (reduce it), but not if you have already added the egg yolks. In that case, blend a teaspoon of flour with a teaspoon of soft butter. This paste, *beurre manié*, is a thickening and binding agent. Beat it into the hot sauce, off the fire, until it is smooth. Then simmer the sauce for a few minutes. That should do the trick.

If you are not going to use the sauce immediately, cover the saucepan tightly with transparent wrap to prevent a skin from forming.

Once you have made this kind of sauce successfully you will see that it is really not so difficult, and there is absolutely nothing that comes out of cans or packages that can compare.

Hot Dilled Cucumbers

Serves four

Here is a delightful summer vegetable, one that is excellent
to serve with fish as well as with the hot chicken mousse.
When you are using a garnish for the center of a ring mold,
always try to have it a different color and a contrasting
texture and flavor from the mold. The soft airy mousse
contrasts well with the slightly crisp pale green cucumbers.
And the fresh dill brings out the best in everything.

PREPARATION TRAY

cucumbers, peeled and cut, standing in cold salt water

dill, chopped

MARKETING LIST

3 small cucumbers
butter
salt
white peppercorns
fresh dill

1   Using a potato parer, skin: **3 small cucumbers**

      2   Cut off the tips first, then the stalk ends, or the cucumbers will taste bitter.

      3   Cut the cucumbers in half lengthwise.

      4   Cut them in inch-thick slices, and if there are large seeds, remove them.

      5   With a small paring knife, round off the sharp edges and carve the chunks to look like large olives.

1   In a heavy saucepan put: the cucumber "olives."

      2   Cover them with **cold water.**

      3   Bring slowly to a boil.

      4   Drain the cucumbers well in a colander at once.

      5   Return them to the empty pan and add:
        3 tablespoons (1½ ounces) of butter
        ¼ teaspoon of salt
        ¼ teaspoon of freshly ground white pepper

      6   Cover the pan with a piece of well-buttered wax paper and then the lid.

      7   Cook over moderate heat for not more than 10 minutes, shaking the pan vigorously every so often.

      8   When the cucumbers are cooked, add:
        2 teaspoons of chopped fresh dill

      9   Pile the cucumbers in the center of the chicken mousse ring *after* the sauce has been spooned over it.

Cucumbers are another vegetable, like lettuce and endive and celery, that we most often eat raw. Like them, they are watery, and the preliminary blanching is important for cooking out most of the excess moisture and any bitter taste. Then you can stew the vegetable in butter without overcooking it, and the result is a slightly crisp, subtly flavored garnish. A completely new taste.

Home Baked White Bread

Makes two two-pound loaves

My mother would never have understood why a recipe for plain white bread should have been included in a gourmet cookbook. She, who did absolutely everything in our home, used to bake bread in the normal course of events once a week. And such bread! But today homemade bread, homemade jam, homemade butter are luxuries. Those things that used to be the basis of our life, really, are now done outside the home on a mass commercial scale. And they have lost their savor. In most households nowadays, a slice of bread spread with butter and jam would be pretty ordinary. Yet it could be the most wonderful thing to eat on earth. I think we must try to get back to that way of doing things.

So here is a recipe for white bread and, as you will see, there is nothing so mysterious or difficult about it after all. You will get two loaves, or one loaf and about a dozen and a half small rolls from this quantity. You will also get an immeasurable amount of satisfaction—the hidden bonus in this recipe.

MARKETING LIST

milk
butter or margarine
sugar
salt
yeast
  (package or cake)
all-purpose flour
butter

PREPARATION TRAY

scalded milk, mixed with shortening, sugar and salt, ready and cooled

tins, well-buttered

1 In a heavy saucepan put: **1 cup of milk**
>   2 Scald it (bring it just to the boil).
>   3 Remove from the heat and add:
>   **4 tablespoons (2 ounces—½ stick) of shortening**
>   (Use margarine or whatever you like but I think but-
>   ter is the nicest.)
>   **1 tablespoon of sugar**
>   **1 teaspoon of salt**
>   (The shortening melts and the salt and sugar dis-
>   solve more rapidly in the scalded milk. Formerly the
>   scalding had to be done in order to kill the bacteria
>   in unpasteurized milk, but that is no longer the
>   reason for scalding the milk today.)
>   4 Fill a 2-cup measure with:
>   **1 cup of lukewarm water** (between 110°-115°)
>   5 Sprinkle on top of it:
>   **1 package of dry yeast**
>   6 After a few minutes, stir well.
>   7 Mix the dissolved yeast into the milk when the milk
>   has cooled. (Wait about 5 minutes. If the milk is
>   more than lukewarm it will kill the yeast.)

1 Put into a large bowl: **3 cups of sifted all-purpose flour**
>   2 Mix the flour well with the combined liquids.
>   3 Gradually stir in:
>   **3 more cups of sifted all-purpose flour**
>   4 When the dough leaves the sides of the bowl you
>   have used enough flour.
>   5 Turn out onto a lightly floured pastry board or slab,
>   and knead thoroughly.

(Many of us have never watched bread being kneaded,
and it is this process that puzzles and inhibits us. Well,
it needn't. Naturally, as with any manual operation, it
will improve with practice—you will acquire a rhythm and
touch after a while.

What you want to do is exercise the dough, which is
sticky at first, so that the gluten in the wheat flour can
develop as the moisture in the dough is pressed into it.
Then your dough will become elastic and smooth. So

185

you press down on the dough with the heels of your hands, lightly, pushing the dough away from you quickly. A light dusting of flour on your hands at the beginning will prevent sticking. Fold the dough over toward you, and press down lightly once more. Then give it a quarter turn to the left, and repeat. Continue this rhythmic pressing, folding and turning for about 8 minutes, or until the dough feels elastic and its surface becomes smooth and satiny. It will no longer stick to the board or to your hands.)

1   Brush your largest bowl with **melted butter.** (The bowl should hold 3 times the capacity of the dough.)
2   Put the smooth ball of dough in the bowl.
3   Brush the top and sides of the dough with a little melted butter.
4   Cover the bowl with transparent wrap and a cloth (my mother used to use a clean square of baby blanket). The dough will rise best in a warm room, carefully protected from drafts. Ideally it should rise to double its bulk in 2 hours. If the dough rises too much your bread will be coarse textured and will taste yeasty. If it rises too little your bread will be soggy.
5   Test to see if your dough has risen the correct amount by pressing a finger into it. If, when you remove your finger, a dent remains, the dough is ready for the next step.
6   Break the rise by punching down the dough with your fist a few times.
7   Turn the deflated dough out on a lightly floured board.
8   Divide it into 2 parts.
9   Knead each part a few times and make a smooth ball from each.

1   Shape one ball into a loaf that will fit your bread loaf tin.
2   Place it in a well-buttered loaf tin.
3   You may make a second loaf with the other ball of dough, or you may make rolls by shaping the dough

186

into balls that will fill greased muffin tins about ⅓ full.

4   In either case, cover the filled tins with a cloth, and allow the dough to rise again until it has nearly doubled in bulk (about 40 minutes).

5   Test by pressing your finger into the risen dough, and if it leaves a dent, your bread or rolls are ready for the oven.

6   Bake in a preheated 375° oven. (If you are baking in oven-glass pans, set your oven for 350° since glass holds heat longer than tin.)

7   The loaf of bread will take from 45 minutes to 1 hour to bake to a lovely golden brown.

8   The rolls will be baked in about 15 to 20 minutes.

9   Remove the loaf and the rolls from their pans right away, and allow them to cool on a rack.

10   Leave them uncovered if you like a crisp crust.

11   Cover with a towel while cooling if you prefer a soft crust.

Be prepared for members of your family to beat a path to your kitchen door, for the smell of baking bread has more magnetic pull than the greatest French perfume. You will be lucky if you are left with enough bread or rolls from your baking spree to serve for dinner that night.

Glace-Crème au Praline

(Praline Ice Cream)

(See recipe on page 212.)

or

Tartelettes aux Fraises

(Strawberry Tartlets)

(See recipe on page 259.)

Ragoût de Boeuf en Daube

Gnocchi à la Romaine

MENU 13

Hot Brioche

Ripe Melon, Peach or Pear

Suggested Wine: Vin Rosé

Ragoût de Boeuf en Daube
(Casserole of Beef with Wine)

Serves six

(See recipe for Ragoût de Veau en Daube on page 65. Note directions for changing it to Boeuf en Daube.)

(See recipe for Ragoût de Veau en Daube on page 65.

MARKETING LIST

farina
Salt
Cayenne pepper
Sweet butter
Parmesan cheese

Gnocchi à la Romaine
(Farina Gnocchi, Roman Style)

Serves six

French gnocchi are generally made with a panade that is like cream puff paste to which potatoes or farina may be added, and then the gnocchi are poached. But the Roman style is simply cooked farina dressed up with butter, cheese and seasonings, chilled and sliced, and browned under a broiler. When you want to serve a starch that is different, follow the Roman road. Start out as though you were going to cook breakfast cereal, and then make a right turn and wind up with these delicious Gnocchi à la Romaine.

PREPARATION TRAY

farina, cooked and chilled

au gratin dish, buttered

Parmesan cheese, grated

190

1   Put into a heavy 4-quart pan: **6 cups of cold water**
   2 teaspoons of salt
 2   Bring to a rolling boil, then reduce it to a simmer (the point at which the liquid is just below boiling, and there is only an occasional bubble).
 3   Slowly mix in: **1 cup of farina** (or you may use white or yellow cornmeal).
 4   Let the farina just trickle into the simmering water and keep stirring with a wooden spoon the whole time to keep it smooth.
 5   Continue stirring over a slow fire for 7 minutes.
 6   Remove from the fire and mix in with a wooden spoon: **a good shake of cayenne**
   3 tablespoons (1½ ounces) of sweet butter
   ⅓ cup of freshly grated Parmesan cheese
 7   Rinse a jelly roll pan out in cold water.
 8   With a rubber scraper spread the mixture evenly on it.
 9   Let it cool, then cover it with wax paper and put it in the refrigerator to set. (Under 30 minutes.)

1   Remove the jelly roll pan from the refrigerator. It will have about a ½-inch layer of cold, firm farina on it.
 2   With a round 2-inch cookie cutter cut small circles. (Or cut 1½-inch squares with a small sharp knife.)
 3   Brush the bottom of a large *au gratin* dish well with melted butter.
 4   Arrange the rounds or squares of *gnocchi*, overlapping, in the dish, in one layer.
 5   Brush them with: **melted butter**
 6   Sprinkle them with: **freshly grated Parmesan cheese**
 7   Sprinkle or dot with: more **melted butter**
 8   Brown under a hot broiler.

There is a moment, in the preparation of *Gnocchi à la Romaine*, when you seem to have an unpromising sheet of cold, gummy breakfast cereal out of which to make a silk purse. Don't despair! The savory rounds browned with cheese and butter do spring from such humble beginnings, but through the alchemy of cooking, something wonderful emerges.

191

Hot Brioche

(See recipe on page 112.)

Ripe Melon, Peach or Pear

When you serve fresh fruit or melon for dessert it must be at the very peak of perfection. A large, handsome peach or pear, exactly at the correct stage of ripeness, or a slice of melon that is properly sweet and juicy—is unbeatable.

But fruit or melons that are below par should not come to the table. Serve well-chilled, on a grape leaf with a wedge of lemon or lime. A small fruit knife should accompany the peach or pear so it can be cut into neat slices or wedges. The melon, of course, needs only a spoon.

If you like cheese with your fruit, there is an excellent dessert cheese faintly flavored with kirsch, called Gourmandise, that is especially good with pears, peaches or apples. The cheese is always served at room temperature, several hours out of the refrigerator.

Still, one perfect piece of fruit is quite marvelous all by itself. It makes a very simple dessert, for which the biggest problem is probably the marketing. As my greengrocer once earnestly explained to me, "Good-a fruit don't grow on trees these days!"

MENU
14

Paella

Crème Renversée au Caramel

Suggested Wine: Sangria
(Madeira mixed with water, sugar and a little nutmeg.)

1 2½ pound chicken
6 hot Spanish
    garlic sausages
½ pound small
    pork sausages
2 small live lobsters
2 dozen large mussels
½ pound sea scallops
1 pound of shrimps
    boiled and cleaned
long-grained rice
Saffron
lemon
1 red, 1 green pepper
4 tomatoes
2 yellow onions
½ pound of white
    mushrooms
celery
carrot
bay leaf
salt
white pepper
tomato paste
meat glaze
potato flour
red currant jelly
chicken stock
butter - salt
    and sweet
white wine
Calvados

Paella
(Spanish Chicken with Rice and Sea Food)

Serves twelve

I should warn you now that this is no simple everyday dish. Nor is it something to prepare for just a small group. Paella is a lot of work, with a lot of ingredients, but it will feed a lot of people and give them a lot of pleasure, which rather evens the score. This is a wonderful dish for a buffet, as the enormous metal Paella dish heaped with the spicy provender of Mediterranean lands is an impressive sight that gives off an exciting aroma. It fairly demands a chorus of oles! for the cook. You will understand why when you read what goes into it.

PREPARATION TRAY

chicken, cleaned and trussed (see directions on page 356)

mussels, scrubbed and cleaned (see directions on page 356)

1 cup all together of celery, carrot and onion, sliced

4 teaspoons of fresh lemon juice

2 yellow onions, chopped fine

chicken stock

1 teaspoon of crushed saffron, mixed with 2 teaspoons of water

1 pound of raw shrimps, shelled and deveined

½ pound of white mushrooms, cleaned and sliced

1 red and 1 green pepper, seeded and cut into squares

4 tomatoes, skinned and quartered

194

Even the longest journey starts with but a single step, and so with this recipe. Taken step by step it is not difficult. Just don't look back and don't look ahead, and before you know it—*paella!*

First, take a 2½ pound chicken and truss it (see page 356).

1 In a deep heavy pan melt:
   5 tablespoons (2½ ounces) of salt butter
   Stir with a wooden spoon until it just begins to color.

2 Put in the chicken, breast side down, and cover the pan.

3 Brown each side of the breast, then each leg, the wishbone, and lastly the back. Turn chicken by inserting a wooden spoon in the cavity and using it as a handle. Do all the browning with pan covered.

4 Brown the **liver of the chicken** and the **6 Spanish sausages** at the same time.

5 Remove sausages, and heat in a tiny pot:
   4 tablespoons of Calvados
   Ignite by tipping pot into flame, and pour burning Calvados over chicken and liver.

6 Remove chicken and liver from pan and stir in, off the fire: **1 teaspoon of tomato paste**
   1 teaspoon of meat glaze
   4 teaspoons of potato flour

7 Mix until quite smooth, then mix in, still off the fire: **2½ cups of chicken stock**
   ½ cup of white wine
   1 teaspoon of red currant jelly
   a very little salt
   ¾ teaspoon of freshly ground white pepper.

8 Stir over the fire until it comes to a boil, then reduce the heat to a simmer.

9 Carefully carve the chicken, including the back (see directions on page 356). Slice the liver.

10 Put the pieces back into the sauce with the liver, the Spanish sausages cut in half, and **½ pound of small pork sausages**

11 Place the pan, uncovered, on the top shelf of a pre-heated 375° oven for 45 to 50 minutes. Baste a few times.

1   While the chicken is cooking, melt in a deep heavy pan:
3 tablespoons (1½ ounces) of salt butter

2   Split in half: **2 small live lobsters**
(Using a sharp heavy knife, start from the small cross in the center of the head, and cut down. Remove the little sac from behind the eyes, and the large vein down the tail.)

3   Remove large claws with a pair of shears, and remove small claws.

4   Place the lobsters, cut side down, in the hot butter. Put claws on top of bodies.

5   Cover the pan and cook briskly for 3 minutes.

6   Remove the cover.

7   Heat and flame: **¼ cup of Calvados**

8   Pour over the lobster, and when flame dies, cover the pan and cook briskly again until the lobster blushes—a result of the heat, not the brandied humidity.

9   Set aside to cool a little. (This might be a good time to baste the chicken.)

You are now ready for your 24 large, well-scrubbed mussels. (See page 356 for how to clean and prepare mussels.)

1   Put into a pan: **24 scrubbed mussels**
1 cup all together of sliced celery, carrot, onion
1 bay leaf
¾ cup of dry white wine
2¼ cups of water
2 teaspoons of salt
a few white peppercorns

2   Cover the pan and bring slowly to a boil.

3   Boil for 3 to 4 minutes—until all the shells are well opened.

4   Strain the liquid and keep it to be used later.

5   Remove the top shell from each mussel and discard,

196

leaving the mussels on the half shell to keep warm in the covered pan.

1 Next, heat in a small sauté pan: **3 tablespoons (1½ ounces) of salt butter**

2 Dry well: **½ pound of sea scallops**

3 Dust them lightly with **flour**

4 When the butter begins to brown, put in the scallops and brown them quickly on each side.

5 Sprinkle with: **2 teaspoons of lemon juice a little salt a little freshly ground white pepper**

6 Cover pan and cook gently for 3 to 4 minutes.

7 Add them to the lobster pan; cover and keep warm. (Have you basted the chicken lately?)

Now we're ready for the rice.

1 Take a small, deep casserole with a tight-fitting lid.

2 Melt in it: **8 tablespoons (4 ounces—1 stick) of sweet butter**
(The Spaniards would use olive oil, but I think it a bit too strong.)

3 When it is just melted add:
2 finely chopped yellow onions
season with **salt and a little freshly ground white pepper.**

4 Cook slowly until onion is soft without browning, then add: **1½ cups of long-grained rice (Patna)**

5 Stir rice with a wooden spoon so that it is well-coated with the onions and butter.

6 Mix in a small oven-glass cup:
1 teaspoon of crushed saffron
2 teaspoons of water

7 Add to the rice and mix well so that it becomes an even bright yellow color.

8 Mix in: 3 cups of the strained mussel stock.

9 Stir over the fire until it comes to a boil.

10 Then add: **1 pound of shelled and deveined raw shrimps**

11   Reduce the heat to a slow simmer.

12   Cover the casserole tightly, and cook for 25 minutes without removing the lid.

13   Fluff up with 2 forks, cover and set aside.

We are now on the last lap—the vegetables.

Your chicken is probably out of the oven by now. Cover the pan and keep it warm with the rest of your collection.

1   Melt in a sauté pan (you can use the one you did the scallops in) :
4 tablespoons (2 ounces—½ stick) of salt butter

2   When it is hot, add:
½ pound of white mushrooms,cut in thick slices.

3   Coat them well with the hot butter and add:
2 teaspoons of lemon juice
a dash of salt and freshly ground white pepper

4   Sauté briskly for only 2 to 3 minutes, then add:
1 red and 1 green pepper, seeded and cut into large squares.

5   Cook another 2 to 3 minutes.

6   Lastly, add: **4 tomatoes,** skinned and quartered.

7   Just mix them with the other vegetables, but do not allow them to cook or they will get too soft and will break up.

To serve: Heat a metal *paella* dish or a very large shallow casserole.

Put all the different ingredients in it in layers. First a layer of rice, then vegetables, then fish, then meat.

Save the nicest pieces of everything for the top, and arrange it so that it will be easy for people to serve themselves a bit of each of this infinite variety of good things without hunting through the entire *paella* for buried treasure.

One more word of warning: A large hot *paella* dish is best transported from kitchen to table on a tray. Better yet, get a strong man to help you, especially if *you've* done all the work up to this moment. Now relax and enjoy your Spanish masterpiece. *Ole!*

Crème Renversée au Caramel
(Caramel Custard)

Serves six
Double this recipe when used for this menu.

A custard is like the little girl in the nursery rhyme—when it is good it is very, very good, but when it is bad it is horrid! Crème Renversée au Caramel is one of the standbys of French restaurants where, if you are lucky enough to have it at its best, it is flawlessly smooth—as shiny as satin, as lush as velvet, served unmolded with a topping of amber caramel. Once you have tasted custard this way, you will never accept the kind that is served in a cup under an ugly wrinkled skin, or one that separates into an unpleasant curds-and-whey texture. In this recipe the extra egg yolks, the slow and careful mixing of hot milk and eggs, the straining of the mixture, and the gentle baking all contribute to the perfection of the finished product. If this seems to you an overly meticulous way to make a simple custard, try it and discover for yourself how the extra ingredient of care transforms the simple into something extraordinary.

MARKETING LIST

Granulated sugar
Cream of tartar
Light Cream
eggs
milk
fresh Vanilla bean

PREPARATION TRAY

custard, strained and warm, but not baked yet

soufflé dish or molds

First I will give you directions for making your caramel and lining either one 8-inch soufflé dish or six individual molds with it. (If you are making this to serve 12, use two 8-inch soufflé dishes or 12 individual molds and double all quantities.)

It is best to make the caramel in a heavy saucepan—copper that is *not* lined with tin is preferable, but heavy aluminum will do.

1   Put into the saucepan: **2 cups of granulated sugar**
    ½ teaspoon of cream of tartar (this will prevent crystallization).
    scant ½ cup of cold water

2   Over a slow fire, stir with a metal spoon until the sugar dissolves.

3   Place next to your saucepan:
    a large bowl of cold water
    2 heavy pot holders

4   Allow the sugar and water to boil until the syrup becomes a lovely amber color (It takes about 10 or 15 minutes, but watch it every moment, for it can darken very quickly. If it gets too dark the syrup will have a burnt taste.)

5   As soon as the syrup is amber color, turn off the heat. Allow the liquid to settle down and stop bubbling.

6   Lift the pan with pot holders—syrup is dangerously hot!

7   Set it in the bowl of cold water to stop the caramel from cooking. (Put it in the cold water at once, if by any mischance you have let the syrup get too dark.)

8   If you are using one large mold, pour in the caramel, tip the mold all around to coat it and when it is all lined, pour the excess caramel back into the saucepan.

9   Add to the caramel in the saucepan:
    ½ cup of water

10   At once, stir it over a slow fire until the caramel and water blend. You must do this quickly, as the caramel is stiffening fast at this point.

11   Chill it to set. You can pour this extra caramel over the unmolded custard later.

12   If you are using individual molds, simply put a good spoonful of caramel on the bottom of each.

Have ready this custard.

1   Put into a mixing bowl:
3 whole eggs
2 egg yolks (A *crème renversée*, which is unmolded, must be firmer than a custard served in its cup, and that is why there are more eggs in a French custard.)
½ cup of granulated sugar

2   Stir with a wire whisk until it is well blended but *not* bubbly. (You want a satin-smooth custard, not one that is lacey and full of holes.)

3   Scrape into the mixture the tiny black seeds from:
½ a fresh vanilla bean (reserve the pod)

4   In a saucepan heat:
1 cup of milk
1 cup of light cream
the empty vanilla bean pod

5   Scald slowly, stirring once or twice.

6   When the milk and cream are scalded, pour in a steady trickle on the egg mixture, stirring with your whisk the entire time.

7   Pour the custard through a fine strainer (a *chinois*, or Chinese strainer, whose conical shape resembles a coolie hat.)

8   Fill the molds just to the top.

9   Stand the mold (or molds) in a shallow pan ½ filled with hot water.

10   Place them in a preheated 325° oven. The water in the pan should never boil, as your custard will separate if it cooks too quickly.

11   The individual custards should bake for ¾ hour, or until a cake wire inserted in one comes out clean.

12   The large custard should bake from 1 hour to 1¼ hours. Test it with a cake wire to be sure it is done.

13   Allow the custard to chill first at room temperature, then in the refrigerator. Then run a knife around the inside of the mold to unmold it.

14   Place a serving dish on top of the mold and quickly reverse them. Lift the mold, and you will have a perfect custard with a shiny smooth caramel top.

You may serve it with the extra caramel syrup, though it is quite rich and sweet enough as it is.

Consommé Julienne

Ris de Veau aux Marrons

Petits Pois à la Francaise

MENU

15

Glace-Crème au Praline

Palets de Dames

Suggested Wine: Chablis

Consommé Julienne
(Consommé with Shredded Vegetables)

Serves four

MARKETING LIST

Chicken Stock
6 chicken wings
6 chicken feet
tomatoes
tomato paste
dry sherry
salt
eggs
white peppercorns
carrot
turnips
string beans
    (young if possible)
white celery
cucumber

In the great old days of gastronomy, an important dinner frequently included two soups—one thin and one thick. Today we are inclined to omit soup altogether, or at best serve just one. A clear garnished soup such as Consommé Julienne is an excellent first course for a fairly rich dinner, especially in this calorie-conscious age. A good strong chicken stock, clear and free from fat, with its own mellow rich flavor, garnished with dainty shreds of firm vegetables, will whet the appetite for the dinner that is to follow. And a tasty homemade soup is enough of a rarity in our time to make it a first course of great distinction.

PREPARATION TRAY

chicken stock

chicken feet, blanched

4 tomatoes, sliced

2 tomatoes, skinned, quartered and shredded

carrots, turnips, string beans, celery and cucumber,
neatly shredded and blanched

1 In a medium-size soup pot of stainless steel or tin-lined copper
    put:
    6 cups of chicken stock (See recipe on page 353. It
    is a good idea always to have a quart or so of stock
    in your refrigerator or freezer.)
    6 chicken wings
    6 chicken feet, blanched (See recipe on page 355.)
2 Bring to a boil and simmer gently for 1 hour with:
    4 tomatoes, sliced with skin left on
    a little salt
    a little freshly ground white pepper
3 If any scum forms, skim it off carefully.
4 Put the consommé through a strainer, into a bowl,
    and allow it to get cold.
5 Remove any fat that rises to the surface.
6 Put the consommé back into the pot with:
    2 tablespoons of tomato paste
    ¼ cup of dry sherry
    3 egg whites, beaten to soft peaks
7 Beat the consommé with a wire whisk, over a slow-
    fire, until it comes to a rolling boil. This is part of
    the clarifying process, and the egg whites will rise
    to the surface, carrying with them all the minute
    particles that would have clouded the consommé.
8 Turn off the heat.
9 Line a colander with a clean towel rung out in cold
    water.
10 Allow the consommé to stand for 15 minutes before
    slowly and gently pouring it through the damp
    towel.

Return the strained (and now clear and sparkling) consommé to
    the pot.
    1 Add: **2 tablespoons of dry sherry**
    2 · The following garnish of julienne vegetables:
        1 very large red carrot
        2 baby white turnips
        a handful of young string beans
        2 pieces of white celery stalk without leaves
        1 small cucumber

Cut the above vegetables into very fine neat shreds and plunge them into boiling water and boil for 2 minutes before draining them well and adding them to the soup.

3   Add too: **2 tomatoes**, skinned, quartered, their pulp removed, and the rest cut into fine shreds.

4   Taste the soup for final seasoning. If your stock was good and strong, it should need very little, if any, as you want its honest flavor to come through.

Be sure with all hot soups that you serve them truly hot. This one should be a transparent amber with bright green, orange and white shreds of vegetables floating in its clear depths. And a curl of fragrant steam should rise from the cup or bowl advising the diners that what awaits them is good—and hot.

Ris de Veau aux Marrons

(Sweetbreads on Chestnut Purée)

Serves four

"Veal sweetbreads may be looked upon as one of the greatest delicacies in meats, and may be served at any dinner, however sumptuous." So said the master chef, Escoffier, before going on to describe the proper procedure for readying sweetbreads for cooking. For this delicacy takes a bit of fussing over in advance of its final preparation. It is very much worth doing properly, you will agree, when you see and taste the exquisite result. And the preliminary work can easily be done the day before, leaving you a fairly simple recipe to prepare, and a resulting dish that is a masterpiece—if you say so yourself.

MARKETING LIST

2 large pair of
Calf's sweetbreads
(to serve four)
butter
brandy
Calvados
meat glaze
tomato paste
potato flour
Chicken stock
white wine
red currant jelly
white pepper
2 Idaho potatoes
2 eggs
1 pound can of
unsweetened
chestnut purée
salt
Cayenne pepper
ground cardamom seed
heavy sour cream

PREPARATION TRAY

sweetbreads, blanched and pressed

1¾ cups of chicken stock

potato and chestnut purée made

207

Choose sweetbreads that are large, very fresh—white and free of bloodstains. Soak them for several hours in cold water, changing it frequently, or leave them under running water, to get rid of any impurities.

1 Put **2 pairs of sweetbreads** in a pan.
2 Cover with **cold water** and bring slowly to a boil.
3 Drain and plunge at once into ice water.
  (This preliminary blanching hardens the surface, and the delicate sweetbreads will now be firm enough to handle.)
4 When the sweetbreads are cool, dry them and carefully trim off fat, sinew and membrane skin.
5 Place them between two jelly roll pans, weighed down with a couple of bricks. (You frequently need weights in the kitchen, and I have found that ordinary bricks, wrapped in foil so they become attractive silver bricks, do the trick admirably. If you live near Fort Knox you might have a better idea.)
6 After an hour or two, the sweetbreads will be well-pressed, flat and of a uniform thickness, ready to be cooked. (The above preparation can be done as much as a day in advance, and the sweetbreads refrigerated until you want to cook them.)

Dust sweetbreads lightly in **flour.** Clap each one between your palms to shake off excess flour and to give it a light, even dusting.

1 Heat in a heavy sauté pan:
  6 tablespoons (3 ounces—¾ stick) of salt butter
2 When it is on the point of browning, put in sweetbreads.
3 Cover with a flat lid that rests on the meat, and place a weight on top of the lid.
4 Brown on one side.
5 Turn sweetbreads over gently with a broad spatula.
6 Brown on the second side, *uncovered.*
7 Flame with **¼ cup of Calvados**
8 When flamed, remove the sweetbreads to a dish.
9 Now, stir into the pan, *off the fire*:
  1 teaspoon of meat glaze

1 level teaspoon of tomato paste

3 teaspoons of potato flour (this will give you a clear sauce).

10 When this is smooth, add and mix in, *still off the fire*: **1¾ cups of chicken stock**
½ cup of white wine
(Although both of the above ingredients will blend into your sauce, they must *not* be added to each other and then poured. It sounds like a good short cut, but it only succeeds in spoiling the flavor of both the stock and the wine. So add them separately.)
2 teaspoons of red currant jelly
1 teaspoon of freshly ground white pepper

11 Stir over the fire until boiling.

12 Reduce the heat to a simmer.

13 Put back sweetbreads.

14 Place on the top shelf of a preheated oven, and cook uncovered for 35 minutes at 375°, basting about four times.

To accompany the sweetbreads, make the following purée:

1 Take: **2 Idaho potatoes**
Skin them, and cut them in half across.
Put into a pan and cover with cold water.

2 Add: **2 teaspoons of salt**

3 Bring to a boil, and boil fairly briskly until potatoes are soft. (Do *not* prick them with a fork to test, or they will get watery. Use an ice pick which will pierce only in one place.)

4 Drain potatoes, and return pan to low heat to dry out all moisture.

5 Strain through a sieve or put through a food mill until smooth.

6 Beat into potatoes: **4 tablespoons (2 ounces—½ stick) of butter,** bit by bit
1 whole egg
1 egg yolk
1-pound can of unsweetened chestnut purée, added teaspoon by teaspoon.
Season with: **salt and cayenne pepper**

½ teaspoon of ground cardamom seed
2 tablespoons of brandy
2 heaping tablespoons of heavy sour cream

7   Smooth the chestnut purée evenly on the bottom of an *au gratin* dish, and with a large metal spatula make a double row of shallow ripples on the surface. Place the sweetbreads on top. Carefully coat them with the sauce.

8   Place under the broiler (on the highest rack) for 1 or 2 minutes, just before serving.

You can then carry to the table in triumph a dish worthy of Escoffier's accolade and your best efforts.

Petits Pois à la Française

(*Braised Baby Peas with Lettuce and Onions*)

Serves four

The tiny peas from a June garden, shelled at the very moment you want to use them, would be the ideal ingredient for this dish. But let us count our blessings. We can still have quite delicious tiny peas, thanks to the frozen food industry. So this dish that used to be a great seasonal delicacy is now ours to enjoy all year round. It is so good it deserves to be eaten as a separate course with no distractions.

MARKETING LIST

3 packages of frozen
    baby peas
  (or 4 cups of
    fresh peas)
Scallions
Boston lettuce
bacon
butter
flour
sugar
salt
white peppercorns
parsley

PREPARATION TRAY

scallions, washed, skinned and trimmed

Boston lettuce, washed, drained, cut into eighths

butter, softened and mixed with flour

parsley, chopped

210

1   Put into a heavy 3-quart saucepan:

> **½ cup of water**
>
> **3 packages of frozen baby peas** or **4 cups of tiny fresh peas** (if you use fresh peas, use about ¾ cup of water).
>
> **1 bunch of scallions,** washed, skinned, and with most of the green skins cut off.
>
> **1 head of Boston lettuce** washed, drained and cut into eighths.
>
> **¼ pound of bacon** cut into strips ¼ to ½ inch wide.
>
> **¼ teaspoon of salt**
>
> **1 heaping tablespoon of granulated sugar**
>
> **a sprinkle of freshly ground white pepper**

2   Cover the pan and simmer gently for 15 to 20 minutes.

3   In a small bowl soften:

> **3 tablespoons (1½ ounces) of butter**

4   Mix in thoroughly:

> **2 teaspoons of flour**

5   Add this *beurre manié* (butter and flour thickening) bit by bit to the pan as a thickening and binding agent.

6   Cover the pan and simmer very, very gently—do not let it boil—for 1 to 1½ hours.

7   Stir the peas occasionally.

These tiny peas will be unwrinkled, their skins intact, even after this long cooking. That is why you can only use the baby variety for this recipe. Full-grown peas would wrinkle and split. The soft peas will be bound together in a creamy sauce, and they are to be served in a deep *au gratin* dish, sprinkled with **fresh parsley.** You are likely to decide, once you have tasted peas in the French style, to become a vegetarian.

Glace-Crème au Praline

(Praline Ice Cream)

Serves four to six

If you have one of the easy new electric ice-cream freezers, homemade ice cream is a rare treat that you will be able to enjoy every day—if you don't have to watch calories. In fact, this ice cream is so superior to even the best commercial product that you may be tempted to make it the hard way in an old-fashioned hand-cranking freezer if you don't have an electric one. Nuisance though that is, it does at least have the advantage of working off in advance some of the calories you're going to get from the ice cream. I wish everyone would try this recipe just once, anyhow, so that you'll all know how truly marvelous a dish of ice cream used to be, and can be again. Better a tiny helping of this creamy-smooth confection than a whole portion of the cardboard carton variety.

MARKETING LIST

granulated sugar
Cream of tartar
eggs
heavy cream
Vanilla bean
praline powder

PREPARATION TRAY

¾ cup of praline powder

3 cups of heavy cream, lightly whipped and flavored

212

1   Put into a small saucepan:
     1¼ cups of granulated sugar
     ¼ teaspoon of cream of tartar
     ¾ cup of water

2   Stir over a slow fire until the sugar dissolves.

3   Let it boil until the syrup will spin a little thread between finger and thumb. (About 225° on a candy thermometer.)

4   In a mixer bowl put: **5 egg yolks**

5   Beat them in the machine until they are light and fluffy.

6   Then, with the machine on high, pour the syrup over the egg yolks in a slow trickle.

7   Continue beating until the mixture is thick and cold.

8   Slowly beat in:
     3 cups of heavy cream, whipped until slightly thick.

9   Add: **the seeds scraped from ½ of a vanilla bean.** (Slit the pod with a small sharp knife, and scrape the little black seeds into the mixture. Put the empty pod into a canister of sugar, if you like, to make vanilla sugar.)

10 Turn the mixture into an ice-cream freezer.

11 Pack around it:
     3 parts of ice to 1 part of rock salt. (See the directions for your particular freezer.) Using too much salt may result in a granular ice cream.

12 Turn the freezer until the ice cream is set. It will not be as hard as commercial ice cream, though it will be quite firm.

13 Mix into the ice cream:
     ¾ cup of praline powder (See recipe on page 351.)

Store the ice cream in a covered container in the freezer compartment of your refrigerator, but do not put it in an ice tray.

   Serve it as you would serve any ordinary ice cream, but be prepared for an extraordinary taste treat!

If you want to be really gala, you can fill a *bombe* mold with the ice cream, and serve it unmolded, surrounded by fresh berries.

1 Rinse your mold out in cold water, pack it with the firm ice cream, cover the top with wax paper (or the metal lid if you are using the special kind of *bombe* mold).

2 Freeze for at least 4 hours.

3 Run a knife around the edges.

4 Reverse the mold on a serving dish and wrap it in a towel wrung out in hot water to loosen it.

5 Knock the mold sharply, and raise it from the ice cream. (If you use a regular *bombe* mold, you turn and remove the screw at the bottom, blow into the little opening, and that releases the ice cream without the necessity of using any heat.)

No matter how you serve it, this is the superb ice cream that caused one Frenchman to say upon tasting it, "What a pity this isn't a sin."

Palets de Dames

(Ladies' Disks)

Makes 36 to 40 small cookies

This is one of the best of the petits fours secs, the wonderful little dry biscuits that grace the tea table or are served with ice cream. Their name comes from the fact that these small disk-shaped cookies resemble the palets of stone or metal used in an old French game. In the game the palets are lagged at a mark, and I suppose that these dainty cookies were considered just about right for girls' rules. They are far too good to be used as playthings, however, and if you have any left over they will keep very well in an airtight container.

When you are making pastry or other baked goods, it is always best to measure your ingredients on kitchen scales. European recipes are always given by weight, and for baking, where absolute accuracy is essential, these recipes are foolproof. I know only too well that many kitchens here do not have scales, so I will give what at best can only be a rough equivalent measure in tablespoons or cups as well as the accurate weight measurement. But I should much rather you went out and got yourself a scale before embarking on any of these pastry recipes. You will find your own product so far superior to store-bought baked goods that you will want to bake often, so you may as well do it up brown right from the beginning.

MARKETING LIST

Sweet butter
Superfine sugar
all-purpose flour
Currants
light rum
egg

PREPARATION TRAY

melted butter

4½ tablespoons (2¼ ounces) of soft sweet butter

2 tablespoons of currants, washed and well cleaned

2 cookie sheets, buttered

First, turn on your oven to 350°.
       1 Brush with **melted butter** 2 heavy cookie sheets.
       2 Set them aside.

1   In a mixing bowl put:
            4½ tablespoons (2¼ ounces) of soft sweet butter
     2 Beat until light and creamy with wooden spatula.
     3 Add: **2¼ ounces (about ⅓ cup) of superfine sugar**
     4 Beat until light and foamy.
     5 Add: **1 egg**
     6 Beat well.
     7 Mix in: **2¾ ounces of flour** (a good ½ cup)
           2 teaspoons of light rum
     8 Beat well.
     9 Mix in: **2 level tablespoons of currants,** carefully cleaned and stemmed.
   10 Put the mixture out onto the greased cookie sheets in very small balls. (Use a small spoon.)
   11 Flatten them out into little disks with the bottom of a wet fork. (If it is wet the dough won't stick.)
       (Here let me suggest that it is the better part of valor to test-bake one cookie first before putting all your dough in one baking. That way, when it has baked, if you find the dough needs to be thicker, you can just add a bit of flour to the bowl. Or if it ought to be thinner, the tiniest bit of cold water will do the trick. And you won't have spoiled the whole batch.)
   12 Bake until the edges of the cookies are a light brown (about 8 or 9 minutes).
   13 Carefully remove the cookies from the cookie sheets with a small spatula and cool them on cake racks.
   14 Store in airtight tins.

Note: The same recipe can be made substituting 1½ ounces of finely ground almonds for the currants. Then the biscuits are called Viscontis and they are put out on the cookie sheet in ovals through a cardboard stencil. Viscontis may be used plain or they may be sandwiched with honey, jam or butter cream filling and their tops lightly dusted with confectioners' sugar.

Quiche Lorraine

Boeuf à la Mode

**MENU
16**

Epinards à la Hambourg

*Macédoine
de Fruits Rafraîchis*

*Suggested Wine:
Châteauneuf-du-Pape*

3 pounds top sirloin
   of beef
1 calf's foot
4 marrow bones
butter
brandy
meat glaze
tomato paste
potato flour
chicken stock
red wine
sherry
red currant jelly
black and white
   peppercorns
salt
celery
bay leaf
18 small white onions
sugar
6 oz. of mushrooms
lemon
2 white turnips
2 carrots
1 package frozen peas
1 package frozen
   string beans
olive oil
vegetable oil
tarragon vinegar
garlic
yellow onion

Quiche Lorraine

(Cheese and Bacon Tart)

(See recipe on page 62.)

Boeuf à la Mode

(Pot Roast of Beef)

Serves six

Some of the best dishes to come out of France are the simple hearty ones that are brought to the table in a large casserole. A loaf of bread, a jug of wine and a beautiful boeuf à la mode are Paradise enow for your true lover of good food.

Because the beef is cooked with a calf's foot, its sauce will jell when it is chilled. Often the leftover meat is served cold in its jelly, and reappears attractively molded and garnished for luncheon or a light supper.

If you want a fine one-dish meal, boeuf à la mode is a classic example.

PREPARATION TRAY

beef, marinated

all vegetables prepared for cooking and in water, except onions

chicken stock

218

1   Remove most of the fat from: **3 pounds of top sirloin of beef.**
2   Tie it tightly several times with fine string.
3   Let it stand in the following marinade for at least 4 hours. Mix together in a saucepan:
¼ cup of olive oil
¼ cup of vegetable oil
1 cup of tarragon vinegar
1 cup of red wine
1 large clove of garlic, bruised
1 onion, sliced
1 stalk of celery, sliced
1 bay leaf
a few black peppercorns
Warm them a little, and pour the marinade in a small deep crock just large enough to hold the meat.
4   After the meat has marinated, remove it and dry it thoroughly.

1   Heat in a heavy pan: **3 tablespoons (1½ ounces) of salt butter**
2   When it begins to brown, sear the beef in it quickly, all over.
3   Brown at the same time: **1 calf's foot cut in pieces**
4 marrow bones
4   Flame with: **¼ cup of brandy**
5   Remove meat and bones from the pan.
6   Stir into pan juices, *off the fire*:
1 teaspoon of meat glaze
1 teaspoon of tomato paste
4 level teaspoons of potato flour
7   And add, *still off the fire*: **2½ cups of chicken stock**
½ cup of good red wine
2 tablespoons of dry sherry
2 teaspoons of red currant jelly
8   Season with: **1 teaspoon of freshly ground black pepper and very little salt** (the meat glaze is salty).
9   Stir over the fire until mixture boils.
10   Put back beef, calf's foot, and bones and **a piece of celery leaf tied to a bay leaf**
11   Put on top shelf of a preheated 375° oven, uncovered, for at least 1½ hours. Baste frequently.

While the beef is cooking:

1 Blanch: **18 baby white onions** (cover them with cold water, bring to a boil, then drain) .

2 In a heavy pan heat: **3 tablespoons (1½ ounces) of salt butter**

3 Add the blanched onions and shake them over a medium fire until they begin to brown.

4 Sprinkle them with: **salt**
freshly ground white pepper
1 tablespoon of granulated sugar

5 Continue shaking till the onions are brown all over, and beautifully glazed. Then set aside.

6 Cut in half, if small, in quarters, if large:
6 ounces of mushrooms

7 Sauté them in: **2 tablespoons (1 ounce—¼ stick) of hot salt butter**

8 As soon as the mushrooms are coated with the butter, add: **1 teaspoon of lemon juice**
salt, pepper

9 Cook for 2 minutes and set aside.

1 Take: **2 medium white turnips** and **2 medium carrots**

2 Cut into ovals about the size of large olives.

3 Cook them in chicken stock until they are just soft.

1 Take: **½ package of frozen green peas**
½ package of frozen string beans

2 Cook them in very little salt water until just soft.

3 Set aside.

1 When beef is done, remove the string.

2 Discard bay leaf and celery leaf.

3 Remove marrow from bones.

4 Remove meat from calf's foot.

5 Replace meat and marrow in sauce.

6 Just before serving, add freshly cooked vegetables.

Serve the entire savory meal in a large casserole, either copper or earthenware, with a long loaf of crusty French bread for mopping up the sauce.

Epinards à la Hambourg
(Spinach with Mornay Sauce)

(See recipe on page 93.)

Macédoine de Fruits Rafraîchis
(Fresh Cut-Up Fruit)

Serves six to eight

A fresh fruit cup can be a delightful finale to a meal, equally good after a heavy or light repast. But it must be memorable in itself, and not just a dull collection of fruit chunks floating in their own juice. There are four rules to follow for a superlative fresh fruit compote.

1. Use fruit that is ripe and flavorful.
2. Take pains to cut it properly.
3. Serve it well chilled.
4. Give it that indefinable something special by adding the marvelous syrup for which the recipe follows.

MARKETING LIST

Oranges
Lemons
Limes
Granulated sugar
Cream of Tartar

SYRUP FOR FRESH FRUIT CUP

(About one quart)

PREPARATION TRAY

the outer rind of

3 oranges

2 lemons

2 limes

peeled and cut into shreds

Have a quart screw-top jar ready to store the syrup in.

1 With a potato peeler, remove all rind from:

   3 oranges

   2 lemons

   2 limes

   (It is very important not to remove any of the inner white skin from the citrus fruits as it is very bitter.)

2 Cut the citrus rinds, a few at a time, on the chopping board. Use a very sharp chopping knife (a chef's knife is ideal) and cut across the strips of rind so you have very fine slivers of orange, lemon and lime skin.

1 Put in a deep heavy pan:

   5 cups of granulated sugar

   3½ cups of water

   1 level teaspoon of cream of tartar

   (This will prevent the sweet syrup from crystallizing.)

2 Stir with a metal spoon over a slow fire until the sugar dissolves, then add the finely shredded citrus rinds and allow to simmer very gently until the rind is quite translucent—like marmalade. This will take about an hour or so.

3 Chill and store in a screw-top jar, but *not in the refrigerator.* Any cool place will do.

This syrup is poured onto the fresh cut up fruit, but not until just before it is to be eaten. Otherwise the sugar draws all the juice out of the fruit and leaves it limp. For buffet service, place a small bowl of the syrup next to your large fruit bowl, and spoon it over each portion as it is served. Never allow the fruit to stand in the syrup.

FRESH CUT-UP FRUIT

As for the fruit cup itself, I will give you one suggestion for a good combination, but much depends upon what fruits are in season, or what looks best in your market on the day you shop. The variations are endless.

The basis for all fruit cups is **grapefruit** and **oranges.**

1 The best way to prepare them is to take a serrated stainless steel knife. Using it like a small saw, remove both the inner (white) and outer (yellow or orange) skin of the citrus fruit at the same time. Be sure there are no little remnants of the white rind still clinging to the fruit.

2 Still using the same knife, carefully remove the sections, taking great care not to cut the dividing skins. Put sections in a large bowl.

3 Cut the **melon** with a small melon baller, and add to the citrus fruit.

4 Skin the **pears,** cut into quarters and then into slices.

5 Add to bowl.

6 Cut the **plums** into sections around the stone, and add.

7 Peel the **bananas,** cut them into thick slices, sprinkle them with **lemon juice** so they won't darken, and add to the bowl.

8 Skin and pit the **grapes,** pit the **cherries,** and add them to the bowl for final accents of color, flavor and texture.

MARKETING LIST

2 white grapefruit
3 navel oranges
1 small melon
2 ripe pears
½ pound of Plums
2 bananas
¼ pound black grapes
3 ripe peaches
¼ pound of cherries
1 lemon

Of course, you can only use the fruits that are in season, but it is nearly always possible to get the citrus fruit. With that as a base, and with the excellent syrup as a flavor brightener, almost any combination is bound to be successful. A glass or crystal bowl sets off the colorful macédoine to perfection.

MENU
17

Crème Olga

Poulet en Demi-Deuil

Boiled New Potatoes
with Dill

Beignets Soufflés Royal

Suggested Wine:
Pouilly-Fumé

Crème Olga
(Scallion and Raw Mushroom Soup)

(See recipe on page 74.)

Poulet en Demi-Deuil
(Chicken in Half-Mourning)

Serves four

(See recipe on page 74.)

There is nothing funereal or even half sad about this chicken when it appears at the table. It is the Merry Widow of roast poultry, elegantly attired in round black slices of truffle showing coquettishly from beneath its skin, hence its fanciful name.

The idea of inserting sliced truffle between the skin and flesh of a fowl is supposed to have originated about fifty years ago in Lyons. It was the specialty of a famous woman chef whose restaurant, La Mère Fillioux, was one of the gastronomic landmarks of that province.

This recipe is an adaptation of hers—our chicken will be roasted rather than poached. It is a fine example of how a little creative imagination can lift a more-or-less commonplace dish to something extraordinary, while still maintaining its basic simplicity.

MARKETING LIST

1 4½ pound chicken
black truffles
garlic
shallots
chives
tarragon
  (fresh if possible)
butter
lemon
meat glaze
tomato paste
potato flour
chicken stock
white wine
Calvados
red currant jelly
white pepper

PREPARATION TRAY

chicken, cleaned, trussed, and with sliced truffles inserted under the skin

shallots, chives, tarragon, garlic, truffle, chopped

chicken stock

226

1 Take a **4½ pound chicken,** remove all fat from it, wash it thoroughly in running cold water, and dry well with paper towels.

2 Rub the inside and outside of the chicken with **½ lemon.**

3 Place the chicken on your board, breast side up, legs toward you. Insert your fingers between the skin and the flesh on one side of the breast bone, and gently loosen the skin over the breast and thigh. Keep your fingertips pressed down toward the flesh, being careful not to poke them through the skin. Repeat on the other side, and when the skin is loosened, carefully insert about: **3 large slices of truffle** along each breast, and 2 on each thigh. Arrange them symmetrically. (Incidentally, you can prepare chicken, turkey or smaller birds for roasting by inserting thin pieces of very cold butter and various seasonings in place of the truffles.)

4 Now truss the chicken with string according to directions on page 356.

1 In a heavy pan heat slowly: **5 tablespoons (2½ ounces) of butter**

2 Stir with a wooden spoon until the butter foams.

3 Put in the chicken, breast side down.

4 Cover pan and brown chicken slowly and carefully on each side of breast.
(Turn chicken by inserting handle of wooden spoon in cavity and flipping it over.)

5 Then brown chicken on each leg, on the wishbone, and lastly on the back.

6 Heat in a small pot: **¼ cup of Calvados**
Ignite it, and pour it flaming over the chicken.

7 When chicken has been blazed, remove it from the pan and set it aside.

1 Add to the juices in the pan: **2 tablespoons (1 ounce—¼ stick) of butter**

2 When it is melted add: **2 level teaspoons of finely chopped garlic**

2 level teaspoons of finely chopped shallots
2 level teaspoons of finely chopped truffle
2 level teaspoons of chopped fresh tarragon
2 level teaspoons of chopped fresh chives
(It is a good idea to do this chopping in advance, or while the chicken is browning. In either case, take the time to look at the beautiful white, black and green bits you have chopped, as they lay on your board like so many mounds of gems. I think one of the great pleasures of cooking is the beauty of the raw materials, especially when they have been enhanced by your own efforts.)

3 Cook for 1 minute before removing pan from fire and adding:
½ teaspoon of meat glaze
½ teaspoon of tomato paste
2 teaspoons of potato flour

4 Stir with a wire whisk.

5 When this is smooth add, still off the fire:
1¼ cups of good chicken stock
¼ cup of dry white wine
½ teaspoon of red currant jelly
a little freshly ground white pepper

6 Stir, over the fire, until sauce comes to a boil.

7 Put back the chicken, whole, and baste it well with the sauce.

8 Place it on the top shelf of a preheated 375° oven for 1 hour, basting several times.

9 Should the sauce separate while in the oven, mix in:
3 or 4 tablespoons of Calvados, and stir well.

To serve: Place chicken on a wooden carving board and carve as needed. If you have a silver platter into which a carving board fits, bring the *Poulet en Demi-Deuil* to the table on it, with the sauce in a sauce boat. Coat each serving with sauce, and try to be Even-Handed Justice in doling out the truffled portions.

Boiled New Potatoes with Dill

These perfectly simple potatoes set off the truffled chicken and its aromatic sauce ideally. And there are a number of other dishes that they are good with too.

It may seem like an elucidation of the obvious to give a recipe for plain boiled potatoes in a gourmet cook book, but the simplest of dishes are so rarely done properly. When the lowly potato is cooked correctly, it can take its place beside many of the more elaborate dishes—and add considerably to their enjoyment.

MARKETING LIST

3 to 6 potatoes per
person (depending
upon size of
potato - not person)
butter
Salt
fresh dill

PREPARATION TRAY

potatoes, scrubbed

fresh dill, chopped

1 Try to choose **tiny new potatoes** of uniform size. Scrub with a brush, but do not peel them before cooking, both for the sake of their flavor and their vitamin content. Cook in enough boiling salted water to cover. (1 teaspoon of salt to 3 cups of water is about right.)

2 When the water is boiling vigorously, put the potatoes in and replace the lid on the pot. (New potatoes are always cooked in boiling water, old ones in cold water brought to the boil.)

3 Boil for about 20 minutes, or until the potatoes are tender but not too soft. It is overcooking that ruins the texture and therefore the flavor of this vegetable (and most others).

4 Drain the potatoes well, and shake them in the pot over the fire just to dry them.

5 Remove the skins.

6 Mix with a **little melted butter** and **chopped fresh dill.**

Serve in an earthenware bowl. Simply perfect, and perfectly simple.

Beignets Soufflés Royal
(Puffed Fritters)

Serves six

This is an unusual dessert to find in the French cuisine where deep-fat frying is usually reserved for potatoes. Beignets soufflés are about as close as French cookery comes to our doughnuts or crullers, but they are lighter and more delicate.

Made of cream puff paste (pâte à choux) that is fried instead of baked, the beignets are delicious eaten just as they are with a generous dusting of powdered sugar. (I have seen one of my cooking classes gobble them up as fast as the cook set them out to drain.) But if you can, serve them hot with one of the fruit sauces or the hot sabayon sauce, the recipes for which will follow the beignet recipe.

MARKETING LIST

sweet butter
salt
all-purpose flour
eggs
vegetable oil
light rum

PREPARATION TRAY

cream puff paste (*pâte à choux*) made up to the point where it is chilled

fruit sauce, if you are using one

1   In a small heavy pan put:

> ½ **cup of cold water** (very accurate measure)
> **3 tablespoons** (**1½ ounces**) **of sweet butter,** cut
> into small pieces so it will melt quickly
> **a pinch of salt**

2   Stir with a small wooden spoon over a slow fire until
the water just comes to a rolling boil. Make absolutely certain that the butter is all melted by the
time the water boils.

3   Throw in: **½ cup of all-purpose flour**

4   Remove the pan from fire at once, and beat the mixture until smooth. Then beat over a slow fire until
it forms a large smooth ball.

5   Put the dough into a mixer bowl and at medium
speed beat in: **2 whole eggs,** added one at a time.

6   Beat until very shiny.

7   Then add: **2 tablespoons of rum**

8   Put mixer bowl in the refrigerator and chill the
batter for ½ hour.

In a deep skillet heat deep fat for frying. Heat to 370° on a fat
thermometer. This is the only accurate way to gauge
the temperature.

1   With a small teaspoon scoop up some of the batter
—about the size of a walnut.

2   Push off into the hot fat with another spoon, and
try to keep it in the shape of a small ball.

3   Now watch your *beignets* puff and swell. They will
turn over in the fat by themselves, for as they brown
on the under side, they become lighter, and the
heavier uncooked side then rolls over into the fat.

4   When the *beignets* are a lovely golden brown all
over, remove them with a fish slice (the flat long-
handled strainer for removing food from deep fat)
and drain them well on paper towels.

5   Roll the *beignets* in **confectioners' sugar,** coating
them heavily, and serve with one of the following
sauces.

APRICOT SAUCE

1 Put into a small heavy pan: the contents of a ½ pound jar of smooth **apricot jam (about ¾ of a cup)**
¼ cup of superfine sugar
the grated rind of 1 lemon
2 tablespoons of lemon juice
3 tablespoons of kirsch

2 Bring slowly to a boil, stirring constantly with a wooden spoon.

3 Allow to simmer for 3 or 4 minutes.

4 Strain and serve hot with the *beignets soufflés.*

Note: As an alternative, the same amount of red currant jelly can be used instead of the apricot. Kirsch or framboise (raspberry liqueur) can be added, and when the sauce has cooled a bit, sliced fresh strawberries or raspberries may be put into the sauce, which will then be served separately with the hot *beignets.*

If, instead of a fruit sauce you prefer a sabayon sauce, the recipe follows.

MARKETING LIST

½ pound jar of smooth apricot jam
Superfine sugar
lemon
Kirsch

SABAYON SAUCE

1 In a small heavy china bowl put: **1 egg**
2 egg yolks
4 rounded tablespoons of superfine sugar
½ an egg shell full of kirsch or framboise liqueur (the larger half, naturally).

2 Stand the bowl in a shallow pan half full of hot water.

3 Place it over a low fire and continue to beat the mixture with a whisk until it thickens—about 7 or 8 minutes. (This sauce does not take kindly to standing around and waiting, so be sure to make it just when you're ready to use it.)

Serve the hot sabayon sauce separately with the *beignets soufflés.* The crisp golden *beignets* are especially good with this creamy custard sauce—an interesting example of two foods that maintain their own individualities while combining beautifully.

MARKETING LIST

eggs
Superfine sugar
salt
Kirsch or framboise

Filets de Sole
à la Bonne Femme

Suprêmes de Volaille
à la Kiev

MENU
18

Rice Pilaf

Soufflé au Citron

Suggested Wine: Chablis

Filets de Sole à la Bonne Femme

(Poached Fillets of Sole with Mushrooms
and Hollandaise)

Serves four

Basically the method of poaching fish fillets in a wine stock with a little mushroom for flavoring is the same in every recipe, but from that point on there are variations in the final sauce and garnish. Onions, cucumbers, shrimp, mussels, cheese sauce, sherry sauce—the variations are limitless. The important thing to remember in every poached fish recipe is never to permit the liquid to boil. Poaching is the art of brinksmanship applied to boiling—the almost but not quite point just below the boiling point. Fish cooked in this fashion will keep their shape and firmness. The tenderness and delicacy of flavor and texture, too often lost in other methods of preparing fish, will be rediscovered when you try poaching your fish. This classic recipe is a particular favorite of mine.

MARKETING LIST

4 fillets of sole
mushrooms
salt butter
sweet butter
salt
flour
cayenne pepper
white peppercorns
light cream
heavy cream
lemon
hollandaise sauce
truffles

PREPARATION TRAY

sole, washed, dried and seasoned

baking dish, buttered

poaching liquid, prepared

mushrooms, sliced

truffles, sliced

hollandaise sauce

fresh lemon juice

1 Wash well in **lemon juice** and **water: 4 fillets of sole**
    2 Dry them on paper towels.
    3 Sprinkle the skin side (the dark side) with:
        a little salt
        a little cayenne
    4 Brush an oblong oven-glass baking dish with a little
        melted butter
    5 Fold the fillets over lengthwise and arrange them on
        the bias along the baking dish.

Now make the following stock:
    1 In a small heavy skillet melt:
        1 tablespoon (½ ounce) of butter
    2 When it foams add: **2 mushrooms, finely sliced**
        (or the stems and peelings from several mushrooms)
    3 Shake the pan until the mushrooms are well coated
        with butter.
    4 Add: **2 teaspoons of lemon juice**
        ½ teaspoon of salt
        a good sprinkle of freshly ground white pepper
    5 Cook briskly for 2 minutes.
    6 Then add:
        ¼ cup of water
        ½ cup of dry white wine
    7 Bring this stock to a boil, then pour it over the fillets
        of sole.
    8 Cover the baking dish with a double piece of but-
        tered wax paper.
    9 Poach in a preheated 350° oven for 15 minutes.
   10 Remove the fillets to a hot flat *au gratin* dish and
        keep them warm until you can cover them with the
        following sauce.

Strain the stock in which the sole was poached.
    1 In a saucepan put: **4 tablespoons (2 ounces—½**
        stick) of sweet butter
    2 When it has melted, stir in, off the fire:
        4 level tablespoons of flour
        ½ teaspoon of salt
        a dash of cayenne pepper

3 When this mixture is smooth, add the strained fish stock.

4 Now stir over a medium fire until sauce thickens.

5 Then add: **½ cup of light cream**

6 Bring to a boil and stir in:
2 or 3 tablespoons of heavy cream

7 Simmer for 5 minutes.

8 Remove the pan from the heat, cover it tightly with transparent wrap and set it aside.

1 In a small sauté pan melt:
3 tablespoons (1½ ounces) of salt butter

2 Add: **4 hard firm mushrooms,** sliced but not skinned

3 Coat them with butter and add:
1 teaspoon of fresh lemon juice
¼ teaspoon of salt
a dash of freshly ground white pepper

4 Shake over a brisk fire for not more than 2 or 3 minutes.

5 Set the mushrooms aside.

Have about a cup of hollandaise sauce ready. (See recipe page 175.) This should be a little bit thinner than usual, as you are going to use it as a glaze and run it under the boiler. If it is thick, it tends to separate then.

1 To serve this dish, arrange the fillets on the *au gratin* dish, side by side.

2 Coat them with the white wine sauce.

3 Then scatter the mushrooms down the middle.

4 Coat the mushrooms and the center of the row of fish with a broad band of the hollandaise sauce.

5 Brown the dish quickly under a very hot broiler.

6 Place a row of **sliced truffles** down the middle, and serve at once.

Suprêmes de Volaille à la Kiev
(Fried Chicken Breasts Stuffed with Butter)

Serves four

This is a favorite dish of Russian emigré chefs, and it has become quite popular here and in France. When you have it in a restaurant, the waiter will take rather elaborate precautions to cut the chicken breast in such a way that the melted butter inside won't spurt out dangerously like an oil gusher. Chicken Kiev has always seemed a formidable dish to serve and to prepare. (One wonders how they get the bones of the breast out and the melted butter in.)

Well, it is not really so difficult or mysterious after all, and once the chicken breasts have been prepared for frying, the actual cooking time is only about 3 or 4 minutes. The paper-thin crisp layer of chicken, with its center of seasoned melted butter is absolutely delicious. Serve it with a fluffy rice pilaf (see recipe on page 240), so that when you cut into the chicken and strike butter, the rice will absorb the golden liquid. Much more fun than letting a waiter do it for you.

MARKETING LIST

2 whole chicken breasts
(if your butcher is good he can skin and bone them)
Sweet butter (frozen)
fresh tarragon
salt
white pepper
garlic
flour
egg
Dry bread crumbs
Vegetable oil
watercress

PREPARATION TRAY

8 slices of chicken breast, rolled around filling, floured, and put in the freezer until now

water cress, washed and dried

a bowl with 1 beaten egg

a bowl with 2 cups of dry white bread crumbs

237

1 If your butcher has not already done so, carefully remove all skin and bone from the **chicken breasts.** You will have four pieces of breast.

    2 With a small sharp knife, carefully remove all fat and sinew that might still be clinging to the flesh. Be sure you remove the long sinew or tendon that is imbedded in the thick upper side of each breast. Scrape the meat from it with your knife, and pull the sinew gently as you scrape, until it comes out.

    3 Lay each breast on a piece of wax paper with the thick side that came off the ribs uppermost. Put your hand on top, and using a sharp knife as though it were a saw, cut the breast in half parallel with your hand.

    4 The top pieces have a little membrane on their surface. Lay them, membrane side down, on separate squares of wax paper, and cover with wax paper. Cover the bottom halves with wax paper, too. You now have 8 slices of chicken breast, each sandwiched between sheets of wax paper.

    5 With a heavy flat cleaver, pound each slice until it is thin enough to be translucent when held up to the light. Be terribly careful not to get the slices so thin that there are holes in them, as your butter will leak out through any tears or rips.

    6 Remove the top pieces of wax paper.

1 Take: **1 stick** (**¼ pound**) of *frozen* **sweet butter**

    2 Cut it into 8 small fingers of butter.

    3 Place one finger of frozen butter on top of each slice of chicken, on the bias. (The membrane side of the chicken should be down, the cut side up.)

    4 Sprinkle the top of the butter with: **a little salt**
a little freshly ground white pepper
¼ teaspoon of freshly chopped tarragon
a very small amount of finely chopped garlic

    5 Roll each chicken slice carefully around the butter, tucking in the ends. Be sure the butter is completely covered and there are no cracks or openings. The soft chicken will stick together when rolled.

238

6 Roll each piece of chicken in **flour.** Pat it smartly so there is a thin even dusting of flour all over.

(At this point in the preparation, you could, if you wished, freeze the chicken Kiev, individually wrapped in transparent wrap, for use the next day or later.)

1 In a small bowl, beat: **1 egg**

2 In another small bowl place:

2 cups of dry white bread crumbs

3 The chicken must be thoroughly coated with beaten egg and bread crumbs, and I find the following procedure the neatest and most efficient way to do it: I use my left hand for the egg, my right for the bread crumbs, and never the twain do meet.

4 With the pastry brush, coat the palm of your left hand with beaten egg.

5 Place a piece of chicken Kiev on your palm, and brush the top and ends thoroughly with egg. (The bottom will be taken care of automatically.)

6 Then with your dry right hand, quickly and lightly roll the chicken in the small bowl of bread crumbs, being sure that every bit of it is covered.

7 Place on a cookie sheet or plate.

8 Repeat until all 8 pieces are breaded.

Cover with wax paper or transparent wrap and chill in the refrigerator for at least ½ hour.

1 Heat **vegetable oil** about 3 inches deep until temperature registers 375° on a fat thermometer. (You really cannot guess with fat, so please do use a thermometer.)

2 Fry until the chicken Kiev turns golden brown— about 3 or 4 minutes.

3 Drain them well on paper towels, and serve piled up on a hot starched napkin on a warm platter. Garnish with small bunches of **water cress**

Warn your guests to cut into the crisp chicken most carefully or they may be sprayed by a buttery geyser. Guaranteed to delight even the most jaded epicure, especially since this is a dish rarely served by the home cook, and not too frequently in restaurants.

Rice Pilaf
(Rice Cooked in Stock)

Serves four

There are many variations you can ring on this basic pilaf. Rice prepared in this fashion—and we borrowed the idea from the Turks, Persians and other people of the Middle East—is especially good with any dishes where the meat or poultry is cut into small pieces and bathed in sauce. The pilaf and the surplus sauce have a sort of preordained affinity—as if, indeed, they were made for each other.

MARKETING LIST

1¼ cups long grain rice
⅓ cup Pignolias
(pine nuts)
2½ cups light
   Chicken Stock
onion
garlic
Salt
white pepper
yellow onion
Salt butter

PREPARATION TRAY

1 yellow onion, finely chopped

garlic, finely chopped

chicken stock

1. In a small heavy pan melt: **6 tablespoons (3 ounces—¾ stick) of salt butter**
2. Add: **1 *finely* chopped yellow onion**
   2 teaspoons of fresh garlic, finely chopped with salt
   1 teaspoon of salt
   1 teaspoon of freshly ground white pepper
3. Stir over slow fire until onion is soft but not brown.
4. Add: **1¼ cups of long grain rice.** Stir until the rice is well coated.
   ⅓ cup of *pignolias*. Stir until nuts are well coated.
5. Cover with: **2½ cups of light chicken stock**
6. Stir over the fire until stock boils. Then reduce to a simmer. Cover the pan tightly.
7. Cook—*without peeking*—for 25 minutes.
8. Fluff up with two forks

Serve separately in a casserole.

Soufflé au Citron
(Hot Lemon Soufflé with Sabayon Sauce)
(See recipe on page 126.)

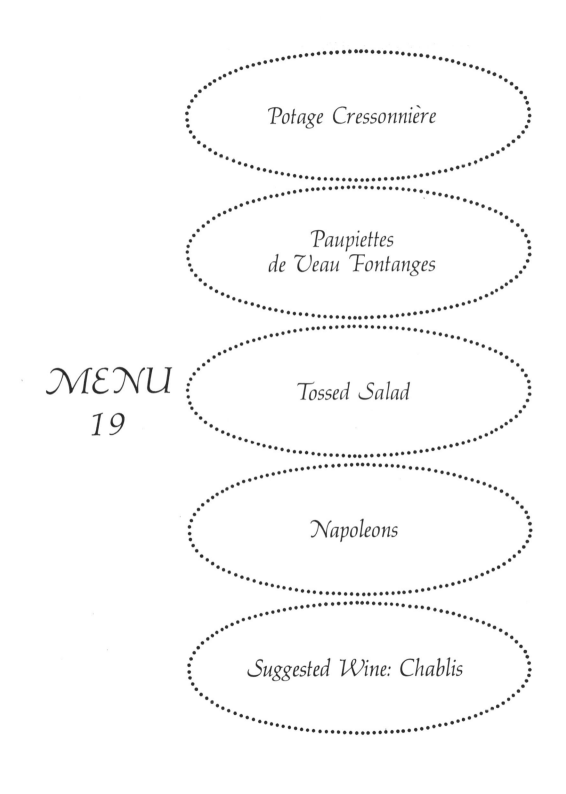

MENU
19

Potage Cressonnière

Paupiettes
de Veau Fontanges

Tossed Salad

Napoleons

Suggested Wine: Chablis

Potage Cressonnière

(Water Cress and Potato Soup)

(See recipe on page 162.)

6 thin slices of veal,
cut from the leg
½ pound finely
ground lean veal
eggs
light cream
salt
white pepper
Calvados
garlic
shallots
6 oz. of boiled tongue
black truffle
salt butter
sweet butter
brandy
meat glaze
tomato paste
potato flour
all-purpose flour
chicken stock
white wine
red currant jelly
3 packages frozen peas
heavy sour cream

Paupiettes de Veau Fontanges

(Veal Birds with Purée of Peas)

Serves six

Paupiettes are thin slices of meat or fish rolled up, frequently around a stuffing. Thrifty French cooks probably invented them originally to use up bits of cooked meat in a tasty filling, but the resultant dishes are so excellent in their own right that they are now their own excuse for being.

Veal paupiettes are known in France as "larks without heads" (alouettes sans têtes), a rather more poetic but less appetizing name than our familiar "veal birds." But there is more than the name to make the difference. First and foremost, the French veal scallops are beaten extremely thin and that gives the dish great delicacy. In this recipe the filling is not only delicious, it is so beautiful that the paupiettes are served cut in half to show their interior design—a mosaic of veal mousse, tongue, truffle and veal. This is a far cry from "something to use up leftovers" and is worthy dinner party fare.

PREPARATION TRAY

6 veal *paupiettes*, stuffed, tied and refrigerated until now

chicken stock

peas, cooked and puréed

1   Put: the **6 slices of veal** between two sheets of wax paper and beat them thin with a heavy cleaver.

2   Remove the top sheet of paper and sprinkle the veal slices with:

a little Calvados (place your thumb over the open bottle top and shake in the best barbershop technique).

a little kosher salt

a bit of freshly ground white pepper

Now prepare the following veal forcemeat (or mousse):

1   In a mixer bowl put:

½ pound of finely ground lean veal

2   Add: **2 raw unbeaten egg whites**

3   Mix well and add slowly:

¾ cup of light cream

(The cream must be added very slowly, almost drop by drop. Slow down the mixer as you add a bit of cream, then speed up the machine until the cream is well incorporated with the veal. Continue adding slowly and beating hard until all the cream is in and the mixture is fairly stiff.)

1 teaspoon of salt (Taste mixture to be sure.)

½ teaspoon freshly ground white pepper

1 level teaspoon of finely chopped garlic

2 teaspoons of finely chopped shallot

1   Spread the mixture on the veal slices about ¼ inch thick. Leave a small margin around the edges.

2   In the center of each slice place:

2 strips of boiled tongue (they should be the size of your little finger).

1 small strip of black truffle between the fingers of tongue

3   Roll the slices up tightly, tucking in the ends so the stuffing is completely sealed in.

4   Tie each end with white string. (The *paupiettes* can be refrigerated at this point, until you are ready to cook them.)

1   In a heavy sauté pan heat:
    2 tablespoons (1 ounce—¼ stick) of salt butter

    2   When it just begins to color, add:
    the 6 veal *paupiettes*

    3   Brown them very quickly on all sides.

    4   In a small pot heat:
    4 tablespoons of brandy
    Tip the pot into the flame and ignite the brandy.

    5   Pour the flaming brandy over the veal.

    6   Remove the *paupiettes* from the sauté pan.

    7   Stir into the pan, off the fire:
    1 level teaspoon of meat glaze
    1 level teaspoon of tomato paste
    2 slightly rounded teaspoons of potato flour

    8   When this mixture is smooth, stir in carefully, still off the fire:
    1½ cups of chicken stock
    ¼ cup of dry white wine (dry vermouth is an acceptable substitute)
    1 teaspoon of red currant jelly
    a little freshly ground white pepper
    (The meat glaze is salty enough to make more salt unnecessary.)

    9   Put the sauté pan back on the fire, stir the sauce until it comes to a boil; reduce the heat to a simmer.

   10   Cut the strings off the *paupiettes* and put the browned meat back in the sauce.

   11   Cover the pan with wax paper (it will cut down condensation of moisture) and the lid.

   12   Simmer gently for about 20 minutes.

PEA PURÉE

1   In a small heavy pan put:
    3 packages of frozen peas
    1 cup of cold water
    1½ teaspoons of salt
    2 teaspoons of granulated sugar

2 Bring slowly to a boil, then cover and simmer gently until the peas are just barely soft. (If green vegetables are overcooked they not only lose their color, but all flavor and food value.)

3 Drain very well. In fact, leave peas in a strainer over a bowl for about 5 minutes so that all moisture has dripped out.

4 Rub through a fine strainer or food mill.

5 In a small heavy pan, melt:
3 tablespoons (1½ ounces) of sweet butter

6 Mix in, off the fire:
3 slightly rounded tablespoons of flour

7 Season with:
a little salt
a dash of freshly ground white pepper

8 Slowly brown the flour.

9 Add the pea purée and mix well.

10 Add and mix in:
3 tablespoons of heavy sour cream

To serve: Heat an oval *au gratin* dish.

With a large spoon put the pea purée down the center.

Smooth out each side with a metal spatula and make small ridges with the same spatula.

With a sharp knife, carefully cut the veal *paupiettes* exactly in half crossways. This will give you an attractive design of veal mousse, tongue and truffle on the cut edge.

Arrange the 12 *paupiettes* on each side of the pea purée. Carefully strain the sauce over the top and serve.

This colorful dish can be prepared well in advance, and need only to be assembled at the last minute. The stuffed *paupiettes* are indeed as delicate and delicious as small birds, and are only a fraction of their cost. But the care of preparation and the quality of minor ingredients are the same for veal birds as they would be for larks, and both are served beautifully. That is one of the secrets of the French cuisine.

245

Tossed Salad

(See recipe on page 69.)

Napoleons
(Puff Pastries with Rum Cream)

Serves six

The delicate flaky pastry that we call puff paste is the most difficult of all to make, but it is well worth the effort. When it is baked it rises in layers of thin crisp leaves (the French name for it is pâte feuilletée or leaved pastry) and is used for patty shells, vol-au-vent crusts, cases for hot pâtés as well as for desserts.

When the crisp layers are sandwiched with a pastry cream you have Napoleons. I am including the recipe for puff paste and Napoleons here because one almost ·never gets the chance to taste them as they ought to be. And it is a shame, really, that in the twentieth century we are disregarding in our home kitchens one of the great culinary delicacies that has come down to us from the Middle Ages —possibly even from ancient Greece. Cakes made of puff pastry have been mentioned that far back in history! I should hate to believe that progress in the kitchen has moved away from quality and toward the dubious goal of instant mashed potatoes. There can't be much satisfaction, either gustatory or creative in that.

The well-known movie star, Joan Fontaine, who took cooking lessons at my school, made Napoleons in class one afternoon. (She was not one to avoid a difficult challenge, that girl!) She was a good cook to begin with, and her Napoleons were superb. First she ate one herself, but her pleasure and pride were such that she had to share her achievement. What did she do? She wrapped one up in a clean white napkin and marched over with it to one of New York's most famous restaurants—Le Pavillon, no less

—which happened to be in the neighborhood. There she presented it proudly to the owner, a man with a formidable background in gastronomy. I think Mr. Soulé's approbation gave her as much satisfaction as an Oscar for her acting ability would have. Certainly her own creativity played as big a part in her cooking as in her acting.

I tell you this to encourage you, too, to try your hand at this recipe. It may be difficult, but you will be rewarded with an artist's sense of achievement when you learn to do it well.

PREPARATION TRAY

pastry made in advance and ready to bake

2 cups of heavy cream, whipped

4 egg whites in a bowl

2 eggs, 2 yolks in a bowl

2 cups of milk in a heavy pan

MARKETING LIST

all-purpose flour
salt
butter
eggs
granulated sugar
plain gelatine
milk
light rum
heavy cream
confectioners' sugar

Make the following puff pastry the day before.

1   In a bowl put:
    4 cups of all-purpose flour
    2 teaspoons of salt
2   Work this up quickly to a paste with:
    1½ cups of ice cold water
    (Handle it as little as possible, because you don't want the dough to have any elasticity, and kneading makes it elastic.)
3   Turn out on a lightly floured board.
4   Roll it out to the size of a large pocket handkerchief.
5   Have standing at room temperature until soft:
    1 pound (4 sticks) of butter
6   With your hands, work the butter to spreading consistency—it should be the same temperature as the dough.
7   Put the butter in the middle of the rolled-out dough.
8   Fold up the dough as though you were wrapping a package. Bring the right and left edges together, and then the top and bottom edges folded to meet.
9   Wrap the package in transparent wrap and then in a cloth.
10 Refrigerate it for 30 minutes.
11 Remove the dough and roll it out on the board in a long strip (about 20 inches long, 8 inches wide).
12 Fold it in 3 evenly. (Bring the top end down toward you and fold the bottom end up over it.)
13 Turn it around so the open edges are at top and bottom.
14 Roll it out once again into a long strip.
15 Fold it in 3 again, and wrap in transparent wrap and a cloth.
16 Put the dough into the refrigerator for 30 minutes.
17 Remove it from the refrigerator, and repeat the process—2 rollings, 2 foldings. (Chefs make dented marks with their fingers on the folded dough to indicate how many turns the dough has had. It must have 6 rollings and foldings [called *tourage* in French] before it is ready to bake. This way butter is spread evenly through the paste in thin layers.)

18 The dough now has had 4 turns. You could wrap it and refrigerate it overnight, and give it the final 2 turns before baking the next day.

19 Remove it from the refrigerator, roll it out, fold it and turn it, roll it out, fold it and turn it the last 2 times.

20 Then, at once, roll the dough out as thin as possible.

21 Cut it in half and roll out each half as long as an ordinary pastry board.

22 Cut the two pieces again so you have 4 pieces, each 20 inches long and 5 inches wide.

23 Place the strips on wet jelly roll pans.

24 Roll out any scraps as thin as possible and lay them on each side of the main pastry strips.

25 Deep freeze the pans for 1 hour before baking.

26 Bake in a preheated 400° oven for 25-30 minutes until the pastry is well risen.

27 Remove and let the pastry cool.

Sandwich the 4 long layers with the following rum pastry cream:

1 In a bowl put:
   2 eggs and 2 egg yolks
   6 tablespoons of granulated sugar
   6 tablespoons of flour
   a pinch of salt

2 Beat with a wire whisk until light and fluffy.

3 Stir in: **4 level teaspoons of plain gelatine**

4 Mix in: **2 cups of scalded milk**

5 Stir this mixture over a moderate fire until it is thick and smooth. (Be sure when you stir you thoroughly scrape the bottom of the pan so it doesn't scorch.)

6 Pour into a large bowl over another bowl of ice and let it cool a little.

7 Add: **3 tablespoons of light rum**
   4 egg whites, beaten to stiff peaks

8 Stir over a bowl of ice until the mixture is very thick and on the point of setting.

9 Then add, bit by bit:
   2 cups of heavy cream, whipped but unflavored

10 Spread this pastry cream between the 4 layers of puff paste.
11 Spread a little on top.
12 In a bowl crumble the scraps of cooked pastry.
13 Sprinkle these crumbs all over the top of the Napoleon.
14 Dust heavily with **confectioners' sugar**

You can serve the Napoleon in one long strip, or you can cut it into individual slices.

It is a real triumph to make a good Napoleon, yet there is no last minute effort involved in the victory. The puff paste can be baked in the morning, the pastry cream can be stored in the refrigerator, and the Napoleon can be assembled a few hours before you want to serve it. The homemade product will have a melt-in-the-mouth delicacy, the flavor of good butter and fresh eggs that you simply cannot find in most commercial products. And once you have mastered the art of making puff paste, there are any number of other desserts and entrées that will be possible as a result of your new skill.

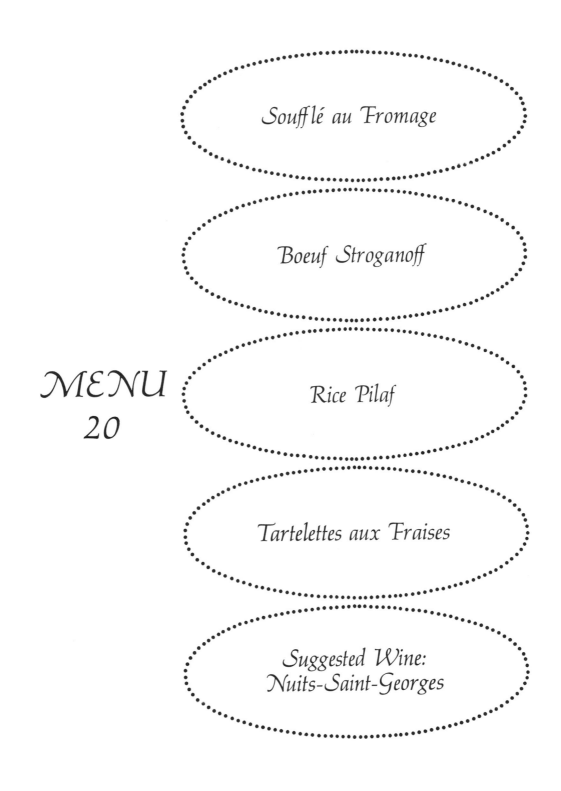

Soufflé au Fromage

Boeuf Stroganoff

MENU
20

Rice Pilaf

Tartelettes aux Fraises

Suggested Wine:
Nuits-Saint-Georges

Soufflé au Fromage

(Hot Cheese Soufflé)

Serves six for a first course, four for a main course

A cheese soufflé is nothing more nor less than a béchamel sauce to which cheese and egg yolks have been added, mixed with stiffly beaten egg whites and baked until it puffs up spectacularly. For all its popularity—and cheese soufflé is almost universally admired—it is not attempted as frequently as it might' be. The fear of a soggy soufflé that fails to rise is one deterrent. Another is that time, tide and soufflés wait for no man. I believe you will find that this recipe gets around both of those drawbacks very neatly. It will also give you a cheese soufflé with a unique flavor that sets it quite apart from any others you may have tasted. If you follow the instructions to the letter, your soufflé will rise to new heights, and so will you!

MARKETING LIST

1½ quart straight-sided Souffle dish
sweet butter
flour
1¼ cups light cream
salt
Cayenne pepper
Dijon Mustard
Dry mustard
Swiss gruyère cheese
Parmesan cheese
Camembert cheese
heavy Sour cream
dry Sherry
7 eggs
fine dry bread crumbs

PREPARATION TRAY

soufflé dish, buttered and cuffed (see directions on page 352)

½ cup of Gruyère cheese, grated

⅓ cup of Parmesan cheese, grated

½ a Camembert, rubbed through a strainer

252

It is a wise idea to have the soufflé dish prepared ahead of time, as once your mixture is made it must be poured into the dish and popped into the oven with no delay. The white porcelain bowls with straight fluted sides are the best.

1 Take a 7-inch dish (1½ quart capacity) and brush the inside with a little **cool melted butter.**

Because I am an eternal optimist, at least about how high my soufflés will rise, I tie a cuff of doubled wax paper around the bowl, giving it a few extra inches of height. (See directions on page 352.) Brush inside of cuff with butter, too.

2 Dust out the inside of bowl and wax paper cuff with **fine white bread crumbs,** tilting the dish and slapping it to make sure the coating is even and thin.

3 Set aside until needed.

1 In a small heavy pan, over a slow fire, melt:
> **3 tablespoons (1½ ounces) of sweet butter**

2 Off the fire add:
> **3 tablespoons of flour,** stirred into the butter all at once with a wire whisk
> **½ teaspoon of salt**
> **a pinch of cayenne pepper**
> **1¼ cups scalded light cream** (Mix this in carefully so you have a smooth *béchamel*.)

3 Stir over a moderate fire until it only just comes to a boil (the sauce must at all times be thoroughly mixed while it thickens as it has to be very smooth and satiny).

4 Remove from heat and mix in well:
> **1 level teaspoon of Dijon mustard**
> **½ teaspoon of dry mustard**
> **½ cup of freshly grated Swiss Gruyère cheese**
> **¼ cup of freshly grated Parmesan cheese**
> **½ a ripe Camembert cheese,** rubbed through a strainer
> **2 tablespoons of heavy sour cream**
> **2 tablespoons of dry sherry**

(It is these last three most unorthodox ingredients, I believe, that make this an extraordinarily delicious soufflé.)

5 Now add, one at a time:
4 egg yolks, beating well each time.

Up until this point the soufflé can be prepared in advance, and can wait very nicely, covered tightly with transparent wrap, until *you* are ready.

About an hour and a quarter before you want to serve the soufflé, light your oven and preheat it to 375°.

1 In a large metal bowl put:
7 egg whites (the 4 whites from the yolks used in the cheese mixture, plus 3 extra egg whites).

2 Beat with a large wire whisk until the egg whites are stiff enough to stay in the bowl when it is turned upside down. (The bowl and beater must be absolutely dry and free of any grease. The egg whites will not rise if there is any grease or fat in them, so if there is even a speck of fatty egg yolk it must be removed before you start beating. Beating in a metal bowl with a large whisk is the best way to aerate the egg whites. You will have much more volume than if you had used a mixer or egg beater. Also, you want to be careful not to overbeat the egg whites for a soufflé or they will collapse when mixed with the rest of your ingredients, and will lack the air power to boost them above the top of the dish.)

3 When the egg whites are sufficiently stiff, immediately pour the lukewarm sauce over them, and fold together carefully with a rubber scraper. The aim is to pass the sauce gently through the egg whites without breaking them down. Do this as quickly and lightly as possible, and at the end of a minute consider the job done, even if there are still a few spots not thoroughly mixed together.

4 Fill the prepared mold with the soufflé mixture.

5 Sprinkle the top with:
a little grated Parmesan cheese

6   Stand the dish in a shallow metal pan half full of hot water.

7   Bake in a preheated 375° oven for about 1 hour or until the top is firm to the touch. (Note: Be sure to leave plenty of room above the dish for the soufflé to rise. One of my students was taken by surprise once in class when hers rose and pushed against the top of the oven from the middle shelf! It *can* happen.)

8   Remove the soufflé from the oven, cut off the string around the wax paper cuff. Carefully peel off the paper.

Tie a folded white starched napkin around the bottom of the dish and serve *at once*. Excellent!

Boeuf Stroganoff
(Fillet of Beef with Sour Cream)

Serves six

There are so many ways to prepare Boeuf Stroganoff that no two cooks seem to agree on anything but the beef and the sour cream. However, there is one very important "must" for this dish. The fillet of beef must be brown on the outside yet beautifully rare within, the whole point being that you can enjoy rare meat in a fine rich sauce. This is not a dish for long cooking, and if it is to be served on a buffet—as it frequently is—care should be taken to keep it hot without continuing the cooking process. Other-wise you will have a beef stew with sour cream instead of a rare and elegant repast fit for a tsar.

MARKETING LIST

2 pounds fillet
of beef
(center cut)
Salt butter
brandy
garlic
½ ounce (1 package)
dried mushrooms
meat glaze
tomato paste
flour
1½ cups heavy
Commercial
sour cream
fresh dill

PREPARATION TRAY

meat, trimmed and cut into pieces

garlic, chopped

dried mushrooms, soaked, drained and chopped

mushroom stock, strained

fresh dill, chopped

1   Remove any skin, fat and sinew from the meat, and cut it into thin fingers 2½ inches long, 1 inch wide.

2   Heat in a heavy pan:
    4 tablespoons (2 ounces—½ stick) of salt butter
    Stir it until it is golden and sizzling.

3   Now, put in your beef, *a few slices at a time*, being careful that the pieces do not touch. This is the trick to browning meat quickly and evenly without allowing any juice or steam to form, thereby stewing instead of sautéing your meat. Remove browned pieces with a slotted spoon or tongs—*never* stab with a fork!—and set aside until all the beef has been cooked.

4   When all the meat is brown, put it back in the pan and flame it with: **¼ cup of brandy**

5   Remove the meat from the pan again and stir into the juices:
    2 tablespoons (1 ounce—¼ stick) of salt butter

6   Remove the pan from the heat and add:
    2 teaspoons of finely chopped garlic (Chop garlic in a little salt with a sharp knife.)
    ½ ounce of chopped dried mushrooms (These give a completely different flavor from our fresh mushrooms, and the two are not interchangeable. Put the ½ ounce of dried mushrooms to soak in ½ cup of warm water for at least ½ hour. Drain the mushrooms, saving the liquid, chop them very fine and add them to the garlic sauce.)

7   Stir slowly over heat for 2 minutes, but don't brown the garlic.

8   Stir in, off the fire:
    1 level teaspoon of meat glaze
    1 level teaspoon of tomato paste
    3 tablespoons of plain flour
    the strained mushroom stock

9   Stir over the fire until it thickens, but don't let it boil.

10   Beat in, a dab at a time:
    1½ cups of heavy sour cream, using a wire whisk.

11   Mix in: **2 good tablespoons of freshly chopped dill**

257

12 Heat the sauce, but keep it below the boiling point or the sour cream will curdle. It should just be steaming. Then put your meat in, but do not keep it in the sauce over a flame or it will continue to cook. It can stay warm indefinitely over hot water, with a cover on, or on an electric hot tray.

If you want to be a thoroughly unruffled hostess, you can brown your beef and make your sauce in the morning, refrigerating them in separate bowls until about an hour before you serve. At the last minute, you can heat the sauce gradually, stirring it to keep it smooth and watching that it doesn't boil. Then add the meat, which will be room temperature by this time, and add your fresh dill to the sauce now, heat the two together, and there's your perfect *Stroganoff*, prepared in advance, yet served precisely *au point*.

Rice Pilaf
(Rice Cooked in Stock)

(See recipe on page 240. Increase recipe by one half
to serve six.)

Tartelettes aux Fraises
(Strawberry Tartlets)

Makes sixteen tartlets

Fresh fruit tartlets are one of the most delightful finales to a meal that I know. If you make the little tarts both round and boat shaped, and further vary them by using several fruits—make some strawberry, some sliced banana, some peeled seedless grapes, and some blueberry—you will have a colorful platter to serve. Just be sure to use the red currant jelly glaze for red fruits and the apricot glaze for the others, as the recipe tells you.

The pastry cream on which the fruit rests may be made in advance and kept in the refrigerator for several days. It is also an excellent filling for cream puffs (see recipe on page 306) or Savarin ring (see recipe on page 118). So when you make it, plan to store some and use it in a very different dessert a few days later. This is a labor-saving restaurant technique that could work well (or save work well) for the home cook.

MARKETING LIST

pastry dough
fine bread crumbs
granulated sugar
ground cardamom
pastry cream
fresh strawberries
red currant jelly
dry sherry

PREPARATION TRAY

pastry dough, chilled

pastry cream, refrigerated

strawberries, washed and hulled

fruit glaze

259

Tartelettes aux Fraises

1   Make up the pastry dough in the recipe on page 63. This will be enough for about 16 to 18 tartlets.

    2   On a lightly floured board, roll the dough out in a very thin sheet, as the molds it is to line are quite small.

    3   Have ready 8 small round tart molds and 8 little boat molds, unbuttered.

    4   Place them all close together.

    5   Lift the sheet of pastry dough on your rolling pin and lay it over the tops of all the molds.

    6   Take a small ball of dough in your hand and push it down into each of the molds. (It is gentler than your fingers and less likely to tear the pastry.) Now your molds are lined.

    7   With your rolling pin, roll across the tops of the molds. That will automatically cut the pastry around each one, leaving very small scraps.

    8   Prick all over the bottom of the pastry dough with a fork.

    9   Brush the surface with **a little melted butter**

    10   Line each with a piece of wax paper weighted down with **raw rice** (this keeps the pastry crust from buckling when it bakes) .

    11   Place the molds on a cookie sheet and bake in a preheated 375° oven for about 20 minutes.

    12   Remove the rice, wax paper and mold, and put the pastry shells back in the oven on the cookie sheet. Leave them to get crisp for about 5 minutes.

    13   Remove the tart shells from the oven and allow them to cool before filling them.

1   Mix together the following:
        2 tablespoons of fine bread crumbs
        2 tablespoons of granulated sugar
        ¼ teaspoon of ground cardamom

    2   Spread on the bottom of each tart shell:
        1 level teaspoon of the mixture. (This will keep the bottom of the shell crisp as the crumbs will absorb any moisture from the filling.)

Fill the tart shells level with the following pastry cream:

1   In a small bowl put:
    2 eggs
    2 egg yolks
    6 tablespoons of granulated sugar
    6 tablespoons of all-purpose flour
    a pinch of salt

2   Beat with a wire whisk until the mixture is light and fluffy.

3   Stir in: **4 level teaspoons of plain gelatine**

4   Mix in: **2 cups of scalded milk**

5   Transfer this mixture to a heavy saucepan.

6   With a wire whisk, stir over a moderate fire being careful to scrape the bottom of the pan thoroughly to prevent scorching. (Don't use an aluminum pan with a wire whisk or your mixture will turn gray.)

7   Continue stirring until the pastry cream becomes thick and smooth. (It may lump a bit at first, but keep stirring. Once it boils it will smooth out.)

8   Put the pan in a bowl of ice and continue stirring until the pastry cream cools a little.

9   Add: **3 tablespoons of light rum**
    4 egg whites beaten to soft peaks

10 Continue to stir over the bowl of ice until the pastry cream is on the point of setting.

11 Then add, bit by bit:
    2 cups of heavy cream, whipped until stiff
    (You will need only about ⅓ of the above pastry cream for these tarts, and you can store the rest.)

12 Fill the tart shells level with this pastry cream and refrigerate them until it sets. Since it is nearly set at this point, it won't take long.

13 Then cover the surface of the tart with **strawberries** that have been hulled, washed and dried. Set them on the pastry cream, hull-side down, point up, as close together as possible.

Glaze the strawberries with the following glaze:

1 In a saucepan dissolve:
   ½ cup of red currant jelly
   1 tablespoon of dry sherry

2 When this has melted, strain it and let it cool before carefully brushing it on the strawberries.

Note: If you use other fruits for these tarts, be sure to glaze with currant jelly for red fruits, and apricot jam for the others.

Another variation is to make a 10-inch pastry shell in a flan ring (see recipe on page 63) and make one large tart instead of the small individual tartlets. In that case, sprinkle around the edge of the flan with a little confectioners' sugar.

Whichever you do, the final step after glazing the fruit is the simplest and pleasantest of all—eat your tart or tartlet promptly. Filled pastry shells lose their fresh crispness if they wait for more than 2 hours.

MENU
21

Pâté Maison

Homard Boréal

Braised Endive

Poires Meringuées
au Chocolat à la Foyot

Suggested Wine:
Dry Champagne

Pâté Maison
(Cold Meat and Liver Paste)

Serves six to ten

One of the most famous luxury products of France is pâté de foie gras—made exclusively of goose liver—which we import here in tins and terrines at enormous prices. But in nearly every little village of France and in each neighborhood of the larger cities, homemade pâtés of mixed liver and meat are available in the shops that sell sausages and pork products. Most restaurants have their own pâté maison too, and it is this poor relation of the fabulous foie gras that is the most popular pâté in France. It used to be made from the liver of a horse, a calf and a pig, according to a recipe in an ancient cookbook!

Naturally, its quality varies with the ingredients used and the skill of the chef who prepares it. But a good pâté maison can be very good indeed. And in its own informal and robust fashion it can hold its own with the more aristocratic foie gras, which is really only for grand occasions.

Your pâté maison will keep for at least a week under refrigeration, and is good to have on hand for canapés, as a first course, or to serve with a salad for luncheon.

PREPARATION TRAY

garlic, chopped

chicken livers, seasoned and rolled in bacon

aspic, chopped (see directions on page 123)

loaf tin, lined with bacon

Line a 2-pound bread loaf tin with slices of bacon.

1 Put into a bowl: **1 pound of ground raw lean veal**
1 pound of ground raw liver (calves' is the best)
½ pound of ground raw pork

2 Add: **2 beaten raw eggs**
½ cup of heavy cream
1 level tablespoon of finely chopped garlic
½ teaspoon of ground sage
2 teaspoons of dried thyme
1 teaspoon of nutmeg
3 teaspoons of salt
2 teaspoons of freshly ground black pepper
1 level teaspoon of paprika

3 Mix this thoroughly with a large wooden spoon.

4 Ignite: **⅓ cup of brandy** and add it, flaming, to the mixture.

5 Half fill the bread mold with this mixture.

1 Take: **4 chicken livers,** season with **salt** and **freshly cracked pepper,** sprinkle with **a little brandy** and roll each liver in a **thin slice of bacon**

2 Arrange livers in a row down the center of the loaf.

3 Cover with the rest of the mixture.

4 Cover top with slices of **bacon**

5 Put a piece of buttered foil over the top.

6 Stand the tin in a pan half filled with hot water.

7 Put into a preheated 325° oven for a good 3 hours.

8 You can tell when the *pâté* is cooked because it will shrink away from the sides of the tin.

9 Remove the tin from the oven and place a weight on top of the *pâté.* This compresses the *pâté* and it will be firmer textured and easier to slice later.

10 When the *pâté* has cooled, put it in the refrigerator to get thoroughly chilled.

11 Then turn it out on a small platter and surround it with set **aspic** that has been cut into cubes, or some sprigs of **fresh water cress**

When you slice into your homemade *pâté,* it should be moist rather than dry, with just a blush of pink at the center. As someone once said, "It takes your own *pâté maison* to make a house a home."

1½ pounds net of
   ground haddock,
   Cod, or sole.
   (allow at least
   another pound for
   skin and bones.
   If your fishmonger
   grinds it for you,
   have him send you
   the skin and bones.)
2 live lobsters
   (1¾ pounds each)
¼ pound net of
   Cooked, shelled shrimp
eggs
light cream
white wine
onion
carrot
Celery
bay leaf
dill
salt butter
sweet butter
brandy
tomato paste
mushrooms
parsley

Homard Boréal
(Lobster Boreal)

Serves six

This dish consists of a hot fish mousse coated with sauce, surrounded by cooked lobster and garnished with stuffed eggs. It is a handsome and unusual way to serve fish and seafood, and since it has several components, a good deal of its preparation should be done a day in advance.

You might want to use parts of this recipe at other times —the eggs stuffed with shrimp and mushrooms are delicious by themselves, and the sauce and lobster butter are well worth knowing for other dishes. But put them all together and you have the incomparable Homard Boréal—Lobster of the far North—a romantically named dish that is almost as spectacular as the Aurora Borealis of the same neighborhood.

PREPARATION TRAY

fish mousse in mold, unpoached

fish stock (see this recipe)

hard-boiled eggs

mushrooms, diced

lemon juice

We will start with the fish mousse which can be prepared in advance up to the point of poaching.

1. Skin and bone:
2½ pounds of haddock, cod or sole
(You want to have 1½ pounds of meat.)

2. Put the meat through a fine grinder, and save the skin and bones.

3. If you have an automatic mixer, you can use it, otherwise, in a stainless steel bowl, over another bowl of ice, put:
1½ pounds of ground fish

4. Beat in with a wire whisk:
3 unbeaten whites of egg (save the yolks in a covered jar to be used for breakfast next day).

5. When the fish and egg whites are well mixed, rub them through a strainer or put them through a food mill and return the mixture to the metal bowl.

6. Beat in slowly:
1¾ cups of light cream
3 good teaspoons of salt
a good dash of cayenne pepper

7. Butter well a plain oval mold (six-cup capacity).

8. Fill it carefully with the fish mousse. (You can refrigerate this, covered with transparent wrap until you are ready to poach it. This much can be done in the morning, if you wish.)

9. Place the mold, covered with buttered wax paper, in a shallow pan of hot water and poach it in a preheated 325° oven until the fish mousse has set (about 30 to 35 minutes).

1. To prepare the lobsters, put in a deep saucepan:
the skin and bones from the fish
1 cup of dry white wine
2 cups of water

2. Bring slowly to a boil, then reduce the heat to a simmer.

3. Carefully remove any scum that rises to the surface.

4. Add: **a little sliced onion**
a little sliced carrot

    a little sliced celery
    1 bay leaf
    2 sprigs of dill
    1 teaspoon of salt
    a few peppercorns

5 Let this fish stock simmer for 1½ hours. Then strain it. You can make the fish stock well in advance.

6 Heat the fish stock in a pan and add:
    2 live lobsters about 1¾ pounds each.

7 Cover the saucepan and allow to simmer briskly until the lobsters blush (about 6 minutes).

8 Allow the lobsters to cool a little, then remove them.

9 Split the lobsters in half, remove the bag from behind the eyes, remove the vein, and carefully take out the meat. Cut the tail meat into neat slices, keep the claw meat whole. (Save the shells and small claws to be used later for the lobster butter. In French kitchens nothing goes to waste!)

10 Set the meat aside and keep it warm until you are ready to assemble the entire dish.

Meanwhile, prepare the following sauce:

1 In a saucepan (preferably tin-lined copper) melt:
    4 tablespoons (2 ounces—½ stick) of sweet butter

2 Stir in, off the fire:
    4 rounded tablespoons of flour
    a little salt
    a little cayenne pepper
    1½ cups of light cream

3 When smooth, stir this sauce over the fire until it comes to a boil.

4 Reduce the heat to a simmer and add, bit by bit, the following lobster butter:

5 In a mortar or a large wooden bowl place:
    the small lobster claws
    the large claw shells
    the tail shells

6 Crush with a pestle until they are broken into smaller pieces.

7   Add: **1 teaspoon of tomato paste**
    12 tablespoons (6 ounces—1½ sticks) of salt butter

8   Continue pounding this mixture with the pestle until it is ground very fine. If you have an electric blender, you can save yourself a lot of hard work by putting the coarsely pounded mixture into the blender until it makes a fine paste.

9   Rub the paste through a very fine hair sieve.

10   Add this lobster butter to the sauce, bit by bit.

11   Cover the saucepan with an airtight seal of transparent wrap until you are ready to use the sauce.

The following hard-boiled egg garnish can also be prepared in advance:

1   Shell and cut in half lengthwise:
    4 hard-boiled eggs.

2   Carefully remove the yolks and rub them through a coarse strainer. Save for later garnish.

3   Fill the whites with the following mixture:
    Cut into small dice:
    ¼ pound of firm white mushrooms
    In a sauté pan melt:
    3 tablespoons (1½ ounces) of salt butter
    When it foams add: the diced mushrooms
    Coat them well and add:
    1 teaspoon of fresh lemon juice
    salt
    freshly ground white pepper
    Shake over a medium fire for 3 minutes.
    Add: **4 ounces of shrimp,** cooked, shelled, deveined and finely chopped
    any small **scraps of lobster meat,** finely chopped
    Mix the chopped mushrooms, shrimps and lobster with a very little of the sauce—just enough to bind.
    Add: **2 teaspoons of finely chopped parsley**
    Stuff the egg whites and sprinkle the tops with the **coarsely sieved hard-boiled egg yolk**

269

Now you may do the final preparation of the lobster meat, and assemble the *Homard Boréal*.

1   In a sauté pan melt:
    4 tablespoons (2 ounces—½ stick) of sweet butter
2   Add: **the lobster meat**
    a little salt
    a dash of cayenne pepper
3   Flame with:
    ¼ cup of brandy
4   Remove the fish mousse from the oven and allow it to stand for 5 minutes in a warm place.
5   Turn the mold out on a hot oval *au gratin* dish.
6   Arrange the lobster around the mousse.
7   Coat the mousse with the lobster sauce.
8   Arrange the stuffed eggs around the sides of the dish and serve.

Perhaps it was the red lobster, the rosy sauce and the gold-sprinkled eggs that reminded someone of the Aurora Borealis, and so gave this dish its name. In any case it is spectacularly good.

Braised Endive

(See recipe on page 55.)

Poires Meringuées au Chocolat
à la Foyot

(Poached Pears with Meringue and Chocolate Sauce)

Serves six

There are so many wonderful ways to use fruit for dessert, yet we tend to repeat ourselves, over and over. Here is a fruit dessert that looks as festive as pastry, has a most unusual combination of flavors, and is, for all its elaborate appearance, not as horribly calorific as one might suppose. This recipe comes from the fine Parisian restaurant called Foyot's, now alas only a legend of gastronomy.

MARKETING LIST

6 ripe eating pears
3/4 cup chopped
  mixed candied fruit
light rum
eggs
superfine sugar
granulated sugar
dark sweet chocolate
lemon

PREPARATION TRAY

pears, poached and stuffed

(if you serve this cold, you can bake the pears in meringue ahead of time and let them cool)

chocolate sauce

271

Poires Meringuées au Chocolat à la Foyot

1   Carefully skin: **6 whole pears**

    2   Leave the little stalk on top, and remove the core with a potato parer.

    3   Make the following syrup by placing in a saucepan:
1½ cups of granulated sugar
1½ cups of water
½ lemon cut in quarters

    4   Simmer gently until you have a light syrup.

    5   Place the pears in the syrup, and baste them frequently.

    6   Simmer the pears for about 15 minutes, or until they are tender but not mushy.
Do not overcook.

    7   Allow the pears to cool in the syrup. When you remove the pears, save the syrup.

    8   In a small bowl stir together:
¾ cup of finely chopped mixed candied fruit
¼ cup of rum

    9   Stuff this heady mixture into the drained pears.

    10   In a long ovenproof dish, stand the stuffed pears in a row with stems up.

Meanwhile make the following meringue:

    1   Using a large wire whisk, beat to soft peaks in a metal bowl: **4 egg whites**

    2   Slowly add: **12 level tablespoons of superfine sugar**

    3   Continue beating until the meringue is stiff. (Can be done in a mixer if you want to spare your arm.)

    4   Fill a pastry bag with the meringue.

    5   Using a star tube, pipe the meringue around the top ¾ of each pear in a continuous spiral. Leave the stem standing free.

    6   Sprinkle the meringue-covered pears well with ordinary **granulated sugar**
(Dribbling the sugar through your fingers is the best way to achieve a nice even snowfall.)

    7   Place the ovenproof dish in a preheated 325° oven until the meringue is set and has cooked to a lovely tawny beige. (From 3 to 5 minutes—you must watch it and see for yourself.)

When you remove the dish from the oven, have ready the following chocolate sauce:

1 Add to the syrup in which the pears were cooked: **4 ounces of dark sweet chocolate,** cut up into small pieces.
2 Stir with a wooden spoon over a very slow fire until the chocolate has dissolved.
3 Let the sauce simmer for 5 minutes.
4 Pour it around the bottoms of the pears.

This dessert is served—either warm or cold—directly from its baking dish, with each guest helping himself to a meringue-coated pear and some hot chocolate sauce. Be prepared for exclamations of surprised delight when your guests come to the hidden treat within.

The entire dessert can be made earlier in the day, and the meringue-coated pears may be chilled in the refrigerator. This leaves only the chocolate sauce to be reheated at mealtime and poured around the base of the pears.

Note: This is a good dessert, too, if Roman Beauty apples are substituted for the pears. In that case, use a regular apple corer, and proceed with the same recipe.

MENU
22

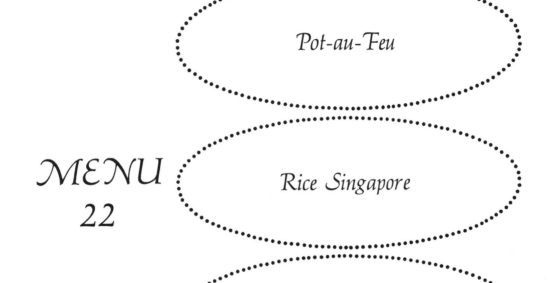

Pot-au-Feu

Rice Singapore

Suggested Wine: Chablis

1 3½ pound chicken, whole
1½ pounds of eye-round of beef
4 Marrow bones
1 Calf's foot (split in half)
lemon
Kosher salt
Carrots
Yellow onions
White Celery
leek
tomato
White turnips
mushrooms
parsley
Italian parsley
Celery leaf
bay leaf
black peppercorns
Salt
tomato paste
dry Sherry
dry white wine
eggs
peas
String beans
parmesan cheese
French bread
cayenne pepper

Pot-au-Feu or Petite Marmite

(Boiled Meat and Bouillon)

Serves six

Mirabeau, the French Revolution's great orator, called pot-au-feu "one of the foundations of the Empire." Used in every French household, the large pot in which meat, poultry and vegetables simmer for hours over the fire produces the stock that is the foundation of most consommés, aspics and a number of sauces in French cooking. This "pot-on-the-fire" has been a fixture of French gastronomy since the Middle Ages, and it was dramatized by King Henri IV who wished that every one of his subjects might put a chicken in their pot every Sunday.

Strangely enough, the meat and vegetables are really only by-products necessary to the making of a good consommé. But as a result of producing several extra quarts to be used in the kitchen throughout the week, you also have a full-course dinner to be served that night. Pot-au-feu is frequently served piecemeal—the clear broth first, the boiled meat and vegetables separately.

Petite marmite is almost identical with pot-au-feu except that its primary purpose is to be served and eaten all together and at once. Its name comes from the marmite, or tall earthenware pot, in which it is cooked. In the case of petite marmite a smaller quantity can be made in a smaller pot. You may call the following dish by either name, and serve it which ever way you prefer. In either event you will be eating one of the basic preparations of French cuisine, refined over the centuries, the epitome of care and fine ingredients.

PREPARATION TRAY

chicken, washed, dried, seasoned and trussed

beef, trimmed and tied

vegetables, cleaned and sliced or cut

bouquet garni, tied

Parmesan cheese, grated

276

To make a good *pot-au-feu*, you must first get a good pot. The tall earthenware cylinders, known as *marmites*, are ideal. They allow very little evaporation, as a result of their shape. Enameled cast iron is good, too, but neither aluminum nor stainless steel will give you as happy a result, since they are not heavy or deep enough. The pot must be at least 2-gallon capacity.

1   Wash, dry and truss:
> **a 3½ pound chicken** (See directions on page 356.)
2   Rub the inside with: **lemon**
3   Season with: **kosher salt**
4   Place the chicken in a double band of aluminum foil about 6 inches wide and 20 inches long, that will be like a hammock or a sling for it when it is put into the pot.

1   Wipe with a damp cloth and remove the fat from:
> **a 1½-pound piece of eye round of beef**
2   Tie it tightly 2 or 3 times with string so it won't dry out or fall apart when cooking.
3   Put into a deep heavy pot:
> **the beef**
> **3 or 4 marrow bones**
> **1 calf's foot,** split in half
> **the veal knuckle**
> the chicken in its foil sling (Bend the ends of the foil over the edges of the pot.)
4   Cover with cold water (about 4 quarts).
5   Bring to a boil very slowly.
6   Reduce the heat to a simmer and carefully skim off the scum. (This must be done whenever raw meat is boiled. The liquids in the meat, which consist in large part of albumen, join with the hot water and then coagulate. These particles expand and rise to the surface as scum. The more carefully you skim this off, the clearer your consommé or bouillon will be. When you have removed it all, wipe away any scum that has formed a ring around the pot.)
7   To the liquid add for flavor: **1 very small carrot**

1 large yellow onion, peeled

1 large piece of celery, the white stalk only, cut into thick slices

1 leek, cut in quarters

1 tomato (with skin on), cut in quarters

1 very small white turnip

a few mushroom peelings and stalks (If you don't have any, use the stalks from ¼ pound of mushrooms and put the caps away for another day.)

8   In a small sauté pan heat:

1 tablespoon (½ ounce) of butter

9   When it is hot, add:

1 thick slice of yellow onion

10   Brown it until it is very dark and glazed, then add it to the pot.

11   Tie together:

1 large sprig of parsley

1 sprig of Italian parsley

1 celery leaf

1 bay leaf

12   Tie one end of the string around the handle of the pan so you can remove this *bouquet garni* easily.

13   Add to the pot:

12 peppercorns

1 tablespoon of salt

14   Cook gently for about 2 hours.

15   After the first 45 minutes, remove the chicken (now you know why it was in a sling). Just lift the foil sling, chicken and all, and set it aside.

16   At the end of the 2 hours, put back the chicken and allow it to cool in the stock.

17   When the stock is just warm, strain it carefully into a large clean bowl.

1   If you want to clarify the consommé, let it get cold.

2   Remove all fat that rises to the top.

3   Into a large tin-lined copper saucepan put:

the degreased consommé

1 tablespoon of tomato paste

¼ cup of very dry sherry

278

½ cup of dry white wine
3 egg whites beaten to soft peaks

4   Heat over a slow fire, beating with a wire whisk, until the consommé comes to a rolling boil.

5   Draw the pan aside and let it stand for at least 15 minutes without touching it.

6   Rinse out a cloth in cold water and line a colander with it.

7   Slowly pour the consommé through it. The egg whites and any particles that clouded the liquid will remain.

8   What comes through is clarified consommé, the aristocrat of them all. (You may serve it hot or use it for aspic.)

To serve this as *petite marmite*:

1   This can be brought to the table in the earthenware *marmite* in which it was cooked, or in a tureen. It will then be ladled into large shallow soup plates that have been warmed.

2   Put into the *marmite* or tureen for each person:
2 small pieces of white meat of chicken
2 small pieces of dark meat of chicken
2 squares of beef (cut about 1 inch square)
a small piece of marrow
a little of the calf's foot cut into strips

3   Just before serving, add to the hot consommé:
24 baby carrots, cut into very small olive shapes and cooked in a little water until soft
24 baby turnips prepared the same way
¾ cup of freshly shelled young peas, cooked until just tender
1 cup of finely shredded string beans, cooked until just tender
a little shredded celery, just cooked

Serve this as *petite marmite* with:
A separate bowl of **freshly grated Parmesan cheese.**
A basket filled with **very thin slices of French bread,** sprinkled with the **cheese** and **cayenne** and lightly browned in the oven.

279

Serve this as *pot-au-feu* by presenting the stock as soup garnished with a few vegetables. Slices of French bread browned in the oven with a coating of fat skimmed from the soup or spread with marrow are the classic accompaniment.

The boiled beef and chicken are then served as a separate course, with the rest of the vegetables.

The stock you get from *pot-au-feu* is superlative, and the delicious dinner is just a secondary benefit. Put the extra stock, cooled, in plastic containers holding 2 cups each and freeze or refrigerate for future use.

In cooking as in families, if one's stock is good the results are bound to be good too. So when you make *pot-au-feu* you are laying the groundwork for future culinary successes, as well as enjoying it that day. A rare instance of eating one's cake and having it too.

Rice Singapore

Serves six

If you hated the gummy, lumpy rice pudding of your child-hood, don't, please, shut your mind against all other rice desserts—though I should hardly blame you if you did. Rice Singapore is a creamy-smooth confection that tastes so delicious it's hard to believe that it's good for you into the bargain. In appearance and flavor it is much like the classic Riz à l'Impératrice, though its preparation is much simpler. Fit for an empress, recommended for the children (without the sprinkling of liqueur on the fruit), this is a magnificent dessert to have in your repertoire.

MARKETING LIST

2 quarts of milk
heavy cream
Carolina rice
plain gelatine
granulated sugar
½ vanilla bean
   (fresh)
lemon
1 pint of fresh
   strawberries
red currant jelly
framboise or Kirsch

PREPARATION TRAY

rice mold, refrigerated

strawberries, hulled and washed

red currant glaze

chilled round platter

1 Wash well and drain: **½ cup of Carolina rice**

2 In a large, heavy pan pour:
   1 quart of cold milk

3 Add:
   the ½ cup of washed rice
   the empty pod of ½ fresh vanilla bean.
   (Scrape out the tiny black seeds and reserve them to flavor the whipped cream later.)

4 Place the pan on an asbestos mat over a very low fire. The slower this cooks, the better. If it cooks for at least 2½ hours it will be delicious.

281

5 Stir frequently until the rice begins to absorb the milk. Then each time you stir, add a little more milk.

6 In this manner you will gradually add:
1 quart of cold milk

7 Continue to stir until the rice has absorbed all of the milk. Again, the slower this is done, the better your results will be.

8 Stir into the thick rice mixture:
1 cup of granulated sugar

9 Rub the mixture through a strainer or put it through a food mill.

10 Soften: **2 tablespoons of unflavored gelatine (2 envelopes) in ¼ cup of cold water, 2 teaspoons of fresh lemon juice**

11 Add to the strained rice mixture.

12 Stir until the gelatine is completely dissolved.

13 Put a large metal bowl over another bowl of ice.

14 Turn the rice and gelatine mixture into it.

15 Stir over ice until the mixture becomes very thick.

16 In a metal bowl, over ice, beat:
1 pint of heavy cream
scrapings from ½ a vanilla bean

17 When the cream is thick, fold it into the rice mixture and quickly fill the mixture into a lightly oiled 8-inch ring mold.

18 Cover it with oiled wax paper.

19 Place the mold in the refrigerator to set for at least 4 hours. (You can make this the day before and refrigerate it overnight, if you wish.)

20 Wash and hull: **1 pint of fresh strawberries**

21 Heat and strain: **½ cup of red currant jelly**

22 Sprinkle the berries with:
2 tablespoons of framboise or kirsch

23 Mix the berries well with the strained jelly to give them a glaze.

To Serve: Dip the mold in hot water for the count of one. Slide a knife blade around the edges. Turn the Rice Singapore out on a chilled round platter.

Fill center of mold with the glazed strawberries.

MENU
23

Petite Marmite

Hot Salmon Mousse

Charlotte de Pommes

Suggested Wine: Marsala

Petite Marmite

(Boiled Meat and Bouillon)

(See recipe on page 276.)

Hot Salmon Mousse

Serves four

MARKETING LIST

1½ pounds of ground
Salmon (net wt.)
(allow about 1 lb.
extra for skin
and bones)
Salmon skin and
bones and a few
extra sole bones
eggs
heavy cream
light cream
flour
milk
dry sherry
carrots
onions
celery
bay leaf
dill
white peppercorns
sweet butter

More and more today people want to eat lightly and at the same time dine well. A fish mousse with a delicate mousseline sauce fills the bill on both counts. "Mousse" comes from the French word for froth or foam, and "mousseline" is that airiest and most delicate of fabrics—muslin. Applied to food, and combined in this recipe the two words are a guarantee of gossamer fare.

When serving salmon mousse in a ring mold, you can follow this suggested menu and leave the center of the mold empty. Or you could instead use the cucumber garnish on page 182 and fill the center of the mold with cooked cucumbers. In either case this is a meal of delicacy and lightness that still satisfies the most epicurean appetite.

PREPARATION TRAY

salmon mousse, except for beaten egg whites

8-inch ring mold, buttered

fish stock (see this recipe)

heavy cream, whipped

1   Put in a mixer bowl: **1½ pounds of ground salmon**
   2   Add, unbeaten:
      1 egg
      2 egg whites
   3   Beat until thoroughly mixed.
   4   Beat in very slowly, almost drop by drop:
      1¼ cups of light cream

Remove bowl from mixer and stir in the following cream sauce:
   1   Melt in a pan: **3 tablespoons (1½ ounces) of sweet butter**
   2   Stir in, off the fire: **3 tablespoons of flour**
   3   Season with:
      a little salt
      a dash of cayenne pepper
   4   Mix in: **1 cup of milk**
   5   Stir over the fire until the sauce comes to a boil.
   6   Let it cool, then stir it into the fish mousse.
      (Recipe can be made in advance to this point, then refrigerated.)

1   Lightly mix in: **2 egg whites, beaten to soft peaks**
   2   Butter an 8-inch ring mold well.
   3   Fill with salmon mixture.
   4   Cover the mold with a piece of buttered wax paper.
   5   Stand it in a pan of shallow water.
   6   Poach the mousse in a preheated 350° oven for 35 or 40 minutes—until it is just firm to the touch.
   7   When the mousse is cooked, remove it from the oven and let it stand for 5 minutes to settle into itself, as it were (you do this with anything that comes out of the oven).
   8   Then turn the mousse out on a hot round serving dish, and cover it with the following sauce.

MOUSSELINE SAUCE

Make the following fish stock (this can be done well in advance):
   1   In a saucepan put: **the fish bones and skin,** well washed.

2 Cover with:

2½ cups of water

½ cup of dry white wine

3 Bring slowly to a boil, then reduce the heat to a simmer.

4 Skim off any scum that forms.

Add: **¾ cup in all of sliced onion, carrot and celery** (very little celery)

1 bay leaf

1 sprig of parsley

1 sprig of dill

8 peppercorns

5 Simmer down gently until the stock is reduced to ⅓ cup. Strain and chill. (If you refrigerate this or any other good strong stock it will jell. You must warm it back to its liquid state before using it.)

6 Put in a bowl:

1 egg

2 egg yolks

1 tablespoon of dry sherry

⅓ cup of concentrated fish stock. (All the flavor for your sauce is in the stock, and that is why it is important to season it well, and boil it down to a strong essence.)

7 Stand the bowl in a shallow pan of hot water. A skillet half-filled with water is excellent for the purpose. Do not let the water boil, or you will scramble the eggs in the sauce.

8 Beat with an egg beater until the sauce thickens.

9 Then, bit by bit, add:

6 tablespoons (3 ounces—¾ stick) of sweet butter

10 Keep beating until all the butter has been added.

11 Now gently fold in without beating:

½ cup of heavy cream, whipped until stiff

12 Pour at once over the salmon mousse, and serve, or if you prefer, you may serve the sauce separately.

Note: You can make this same mousse with other kinds of fish—flounder, halibut or hake are lean and firm enough to use as a substitute.

Charlotte de Pommes
(Apple Charlotte)

Serves four

Those two most homely foods—apples and bread—combine here to make a marvelous dessert. It is impressive looking too, as is anything that comes out of a charlotte mold. Only be careful that your fried bread pieces completely line the mold, and that your apple purée is firm enough to hold up when the dessert is unmolded. As for the rest, the combination of flavors, textures, and the cold sauce on the warm charlotte are absolutely foolproof and unbeatable.

MARKETING LIST

bread
sweet butter
granulated sugar
green apples
apricot jam
lemon
bread crumbs
nutmeg
cinnamon
heavy cream
vanilla bean
confectioners' sugar
sour cream
cardamom

PREPARATION TRAY

charlotte mold, lined with fried bread

apple purée made

sauce, made and refrigerated

1   Remove all the crusts from 1 loaf of good sliced bread. Cut each slice into thirds.

    2   In a sauté pan, melt:
        4 tablespoons (2 ounces—½ stick) of butter

    3   When it foams add:
        several fingers of bread

    4   Fry one side only until it is light golden brown.

    5   Fry all the bread in this way.

1   Take a charlotte mold about 8 inches in diameter and about 3⅓ inches deep.

    2   Grease the inside of the mold heavily with softened **butter.** (Apply it with a wad of paper toweling.)

    3   Dust out the buttered mold lightly with **granulated sugar**

    4   Completely and carefully line the mold with the bread, placing the fried side next to the tin.

    5   Cut out bits to fit the bottom exactly. There must be no cracks for the filling to leak through. Set aside the lined mold.

    6   Skin and core: **8 green apples**

    7   Cut them into quarters and then into eighths.

    8   Put them in a heavy 5-quart pan with:
        6 tablespoons (3 ounces—¾ stick) of sweet butter
        1 small jar of apricot jam
        the grated rind of 1 lemon
        the juice of ½ lemon
        ½ cup of granulated sugar

    9   Cook very slowly until the fruit has become a thick pulp. It should hold its shape in the spoon.

  10   Mix together:
        1 cup of bread crumbs
        ½ cup of melted sweet butter
        ½ cup of granulated sugar
        ½ teaspoon of nutmeg
        a pinch of cinnamon

  11   Mix well, and add this to the apple purée. You must have a very thick fruit purée, or it will soften the crust of bread, and when you come to unmold it, the charlotte will collapse.

12 Fill the purée into the lined mold, and allow it to dome up higher in the center, as it will sink a bit in the cooking.

13 Cover the top with more fingers of bread, fried side up.

14 Place on a small tin and bake in a preheated 375° oven for 35–40 minutes.

15 It is done when the charlotte is just firm to the touch.

16 Remove it from the oven, and allow it to stand and cool for 5 minutes.

17 Slide a knife around the edge of the mold, invert it on a hot round serving dish, and lift off the mold carefully.

Serve the warm charlotte with the following chilled sauce:

1 In a large metal bowl over another bowl of ice, whip: **1 cup of heavy cream**

2 Beat it with a large wire whisk until it begins to hold its shape.

3 Add: **the scraped seeds from a 2-inch piece of fresh vanilla bean.**
2 tablespoons of confectioners' sugar

4 Beat until the cream is thick.

5 Mix in carefully with a rubber scraper:
1½ cups of heavy sour cream
1 level teaspoon of grated nutmeg
the grated rind of 1 lemon
a pinch of cinnamon
½ teaspoon of ground cardamom

Serve this sauce ice cold, in a separate bowl, and spoon it over the warm charlotte. This is a delicious sauce to serve over any warm cooked fruit—baked apples take to it beautifully, for example. Many times a quick family meal can be enhanced by the addition of a quickly made but excellent sauce such as the one above, or the sabayon sauce on page 232.

**MENU
24**

Crêpes aux Fruits de Mer

Boeuf Bourguignon

Salade d'Endive

Rice Singapore

Suggested Wine:
Châteauneuf-du-Pape

Crêpes aux Fruits de Mer
(Pancakes Stuffed with Seafood)

Serves six

There are any number of little French restaurants in New York that have made their reputations on pancakes stuffed with seafood or chicken. The dish is given a fancy name and then it is touted to customers in reverential tones as the "specialty of the house." Your house, too, can have such a specialty, and it will probably taste much better than most of the restaurant versions. For there are very few restaurant kitchens today where one finds the exacting care and top ingredients so necessary to fine cooking. A home kitchen presided over by a devoted amateur cook (like those reading this book or attending my classes—I like to think) is almost the last stronghold of the culinary art. As for this vaunted "specialité de la maison," it is simply that marvelous old stand-by, crêpe batter (see the recipe on page158), which I recommended that you keep on hand at all times in your refrigerator. This time you fill the pancakes with seafood and coat them with a fish velouté sauce, and voilà! Your reputation's made!

MARKETING LIST

Crêpe batter
mushrooms
salt butter
sweet butter
lemon
salt
white peppercorns
cayenne pepper
all-purpose flour
fish stock
light cream
eggs
dry sherry
heavy cream
Parmesan cheese
flaked crabmeat
1 small lobster

PREPARATION TRAY

pancakes, made in advance

seafood stuffing, made in advance

sauce, made in advance

au gratin dish, buttered

Parmesan cheese, grated

melted butter

292

If you are making the pancake batter fresh you can do it in the morning, or even the night before, as it needs to be refrigerated for at least half an hour. You can cook your pancakes way ahead of time, too—in the morning if you want to use them that evening. (See recipe on page 158.) Simply pile them up, one on top of the other, cover them with wax paper, and refrigerate them. They won't stick or spoil, and my only advice is to let them stand at room temperature for a while before filling them so they will not be too chilled when they go under the broiler for the final heating and browning before you serve them.

For the seafood stuffing:

1　Heat in a sauté pan:
　2 tablespoons (1 ounce—¼ stick) of butter

2　When it is hot, add:
　½ cup of flaked crabmeat
　the meat of 1 small lobster, boiled and cut into pieces (about ¾ cup)
　½ teaspoon of salt
　½ teaspoon of freshly ground white pepper

3　Shake over a moderate fire for 1 or 2 minutes.

4　Add: **1 tablespoon of dry sherry**
　2 finely chopped hard-boiled eggs

5　Mix well, remove from the heat, cover the pan and keep warm.

For the sauce:

1　Heat in a sauté pan:
　4 tablespoons (2 ounces—½ stick) of butter

2　When the butter foams, add:
　4 firm white mushrooms cut into thin slices

3　Stir with a wooden spoon until the mushrooms are well-coated with butter.

4　Then add:
　½ teaspoon of lemon juice, drop by drop
　¼ teaspoon of salt
　a good sprinkle of freshly ground white pepper

5　Cook briskly for 2 minutes only. *Don't overcook.*

(These mushrooms will continue cooking in the sauce, and their first syllable notwithstanding, you don't want *mush,* you want a firm, juicy vegetable.)

6 Remove from the fire and stir in:
3 rounded tablespoons of flour
½ teaspoon of salt
a dash of cayenne

7 Still off the fire, mix in with a wire whisk:
a good cup of fish stock (See recipe on page 52.)

8 Stir over the fire until the sauce boils.

9 Then add, bit by bit:
2 teaspoons of sweet butter
¼ cup of light cream

10 Simmer for 5 minutes.

11 In a small bowl mix:
2 egg yolks
2 tablespoons of dry sherry
2 tablespoons of heavy cream

12 This will be used to bind and enrich your sauce. But whenever you have to add raw egg yolk to hot sauce, you add some of the hot sauce to the egg first, and it will never curdle. This is a basic rule.

13 So, add a little hot sauce to the egg, beating with the whisk all the time. When they are thoroughly blended, add the contents of the bowl to the saucepan.

14 Return to the fire and add:
1 tablespoon of freshly grated Parmesan cheese

15 Reheat, but *do not boil* the sauce.
(Once the egg yolks have been added to the sauce, it must not boil again.)

1 Lay out your pancakes with the wrong side up. (The "wrong side" is the second side to be cooked, and it is never as evenly browned as the first side. You want the well-browned side to be on the outside.)

2 On top of each pancake put:
1 tablespoon of seafood filling

3 Spread it out evenly and roll up the pancake like a small cigar.

4 Arrange the rolled pancakes down a buttered *au gratin* dish.

5 Carefully coat with the fish *velouté* sauce. (Use a large spoon; don't pour from the saucepan.)

6 Sprinkle the top with:
a little freshly grated Parmesan cheese
a little melted butter

7 Brown under a hot broiler for only a few minutes.

8 Give it a fancy name, and serve it as the specialty of *your* house.

This is equally delicious filled with chopped cooked chicken, turkey, or ham, in which case you use a *velouté* sauce made with chicken stock. (See recipe on page 353.)

The *crêpes* are good as a sweet, too, rolled around jam and sprinkled with confectioners' sugar, or just rolled up empty, sprinkled with sugar and served with a wedge of lemon. And, of course, there are always *crêpes Suzette* (see recipe on page 157) for a super de luxe dessert. So you see, if you keep a jar of *crêpes* batter always on hand in your refrigerator you are almost as well off as if you had your own genie in a jar for instant kitchen magic.

Boeuf Bourguignon

(Ragout of Beef with Burgundy)

Serves six

French home-cooking is as good in its way as the classic haute cuisine practiced by professional chefs. The dishes that we lump under the uninspired title of "stews" are called variously "ragoûts," "daubes" and "estouffades" by French housewives, and the diversity of names hints at the inventiveness of the home cooks.

These are the dishes that can be cooked in earthenware, copper or enameled cast-iron casseroles and brought right to the table from the stove. They can be kept warm over a low fire, or cooked the day before and, if anything, their flavor is enhanced by waiting.

Red wine, baby onions, mushrooms and salt pork, ham or bacon are the distinctive added ingredients of this beef ragout. They are hallmarks of Burgundian cooking—flavorful country fare steeped in winy sauce that can hold its own with the full-bodied vintages of the region.

MARKETING LIST

2½ pounds of beef
(top round or
top sirloin)
salt butter
brandy
potato flour
tomato paste
meat glaze
chicken stock
red currant jelly
red wine
dry sherry
baby white onions
white peppercorns
granulated sugar
lean boiled ham
tiny button mushrooms
lemon
bread

PREPARATION TRAY

beef, trimmed and cut into pieces

onions, blanched

ham, cut into squares

mushrooms, cleaned and cut

lemon juice

chicken stock

bread, sliced and trimmed

296

In class, where our time is limited, we use fillet of beef cut in squares, and braise it only for 45 minutes. Actually *boeuf Bourguignon* improves with long cooking, and top round or top sirloin is delicious braised for 2½ to 3½ hours, a long, slow, gentle process that brings out the best in all the ingredients and marries them happily forever after. It is a shame to use fillet of beef for anything but roasting or broiling. Still, if for some remarkable reason you wanted to do a ragout of beef in a great rush, I pass on to you this possibility.

1 Remove all fat, skin and sinew from:
>   **2½ pounds of beef (top round or top sirloin)**
2 Cut it into 1½ inch squares.
3 In a heavy sauté pan heat:
>   **3 tablespoons (1½ ounces) of salt butter**
4 When the butter turns golden brown add:
>   a few pieces of the beef at a time.
>   (Be sure the pieces do not touch, as they will stew instead of brown if they touch one another.)
5 Brown the pieces on all sides, then remove them to a warm dish while you thoroughly brown some more pieces. Continue until all the beef is a good rich brown.
6 Assemble all the meat in the pan.

1 In a tiny pan heat: **¼ cup of brandy**
2 Tip it toward the flame and when it ignites, pour the flaming brandy over the beef.
3 When the flames go out, remove the meat with a slotted spoon, and set aside for a few minutes.
4 Stir the pan juices thoroughly, and add:
>   **2 tablespoons (1 ounce—¼ stick) of salt butter**
5 When it has melted, stir in off the fire:
>   **3 good teaspoons of potato flour**
>   **1 level teaspoon of tomato paste**
>   **1 level teaspoon of meat glaze**
6 Mix in, still off the fire: **1¾ cups of chicken stock**
>   (See recipe on page 353).
>   **½ cup of red wine**

> **2 tablespoons of dry sherry**
> **2 teaspoons of red currant jelly**

7   Stir over the fire with a wooden spatula until the sauce comes to a boil.

8   Then add: **a small lump of butter (1 to 1½ ounces)**

9   Put back the pieces of beef.

10   Place the pan, uncovered, on the top shelf of a pre-heated 375° oven.

11   Allow it to cook for 45 minutes if you are using fillet, basting frequently. Let it braise for about 3 hours if you are using top round or top sirloin. Baste frequently and add a little water or stock as the sauce reduces.

While the beef cooks, prepare the following garnishes:

1   Peel the skin from: **2 dozen baby white onions**

2   Place them in a pan and cover with cold water.

3   Bring it slowly to a boil.

4   Drain at once, thoroughly, in a colander.

5   Heat in a heavy sauté pan:
> **4 tablespoons (2 ounces—½ stick) of butter**

6   When it is on the point of browning, add:
> **the blanched onions**
> **a little salt**
> **a little freshly ground white pepper**

7   Sprinkle generously with:
> **granulated sugar (about 2 tablespoons)**

8   Shake over a moderate fire until the onions glaze and turn a golden brown. Then set them aside.

9   Heat in a heavy sauté pan:
> **2 tablespoons (1 ounce—¼ stick) of butter**

10   When it foams add:
> **6 ounces of lean boiled ham,** cut into 1-inch squares.

11   Sprinkle well with: **salt**
> **pepper**
> **sugar**

12   Shake over a moderate fire until you get a good glaze. Then set aside.

13   In a heavy sauté pan heat:
> **3 tablespoons (1½ ounces) of salt butter**

14 When it foams add:
  4 ounces of baby button mushrooms
  (If you can't get them, larger ones cut in quarters
  will have to do.)
15 Coat the mushrooms well with the hot butter.
16 Add: **a little salt**
  a little freshly cracked white pepper
  2 teaspoons of lemon juice
17 Shake for 2 or 3 minutes over a hot fire.

Add these ingredients to the ragout of beef 10 minutes before it is done.

Serve in a casserole (it may be the one in which the ragout was prepared) surrounded by **snippets of fried bread** (See recipe on page 156)

It's funny but the principle of boiling meat in a liquid must have been the first step in a more civilized cuisine. First, man had to be clever enough to make a stewpot. Then he could stop his endless barbecuing and start cooking. And the next great step ahead must have been the substitution of wine for water as the stewing liquid. Nowadays stews appear to be taking a back seat to barbecues as a way of preparing meat, and we've come full circle, back to the caveman. But I think if you'll try one of the French *ragoûts* or *daubes* (and forget that unfortunate word "stew") you will find it as artful and exciting a way to serve meat as any yet devised.

Salade d'Endive
(Belgian Endive Salad)
(See recipe on page 101.)

Rice Singapore
(See recipe on page 281.)

MENU
25

Bouillabaisse

Gâteau Favorite

Suggested Wine: Chablis

Bouillabaisse

(Mediterranean Fish Chowder)

Serves eight to ten

24 large mussels
1½ pounds of bluefish
1 small mackerel
2½ pounds of salmon
  steaks
1 pound of
  sea scallops
2 small live lobsters
1 pound of large
  raw shrimps
onions
celery
leek
carrot
black peppercorns
white peppercorns
Kosher salt
bay leaf
garlic
4 tomatoes
granulated sugar
tomato paste
potato flour
white wine
Sherry
brandy
salt butter
French bread
Saffron
French olive oil

Arguments continue to rage about what goes into the real, the authentic bouillabaisse, and even along the Mediterranean coast, where the fish soup originated, recipes vary. For American cooks there is an even greater to-do about bouillabaisse because, they are told, it is impossible to achieve without the inclusion of certain rockfish that would not be caught dead anywhere but in the Mediterranean.

While the purists argue, the rest of us can do something far more constructive: We can make a bouillabaisse. A very good one can be created from the fish and seafood available here as long as certain essential principles are followed. Olive oil, saffron, garlic, leeks and tomatoes are the traditional flavoring agents, and a wide variety of salt-water fish both soft- and firm-fleshed are indispensable. This is a dish that must not be overcooked. Aside from that, in Milwaukee as in Marseille, the proof of the bouillabaisse is in the empty tureen and the replete diners.

PREPARATION TRAY

mussels, scrubbed and cleaned

onions, sliced

celery, sliced

leek, cut in half

carrot, sliced

tomatoes, skinned and chopped

bluefish fillets, rolled up into *paupiettes*

mackerel fillets, rolled up into *paupiettes*

salmon steaks, skinned, boned and cut into pieces

scallops, washed and dried

shrimps, boiled, shelled, deveined

To prepare the mussels for cooking, see the directions on page 356.

1   In a deep pan put: **24 mussels, scrubbed and drained**
    1½ cups of good dry white wine
    ¼ cup of good dry sherry
    2 cups of water
    2 small onions, sliced
    1 large piece of celery, sliced
    1 leek, cut in half and **1 carrot, sliced**
    7 white, 7 black peppercorns
    a little kosher salt and **1 bay leaf**

2   Bring slowly to a boil and simmer for 5 minutes, or until the mussel shells are all well opened.

3   Remove the mussels with a slotted spoon, discard top shell from each and cover rest to keep warm.

4   Strain and reserve the liquid.

5   In a deep heavy pan melt: **1½ ounces of salt butter**

6   Add: **4 tomatoes, skinned and chopped**
    1 heaping tablespoon of finely chopped garlic
    1 teaspoon of granulated sugar
    a little kosher salt
    a little freshly ground white pepper

7   Cook all together briskly for 3 minutes.

8   Then, off the fire, stir in until smooth:
    1 tablespoon of tomato paste
    1 teaspoon of potato flour

9   Add: the strained stock from the mussels.

10 Stir over the fire until it comes to a boil. Then in this order add: the **bluefish** which has been skinned, boned, cut into 4 long strips, rolled into *paupiettes*.
    the **small mackerel**, treated the same way.
    the **salmon steaks**, skinned, boned, cut into 8 pieces.

Take: **1 pound of sea scallops**

1   Wash them in a little **lemon juice and water**

2   Drain and dry them well on paper towels.

3   Dust them lightly with **flour**

4   Heat in a heavy skillet:
    3 tablespoons (1½ ounces) of salt butter

5   When it foams and just begins to color, add the pound of scallops, a few at a time.

6 Brown them quickly on each side.
7 Add the scallops to the bouillabaisse and simmer for 10 to 15 minutes.
8 Add: the **shrimps, cooked, shelled, deveined**
   Season them with **a little kosher salt , a little freshly ground white pepper and a bit of chopped garlic**

1 In a medium-sized heavy pan heat: **3 tablespoons of butter**
   2 When it foams add: **2 small live lobsters** which have been split in half.
   3 Place lobsters, shell side down in the butter, cover the pan and cook for 3 minutes.
   4 Remove cover, and flame the lobster with:
      ¼ cup of brandy, heated and ignited in a small pot.
   5 Cover lobsters and cook quickly until they blush.
   6 Remove the lobsters and cut each half in two. Remove the large claws and take off the top shells of the claws, so the meat will be easy to get at.
   7 Add the lobster and mussels to the bouillabaisse.

Cut into thick slices: **a loaf of French bread**
   1 Heat in a skillet: **1 teaspoon of French olive oil**
      3 tablespoons (1½ ounces) of salt butter
   2 Stir in: **½ teaspoon of powdered saffron**
   3 When it is hot, brown slowly, a few at a time:
      slices of French bread.

To serve: The steaming bouillabaisse is brought to the table in a large covered casserole or tureen. The slices of fried bread are served separately, and one or two of them are placed in each soup plate. The bouillabaisse is then ladled over them, with care being taken to give everyone a little of each of the seven varieties you have merged into one glorious whole.

Gâteau Favorite

(Favorite Cake)

Serves six
(Double this recipe if you are using it for this menu.)

This is the favorite cake in Alsace-Lorraine at Easter time. Then you see the sugar-dusted cream puff rings filled with cream in every bakery window. In each cake a tiny figurine of the Virgin Mary is hidden, and whoever finds it in his or her portion will have good luck for the rest of the year.

Gâteau Favorite is made with cream-puff dough (pâte à choux), which means that it is one of the simpler pastries to make. When you study to be a chef in France you are not allowed to touch pastry for the first six months of your apprenticeship. Then you are permitted to begin with pâte à choux. So Gâteau Favorite is an excellent and impressive looking French pastry for you to make if you are an inexperienced baker. It is certain to turn out well, and it tastes and looks magnificent.

MARKETING LIST

sweet butter
salt
all-purpose flour
eggs
blanched almonds
granulated sugar
plain gelatine
milk
dark sweet chocolate
heavy cream
fresh vanilla bean
confectioners' sugar

PREPARATION TRAY

cream puff dough, made and chilled

pastry cream, made and refrigerated

almonds, blanched and shredded

cookie sheet, marked with an 8-inch circle

heavy cream, whipped

If you are making this recipe for 12, double all quantities and make 2 cakes.

1 To make cream puff dough (*pâte à choux*) you put into a heavy pan: **2 cups of water**
¼ teaspoon of salt
8 tablespoons (4 ounces—1 stick) of sweet butter that is slightly soft

2 Stir over a slow fire with a wooden spoon until the water comes to a rolling boil.

3 Then at once throw in:
2 cups of all-purpose flour (measured most exactly)

4 Stir vigorously with a wooden spoon, off the fire, until the mixture forms a ball and comes away clean from the sides of the pan.

5 Turn the pastry into a mixer bowl.

6 Turn the mixer to medium speed and add, one at a time: **6 eggs**

7 If the pastry is still stiff, beat an extra egg in a small bowl and add what you need to get a dough that is shiny, sticky, and holds its shape. (Up to this point this is very much what you do when you make a *panade* for *quenelles* or other fish or meat mousse. This is also the procedure for *gnocchi*, so you see, you now have the fundamentals for a variety of dishes.)

8 Put the pastry in the freezer for 10 minutes, or in the refrigerator for a few hours.

1 Meanwhile, on a heavy cookie sheet mark a circle with an ice pick. (Draw around an 8-inch pie or cake tin, making a light scratch with the pick.) Do *not* grease or butter the cookie sheet.

2 Fill a pastry bag with the chilled *pâte à choux*.

3 Using a ¾-inch plain tube, pipe a thick circle of the dough following the marks on the cookie sheet.

4 Pipe a second circle on top of the first.

5 Brush all over the top lightly with:
whole beaten egg

6   Cover all over the top with:
   6 ounces of blanched, slivered almonds

1 Bake in preheated 375° oven for 45 minutes, then turn off the heat and leave the cake to set. It will be a golden cream puff ring, hollow inside.

2   Remove the cake and let it cool. Then cut it in half across, very carefully. Set the top aside, and fill the bottom of the ring with the following Saint-Honoré cream, which is a pastry cream lightened with beaten egg whites.

3   In a mixer bowl put:
   1 whole egg
   1 egg yolk
   3 tablespoons of all-purpose flour
   3 tablespoons of granulated sugar
   a pinch of salt

4   Beat until the mixture is light and fluffy.

5   Then stir in, do *not* beat:
   1½ packets of plain gelatine
   1 cup of scalded milk
   6 ounces of melted dark sweet chocolate
   (Break the chocolate into pieces and place them on an oven-glass pie plate over a pan of hot water. Stand the pan over a slow fire until the chocolate dissolves. Stir it occasionally.)

6   Put this chocolate mixture into a pan over a slow fire.

7   Stir until it thickens and *almost* boils.

8   Cover the pan with transparent wrap and set it aside to cool a bit.

1   Meanwhile, put into a metal bowl over another bowl of ice:
   2 cups of heavy cream

2   Beat with a wire whisk until it begins to thicken.

3   Then add:
   3 tablespoons of confectioners' sugar
   3 inches of scraped vanilla bean
   (Slit the pod, scrape the tiny black seeds into the

cream, use the pod in a canister of granulated sugar to give it a vanilla flavor, if you wish. Or put it in the milk before scalding it for the *crème St.-Honoré*. Remove before using the milk.)

4   Beat until the cream is thick and holds its shape.

1   Stir the chocolate pastry cream over a bowl of ice until it cools a bit.

2   Beat until they reach soft peaks:
    2 egg whites

3   Stir them into the chocolate pastry cream carefully with a wire whisk.

4   Stir the mixture over ice until it gets quite cool.

5   Then add, teaspoon by teaspoon:
    2 cups of the whipped cream (Half of the amount you have—the heavy cream has doubled in volume as a result of being whipped. The slower you add this, the better.)

6   Beat the mixture over ice with a wire whisk, keeping it stiff the entire time.

7   Place the bottom half of the cake on a paper doily on a serving dish.

8   Fill the chocolate cream into a pastry bag with a ¾-inch tube.

9   Pipe it in pyramids, side by side, all the way around the inside of the cake.

10   Fill the remaining 2 cups of whipped cream into a clean pastry bag with a rose tube.

11   Pipe rosettes of plain whipped cream between each chocolate cream pyramid.

12   Dust the almond-studded top of the cake with **confectioners' sugar**

13   Carefully and lightly place it on top of the filled bottom.

Voilà! A beautiful *Gâteau Favorite* that any pastry chef might be proud of.

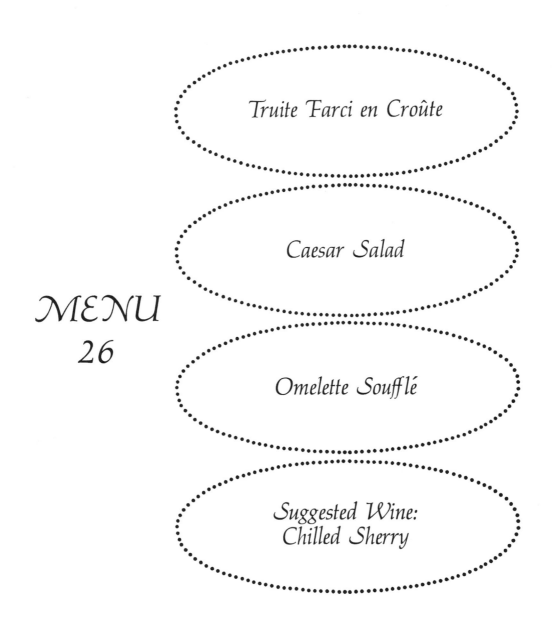

MENU
26

Truite Farci en Croûte

Caesar Salad

Omelette Soufflé

Suggested Wine:
Chilled Sherry

Truite Farci en Croûte
(Stuffed Trout in Pastry Crust)

Serves six

I shouldn't advise doing all this to trout that has just been caught. Any fish that beautifully fresh needs only the simplest grilling or poaching. But fish-market fish, which has not improved with age, can use a bit of help from the chef.

This recipe makes a virtue of necessity, and the stuffed trout is juicy and savory within its flaky crust. Give it the added piquancy of a mustard hollandaise sauce and you have a dish that all but the most severe purists would possibly prefer—but what am I saying? Anyhow, this is a delicious way to serve fish for a change, and especially trout which are usually only worth eating fresh out of a mountain stream or lake.

MARKETING LIST

6 fresh trout
Kosher salt
white peppercorns
½ pound ground
  raw salmon
  (skinned and boned)
raisins
eggs
light cream
Calvados (apple brandy)
fresh dill
shallot
garlic
all-purpose flour
salt
salt butter
Dijon mustard
dry mustard
sherry
cayenne pepper
heavy cream

PREPARATION TRAY

pastry dough, wrapped in wax paper and chilled

trout, cleaned, seasoned and chilled

fish stuffing, made and chilled

310

If your fishmonger can prepare the trout for you, well and good. Otherwise this is how you do it yourself:

1 Carefully scale:
   6 fresh trout (hold them by the tail and scrape the scales off with a knife, going from tail to head).

2 Remove the fins by cutting around them with the point of a knife and then pulling them out, or cut with kitchen shears.

3 Remove the backbone of each trout (the insides will come out with it), starting from the back, not the belly. Cut with a sharp, small, thin-bladed knife on each side of the backbone, and pull out. The entire bony structure and inner organs will come out neatly.

4 Rinse the fish well in cold running water, dry them thoroughly on paper towels.

5 Season the inside of the trout with:
   a little kosher salt
   freshly cracked white pepper

6 Wrap the trout in paper towels and chill them for about an hour. (The reason for doing this is that it is very hard for raw fish to absorb seasoning. If you put the stuffing in immediately after seasoning the fish, it will taste as though it has only been seasoned on the surface. This way, the flavor has a chance to penetrate the flesh.)

Make the following stuffing (enough for 6 trout):

1 Put into a mixer bowl: **1½ pounds of ground raw salmon (skinned and boned)**

2 Add, one at a time: **6 small raw egg whites**

3 Beat in, little by little: **1½ cups of light cream** (Add a few drops with mixer on low, then turn up speed until the cream has been absorbed. Continue until you have added 1½ cups.)

4 Mix in: **6 tablespoons of Calvados**
   6 teaspoons of chopped fresh dill
   3 finely chopped shallots
   ½ teaspoon of chopped garlic
   3 teaspoons of salt

5 Sprinkle the inside of the trout with a little **Calva-dos.** (Place your thumb over mouth of bottle and shake a few drops on the inside of each fish.)

6 Remove the heads and tails.

7 Divide the stuffing evenly, and place on each fish.

8 Fold the fish closed.

Wrap each fish in the following pastry:

1 Put into a bowl: **6 cups of all-purpose flour**
3 level teaspoons of salt

2 Cut up into the flour: **4½ sticks of room-temperature salt butter** (it must be soft).

3 Rub the butter into the flour until it resembles coarse corn meal. (Rub with the tips of your fingers. Lift your hand up out of the bowl and rub your thumb across your fingers, rather than fumbling around deep down in the bowl. It is better to reach up to the heavens than down to the nether regions, and this applies very much to cooking. So lift up your hand and see what you're doing.)

4 When the mixture reaches the coarse corn meal stage, add: **1 scant cup of ice water**

5 Work the pastry up into a ball as quickly as possible, using just one hand.

6 It is a good idea to make your pastry ahead of time, and to chill it, wrapped in wax paper, in the refrigerator until you are ready for it.

7 Turn out the pastry on a lightly floured pastry board.

8 Divide it into six equal parts.

9 Roll out into six large ovals and brush with:
1 whole beaten egg

10 Place a fish on one side of each oval.

11 Fold the dough over and press the edges together to make a tight seal.

12 With a pastry pincer (or a sharp knife) mark the dough with a herringbone pattern on top of each fish.

13 With a knife edge, make a few lines to resemble fins.

14 Put a **small raisin** in place for an eye.

312

15 Cover and chill in the refrigerator for ½ hour.

16 Brush the top side with: **whole beaten egg**

17 Bake in a preheated 375° oven for 40 minutes. (The pastry needs to bake this long, but that final chilling in the refrigerator will keep the fish and stuffing from overcooking.)

Serve on an oval platter with a separate bowl of the following mustard hollandaise:

1 In a small china bowl put:

6 egg yolks

3 teaspoons of Dijon mustard

1½ teaspoons of dry mustard

3 tablespoons of dry sherry

salt

a little cayenne pepper

2 Mix in: **6 tablespoons of heavy cream**

3 Stand the bowl in a small frying pan of hot water over a slow fire.

4 Do not let the water ever come to a boil while you beat the sauce with a small wire whisk. Too much heat will curdle the eggs.

5 Continue beating until the sauce begins to thicken.

6 When the sauce is thick enough to coat a spoon you can start to add, a little at a time:

3 sticks (12 ounces) of very cold salt butter

7 Beat each bit in with the wire whisk until it has been absorbed.

8 When the butter is completely incorporated in the sauce add:

6 drops of lemon juice

9 Serve in a separate bowl.

This mustard hollandaise is a delicious sauce for almost any broiled or sautéed fish. It can be made up several hours in advance, and if the bowl is tightly covered with transparent wrap and left to stand in the pan of warm—not hot—water the sauce will keep perfectly. Too much heat will cause it to separate or curdle, and even when you serve it, remember to have it just warm.

Caesar Salad

Serves six

California is the undisputed champion of salad recipes, and this one, named for the West Coast chef who invented it, is probably the most popular of them all. You can serve it as a salad course with dinner, as I suggest here. But it makes a very satisfactory lunch all by itself, with just a loaf of crusty French bread and a glass of wine.

So many things go into this salad that it is rather time-consuming if you have to toss it together at the last minute. I have found that you can make the dressing early in the day and leave it in the bottom of your salad bowl. Cover it well with a large sheet of foil; put your romaine lettuce, washed, dried and torn into pieces on top of the foil, and set the whole thing in the refrigerator to chill. The bacon, croutons, hard-boiled eggs, grated cheese and chopped parsley can all be prepared in advance and ready to go into the salad bowl at the very last. You can then break the track record with a two-minute Caesar Salad.

MARKETING LIST

2 heads of romaine lettuce
Kosher salt
black peppercorns
white peppercorns
dry mustard
Dijon mustard
granulated sugar
lemon
tarragon vinegar
French olive oil
Vegetable oil
eggs
garlic
croutons
bacon
parsley
Parmesan cheese
anchovies

PREPARATION TRAY

lettuce, washed and dried

fresh lemon juice

tarragon vinegar

garlic, chopped

bacon, fried and crumbled

croutons, fried

Parmesan cheese, grated

parsley, chopped

eggs, hard-boiled and chilled

1   Into a large wooden salad bowl put, in the following order:

1 level teaspoon of kosher salt

¾ teaspoon of freshly cracked black and white pepper combined

¼ teaspoon of dry mustard

1 level teaspoon of Dijon mustard

¼ teaspoon of granulated sugar

1 teaspoon of fresh lemon juice

2 tablespoons of good tarragon vinegar. (I always specify "good" because the commercial tarragon vinegars are *not.* Make your own by adding fresh tarragon to plain cider vinegar. See recipe on page 352.)

2 tablespoons of French olive oil

6 tablespoons of vegetable oil (corn oil, safflower oil, peanut oil)

1 small raw egg, unbeaten

½ teaspoon of finely chopped garlic (Chop it in a little salt.)

2   Stir all of these ingredients well with a wooden spoon. (If you are making this in advance, cover this part of the bowl with a large sheet of foil.)

3   Wash well: **2 heads of romaine lettuce**

4   Shake them thoroughly in a salad basket to get rid of excess moisture.

5   Separate the leaves, and dry each carefully in a towel.

6   Never cut lettuce with a knife. Tear the leaves into convenient pieces.

7   Put the pieces of romaine on top of the dressing (or on top of the foil if you are an early bird).

1   In a large skillet fry until crisp:

½ pound of bacon, cut into thin strips across

2   Drain the strips on paper towels.

3   In the bacon fat put:

¾ cup of croutons (good white bread, cut into small cubes).

4   Fry them to a golden brown.

5 Drain them.

6 Sprinkle them on the romaine.

7 Add: **the crisp bacon**
2 tablespoons of freshly chopped parsley

8 Sprinkle with:
2 tablespoons of freshly grated Parmesan cheese
(The bacon, croutons, parsley and cheese can be wrapped and stored if you are doing this ahead of time. When you are ready to serve the salad, simply pull the piece of foil out of the bowl and let the romaine drop down into the dressing. Add these other goodies, and proceed.)

9 Surround the salad with:
2 hard-boiled eggs, cut into sixths

10 Drape on top of each egg section:
1 fillet of anchovy (Some recipes mash the anchovies into the dressing, but I have borrowed this method from Mike Romanoff. This way, people who dislike or cannot eat anchovies can put them aside, and for the others the flavor is the same, no matter how the anchovies are used.)

11 When you bring the bowl to the table, mix the salad thoroughly so the dressing on the bottom coats all of the other ingredients. If you mix it too early, the croutons and bacon will lose their crunchiness, and that is one of the distinctive features of the Caesar Salad.

When this salad is served in restaurants, the headwaiter makes a big to-do about adding each ingredient and tossing the final conglomeration. If anyone at your house wants to make a production of it, the bacon, croutons, cheese, parsley, eggs and anchovies can be added at the table and the salad tossed with real Hollywood histrionics. It tastes good either way.

Omelette Soufflé
(Puffy Sweet Omelet)

Two omelets serve six

For a quick, easy and impressive dessert you can't beat an omelette soufflé. Unlike the savory omelet, this one takes no special skill, no artful sleight-of-hand, and it is a marvelous dessert for the beginning cook to try. If you have an oval metal or fireproof platter, you can bring it to the table flaming, which is a great deal of spectacle for five minutes of work!

MARKETING LIST

eggs
superfine granulated
      sugar
salt butter
preserves or
   strawberries
   and currant
      jelly (optional)
Confectioner's sugar
rum, Kirsch or brandy

PREPARATION TRAY

eggs, separated

fruit filling (if used)

Depending upon their appetites, you will have to make 2 or 3 omelets to serve 6 people.

1 For each omelet separate: **3 eggs**
2 Add to the yolks:
   3 teaspoons of superfine granulated sugar
3 With a small whisk, beat until light and fluffy.
4 In another bowl beat to soft peaks:
   3 egg whites
5 Add the yolks to the whites, folding in carefully and gently.
6 Use your special omelet pan. Two omelets will have to be made, unless you have two pans and can make the omelets simultaneously.

317

7 Get it hotter than you do for the savory omelets.

8 Rub it out with:
½ tablespoon (¼ ounce) of salt butter in each pan (Use a thick wad of paper towels and coat the hot pan quickly with the butter.)

9 Pour in the egg mixture.

10 Quickly spread it evenly over the whole inside of the pan. The beaten eggs will be stiff, so the mixture will not run.

11 Stir the *top surface only* with the bottom of a fork.

12 Slip the fork around the outside edge, and when you see that the outside is golden, fold the omelet over once, using your fork.

13 If you want to use a filling, put it in before you fold the omelet. You may use about 4 heaping table-spoons of fruit preserve for each omelet, or a like amount of fresh strawberries that have been heated in red currant jelly. Spoon them on the surface of the omelet, then fold it over.

14 Turn the puffy omelet out on a hot metal serving platter.

15 Sprinkle the top heavily with:
confectioners' sugar

16 Take a metal skewer and heat it on the stove burner.

17 When it is red hot, lay it across the sugar topping twice to form an X. The sugar will sizzle and car-amelize, and your omelet will be beautifully branded. (The burnt sugar flavor is what we're after, too.)

18 Heat: **4 ounces of rum, kirsch or brandy**

19 Flame it, and pour the flaming liquor around the edges of each omelet when you are ready to serve them.

This *Omelette Soufflé* is soft and almost runny inside, with a firmer golden crust on the outside. It is an ideal dessert for two or three people. If you wanted to serve six, you could double the amount, cook two separate omelets, but serve them both on the same platter as a flaming duet.

Omelette aux Fines Herbes

Poulet Majorca

MENU
27

Pommes de Terre Sautées

Roulage Léontine

Suggested Wine:
Portuguese Lancers

Omelette à la Française
(French Omelet)

In this menu the omelet is used as a first course and one omelet will serve two. Ordinarily, for supper or for lunch, one omelet serves one. The Dictionary of the Academy of Gastronomes lists over a hundred different kinds of omelets, which gives you some idea of the scope of this most popular egg dish. The basic omelet is always the same, but taking off from the original eggs, seasoning and butter, you can add almost anything else that is edible as garnish or stuffing. Mushrooms, chicken livers, onions, cheese, ham, truffles, bacon, vegetables, chopped meats, seafood, herbs —these foods, alone or in every possible combination, can go into or on top of an omelet. The ancient Romans used to beat eggs with honey and cook them in a pan, and their name for this delicacy was ovamellita (literally egg-honey), from which our omelet probably evolved.

Nothing could be simpler than cooking a few eggs in a pan for a minute and then serving them, with or without an additional garnish. Simple it is, but for beginners difficult too, because it involves a bit of legerdemain that takes practice. I will tell you exactly what to do and how to do it, and then you will have to try it a few times, while you and your patient family consume the not-quite-perfect omelets. Suddenly you will get the knack and your two hands, the omelet pan and the eggs will work together like a charm. There will be a lovely yellow oval on the serving plate, and presto! you will be a full-fledged omelet chef.

PREPARATION TRAY

all fillings prepared in advance

(if you are going to make a number of omelets you can have a large bowl of the egg mixture chilled, and a ladle that will give you the correct quantity for 1 omelet)

butter pats, 1 tablespoon (½ ounce) each

To begin with:

> To make a proper omelet you must first have a proper omelet pan. Cast iron or heavy cast aluminum are best —the metal must be porous, so that rules out copper, tin or stainless steel. A pan with sloping sides about 2 inches deep is preferable. And for a 3-egg omelet, which is the ideal size, a pan measuring 7 inches across the bottom is just right. (If you are preparing omelets for a number of people you will get better results making individual ones in rapid succession instead of cooking several large omelets. Their texture is never as good. It takes only a minute to cook each small omelet, and you could have 2 pans going simultaneously as I do in my restaurant.)

> Once you have your omelet pan, don't use it for anything else, and don't ever wash it or let water touch its cooking surface. The success of your omelet depends upon how smoothly the eggs will slide around in the pan, and how easily you can tip the finished omelet out onto a serving dish. So once you get your new pan seasoned (just as you would a waffle iron), use it only for omelets, wipe it clean with dry paper towels, and it will never stick.

> To season a new omelet pan, rub it with dry steel wool first. Clean it thoroughly with oil. Heat it a little and then fill it with oil and let it stand for 48 hours. Pour off the oil (you can use it again), rub the pan out hard with paper towels, get it very hot for a few minutes, and then it is ready to use. (I have one pan that I've been making omelets in for 20 years, and it has never been washed.)

Now we're ready to make an omelet.

1 In a small bowl break: **3 eggs** (They should be cool, not at room temperature.)
2 Add: **¼ teaspoon of salt**
   1 teaspoon of cold water
3 Beat with a small whisk until the eggs are well mixed but not frothy.
4 Heat the omelet pan over a high fire. When it seems fairly hot, test it first with a pat of butter

MARKETING LIST

eggs
salt
butter
white peppercorns

held on a fork. It should sizzle the moment it hits the pan, but it must not color.

5 Wipe out the test butter with a wad of paper towels. If the pan temperature was correct, you are ready to play for keeps now.

6 Put into the hot omelet pan:
1 tablespoon (½ ounce) of butter

7 Follow it *at once* with: the omelet mixture.

8 Immediately agitate the pan by shaking the handle back and forth with your left hand.

9 With your right hand hold a fork, flat side down, and stir the eggs quickly, moving them all over the bottom of the pan. It will seem as though you are scrambling them, and indeed you are. (Escoffier on omelets might help you here—"it should be borne in mind that an omelet is really scrambled eggs enclosed in a coating of coagulated egg.")

10 When the eggs begin to set, lift your fork and slowly stir only the top surface. (It is now that you add your filling if you are using one.)

11 Let the omelet set for a second, then slide the fork all around the edge.

12 With your left hand raise the handle of the pan, keeping your palm upward. Fold the omelet over so it is huddled at the far edge of the pan, which is tipped away from the raised handle.

13 Knock the pan smartly on the stove to loosen the omelet.

14 With your right hand bring a warm serving plate up to the far edge of the pan.

15 Raise the handle higher, and roll the folded omelet onto the serving plate. Its surface should look like yellow velvet, and it should form a plump oval on the plate.

16 Now sprinkle over it:
a little freshly grated white pepper

17 On top of it place:
a small pat of frozen butter (to give it a gloss)

18 The inside of the omelet should be creamy and soft, but a French omelet is never dry and tough.

That is your basic omelet, and once you know how to do it there are a hundred possibilities open to you. Here are the recipes for a few of the better known omelet variations.

OMELETTE AUX FINES HERBES
(Chopped Herbs)

1   For two omelets, chop very fine about:
2 tablespoons of fresh parsley
2 teaspoons of chives
2 teaspoons of fresh tarragon
2 teaspoons of fresh thyme
2 teaspoons of shallot
a smidgen of garlic

2   Now chop all the herbs together so they borrow one another's flavor.

3   Put these herbs in the hot butter just the instant before adding the eggs. That tiny second of heat will bring out the full flavor of the herbs.

4   Make your omelet as indicated.
(If you wish, you may add, along with the herbs, 3 tablespoons of small croutons that were fried in bacon fat. They will give your omelet a nice crunchy texture.)

MARKETING LIST

Parsley
Chives
tarragon
thyme
Shallot
garlic
Croutons

MUSHROOM OMELET

1   For two omelets, wash: **¼ pound of mushrooms**

2   Save 2 mushroom caps for each omelet, and slice the rest.

3   In a sauté pan heat:
3 tablespoons (1½ ounces) of butter

4   When it foams add: the mushrooms

5   Coat them well with the butter.

6   Add: **1 teaspoon of lemon juice**

7   Cook briskly for 2 minutes.

8   Add ½ the cooked mushrooms to each portion of egg mixture and make the omelet as indicated. When it is turned out on the serving dish, put 2 sautéed mushroom caps on top of each omelet.

MARKETING LIST

mushrooms
lemon

323

(Some people use the sautéed mushrooms as a filling, but I prefer them mixed into the uncooked eggs so their flavor goes all through the omelet as it cooks.)

9 You can also add a band of the sauce from the following recipe, spooned across the top of the mushroom omelet.

CHICKEN LIVER OMELET

1 For two omelets, heat in a small sauté pan:
2 teaspoons of salt butter
2 Quickly brown on each side: **4 chicken livers**
3 Flame with: **4 tablespoons of brandy**
4 Remove the livers.
5 Stir into the pan: **2 teaspoons of butter**
6 Mix in, off the fire: **½ teaspoon of tomato paste**
½ teaspoon of meat glaze
1 teaspoon of potato flour
7 Stir in, still off the fire: **¼ cup of red wine**
½ cup of chicken stock (See recipe on page 353.)
½ teaspoon of red currant jelly
a little freshly ground black pepper
8 Stir this sauce over the fire until it boils.
9 Slice the livers and put them back in the sauce.
10 Simmer it very gently for 10 minutes.
11 Make a basic omelet, and just before you fold it over, put the livers in the center, but *no sauce*. (Use a slotted spoon to take the livers out.)
12 Fold the omelet, turn it out on a warm plate.
13 Spoon a little sauce over the omelet.
14 Sprinkle with **freshly chopped parsley**

OMELETTE BONNE FEMME
(Potato, Bacon and Onion Omelet)

(This potato, bacon and onion filling can also be used alone as a very delicious vegetable. This recipe is enough to fill four omelets.)

1 Cut into ½-inch pieces:
½ pound of sliced bacon (cut the slices across)

2 In heavy sauté pan put: the bacon pieces
   3 tablespoons (1½ ounces) of butter
3 On top of the bacon put:
   2 large onions, sliced and separated into rings
4 On top of the onion rings put:
   2 large Idaho potatoes peeled and cut into ¼-inch slices
5 Sprinkle on top with: **1 level teaspoon of salt
   ½ teaspoon of freshly ground white pepper**
6 Cover with a lid and cook over a moderate fire for 20 minutes, stirring frequently.
7 Place several tablespoons of this filling on an omelet before folding it over.
8 Sprinkle the top with a little **chopped parsley**

CHEESE OMELET

MARKETING LIST

*imported Swiss gruyère cheese
imported Parmesan cheese*

Just before folding the omelet, put in the center:
   3 tablespoons of freshly grated imported Swiss Gruyère cheese
Fold the omelet, turn it out on a warm plate and sprinkle the top well with:
freshly grated Parmesan cheese

Note: If you want to have an omelet supper or luncheon and serve a variety of omelets, make up your fillings in advance. Keep the hot ones warm in double boilers, and have the chopped herbs and grated cheeses in small bowls next to the stove. I also like a bowl of butter pats handy for cooking the omelets (½-ounce pieces save me the trouble of measuring and cutting each time) and for placing on top of the finished ones.

If you have a ladle that measures out the right amount for each omelet, you can have a large bowl with all the eggs, salt and water you will need mixed in advance. Keep it refrigerated until you are ready to start cooking. This is a delightfully informal kind of short-order cookery, yet the advance preparations raise it to a gourmet level.

Poulet Majorca

(Chicken with Orange and Peppers)

Serves four

It was on the island of Majorca off the Mediterranean coast of Spain that I first discovered this recipe. It is one of the best-tasting and most attractive chicken casseroles I know, and the colors and flavors create a fresh, original treatment for a time-honored dish.

If you like brown pieces of chicken in a good brown sauce, garnished with colorful slices of orange, rosy pieces of tomato, and green and red peppers, this is your dish. The art of making it well lies in cooking the chicken for some time, the fruit and vegetables hardly at all. They are added at the last to bring their separate flavors and bright colors to the savory chicken and sauce. The result—the vividness and tang of the Mediterranean world.

MARKETING LIST

3½ pound whole chickens
butter
Calvados
meat glaze
tomato paste
potato flour
Chicken stock
dry white wine
red currant jelly
whole black peppercorns
whole white peppercorns
oranges
garlic
mushrooms
lemon
red pepper
green pepper
French olive oil
tomatoes
(For garnish:
3 Idaho
potatoes)

PREPARATION TRAY

chicken, cleaned and trussed

orange rind, slivered

oranges, sectioned

garlic, chopped

mushrooms, sliced

red pepper and green pepper, blanched and diced

tomatoes, skinned, pipped and diced

potatoes, peeled, blanched and sliced

chicken stock

326

1   With white string truss up:

        a 3½ pound chicken (See instructions on page 356.)

  2   In a heavy sauté pan heat:

        4 tablespoons (2 ounces—½ stick) of salt butter

  3   When it is almost coloring, put in the chicken, breast side down. Cover.

  4   Brown the chicken slowly. (Remember, red meat must be browned quickly, uncovered; poultry and veal are to be browned slowly and covered.) Brown each side of breast, each leg, the wishbone, and lastly the back. Insert a wooden spoon in the cavity and use it as a handle to turn the chicken. Never use a fork as that pierces the flesh and allows the juices to escape.

  5   When the chicken is browned, remove the cover.

  6   In a tiny pot heat: **4 tablespoons of Calvados**
Tip the pot into flame, igniting the brandy.

  7   Pour flaming Calvados over the chicken.

  8   Remove chicken from pan and set on a board.

  9   Add to the pan juices, off the fire, stirring well:

        1 teaspoon of meat glaze
        1 teaspoon of tomato paste
        3 teaspoons of potato flour

10   When the mixture is smooth, stir in:

        2 cups of chicken stock
        ½ cup of dry white wine
        1 teaspoon of red currant jelly
        a little freshly ground black pepper

11   Stir over the fire until sauce boils.

12   Carefully carve the chicken for casserole. (See directions on page 357.)

13   Put pieces back in sauce.

14   Place pan on top shelf of a preheated 375° oven for 45 minutes, basting occasionally.

1   While the chicken is cooking, put in a sauté pan:

        3 tablespoons (1½ ounces) of butter

  2   When it has melted add:

        finely shredded rind of 2 large oranges. (Pare the thin orange skin [also known as the zest] from

oranges with a potato peeler, being careful to get none of the bitter white underskin. Cut strips of rind across with a chef's knife into fine slivers.)
2 teaspoons of finely chopped fresh garlic, chopped in a little salt.
a little salt
a little freshly cracked white pepper

3   Cook slowly and carefully for only 2 minutes. (Never cook garlic fast. Never cook it alone.)
4   Add: **3 sliced mushrooms**
1 teaspoon of lemon juice
5   Cook briskly for 2 minutes.
6   Add: **1 red pepper** and **1 green pepper**
These must first be blanched (plunged into boiling water), drained and cut into large dice.
7   Cook for 2 minutes more.
8   Add: **2 tablespoons of French olive oil**
2 tomatoes, skinned, pipped, cut in large dice.
2 oranges in sections
These must be completely skinned (you have already pared off the orange zest) and sectioned.
9   Set aside vegetable and fruit mixture. (But not without first admiring the vivid colors of the pieces in the pan!)
10   Remove the chicken from the oven.
11   Place the chicken carefully in a serving casserole.
12   Add the vegetable and orange mixture to the chicken sauce and neatly cover the chicken with it.

If you are going to serve this casserole later, I should advise you to keep the chicken and the vegetable mixture in their own pans, reheat them, and then combine them, lest the peppers, tomatoes and oranges lose their original brightness of flavor and color. This interesting and novel combination of flavors in the casserole and in the rosemary-seasoned potatoes that follow, makes something unusual out of ingredients that are in themselves quite commonplace. For me this is far more challenging cookery than an exotic dish concocted from rare and outlandish materials.

Pommes de Terre Sautées
(Potatoes Fried in Butter)

Serves four

A simple potato garnish is good to know. This one profits from the addition of rosemary that gives it a memorable flavor. Though the French did not accept the potato as a safe edible until the eighteenth century, once the economist Parmentier convinced them of its harmlessness, they became enthusiasts. Now there are numerous varieties of potatoes grown, each suitable for certain kinds of preparation. Pommes frites, French fried potatoes, are the great national favorite. But there are hundreds of other ways that inventive French chefs have dreamed up in the past two centuries to serve forth the simple tuber. If you like them done up brown with a fragrant herbal whiff, this one is for you.

MARKETING LIST

2 or 3 Idaho potatoes
(depending upon size)
salt
butter
black peppercorns
rosemary

PREPARATION TRAY

potatoes, blanched and sliced

fresh rosemary, cut into snips

Firm Idaho potatoes are the best kind to use for sautéeing.

1   Peel: **2 pounds of Idaho potatoes**
2   Place in a heavy pan and cover them with **water.**
3   Bring slowly to a boil.
4   Drain the potatoes well, dry them carefully in a clean towel.
5   Cut the blanched potatoes into thin slices (⅛-inch).
6   In a heavy sauté pan melt:
    5 tablespoons (2½ ounces) of butter
7   Add: the sliced potatoes
    1 teaspoon of salt
    a good sprinkle of freshly ground white pepper
8   Shake the pan vigorously over a moderate heat. Don't forget, *sauté* means "jump," so keep the potatoes hopping to prevent them from sticking.
9   When they begin to brown, you can stop shaking them.
10 Turn the slices over, and when they are nicely browned add the **rosemary** (Fresh rosemary is best, cut into snips, but if you can only get the dried herb, be sure it is not stale and flat. Rub dried herbs between your two hands before sprinkling it over food. This releases the flavor.)
11 Don't overdo the rosemary. Herbs are only meant to accent, not to overpower the basic flavor, and the cooking heat will increase their strength.
12 Turn out the sautéed potatoes on a hot serving dish, and add a **slight additional sprinkle of rosemary,** if the potatoes can stand it.

"There's rosemary, that's for remembrance," said Hamlet's Ophelia. And indeed, even a simple potato dish can become memorable with its help.

Roulage Léontine
(Chocolate Roll)

Serves eight to ten

Of all the dishes I have prepared on television, served in my restaurant and taught in my classes, this special chocolate roll wins the popularity contest forks down. Its acclaim is not undeserved. It tastes delicious, looks attractive and in spite of the fact that it is really a soufflé made in a jelly roll pan, the recipe is practically foolproof. For the relatively small and simple amount of work involved, the result verges on the spectacular. A beautiful dinner party dessert when the rest of the food is not overpoweringly rich.

MARKETING LIST

8 eggs
superfine sugar
Confectioners sugar
½ pound dark
    sweet chocolate
Cocoa
1½ cups heavy cream
fresh vanilla bean

PREPARATION TRAY

eggs, separated

chocolate, broken into small pieces

jelly roll pan, prepared

heavy cream, whipped and flavored

1   Separate: **8 eggs**
    (The neatest way to arrange this so that your work-
    ing space is not cluttered with a mess of sticky egg
    shells is this: Have your 8 eggs in a large bowl, and
    have two other good sized bowls to receive the
    whites and yolks. Discard the empty shells into the
    egg bowl, from which you can dispose of them in
    one fell swoop, and your work space remains clean.)

2   Add: **1 cup of superfine sugar** to the yolks and beat
    them, preferably with a large wire whisk, until they
    are very pale and fluffy.

3   Put into a small, heavy pan:
    ½ pound of dark sweet chocolate, broken into
    pieces
    ⅓ cup of cold water
    Stir with a wooden spoon over a *very low* fire, watch-
    ing it carefully until the chocolate has melted.

4   When the chocolate has cooled, mix it gently but
    thoroughly with the beaten egg yolks, using a rubber
    scraper.

5   Beat the 8 egg whites on your mixer machine until
    they form soft peaks. Don't over-beat!

6   Fold your chocolate mixture into the egg whites
    very softly with a rubber scraper. You don't want to
    break down the air you have so carefully beaten into
    the eggs, therefore you use a long sweeping circular
    motion of the scraper, lifting the contents from the
    bottom of the bowl and blending it with the newly
    added chocolate mixture. To ensure a happy mar-
    riage of the two, you occasionally swirl lightly at the
    surface until the color is even and unstreaked and
    the two are as one—a lovely smooth light brown
    mixture.

1   Oil a jelly roll pan (18 x 12 x 1). Cover it with wax paper,
    letting the paper extend ½ inch beyond the narrow ends
    of the pan. Do not oil the paper.

2   Spread the batter evenly over the pan, smoothing it
    lightly with your scraper.

3   Put it in a preheated 350° oven for 17 minutes. It

will puff up and its surface will just have lost its shine, when it is done. *Do not overcook.*

4   Remove the pan from the oven and immediately cover the top of the roll with 2 layers of paper toweling rung out in cold water, and one layer of dry paper towel. Chill at room temperature for 20 minutes.

5   When cool, peel off the paper towels carefully.

6   Loosen the roll a bit by taking a small, sharp knife and cutting along the long sides. Then lift the extension of waxed paper, first at one end, then the other, but only a little way.

7   Dust all over the top with **dry cocoa.** (The best way to do this is to sprinkle the cocoa powder evenly through a strainer.)

8   Now comes the moment of truth. It is time to turn out your chocolate roll onto two overlapping pieces of wax paper. Tear off two pieces of wax paper the length of your jelly roll pan. Lay them on your table top overlapping with the one nearest you on top. Hold the ends of the tin in either hand and flip the pan over quickly—before you can begin to worry about it. Lift the pan, and gently peel off the wax paper on which the roll baked.

Spread the top with the following whipped cream:

1   Put a large metal bowl over another bowl of ice. Cream must always be whipped at refrigerator temperature. Pour in: **1½ cups of heavy cream.** Beat with a large whisk until the cream begins to thicken. (This takes a good amount of elbow grease, but you will find that cream whipped in this way holds up better and has a richer yet lighter texture. Besides, it is good exercise and is one of the living proofs that everything you've got goes into good cooking—brawn as well as brains and creativity.)

2   Add:
    2 heaping or 3 level tablespoons of sifted confectioners' sugar
    2 inches of scraped fresh vanilla bean

When you want the truly superb flavor of vanilla to come through because it is the only flavor in the cream, use fresh vanilla. You can store the soft beans in the refrigerator, tightly wrapped in foil. Cut off a two inch piece of bean, slit it along its length on one side, and with your knife scrape the 3,751 miniscule specks of vanilla into the cream.

3   Continue whipping until the cream holds its shape.

1   Put 9 gobs of whipped cream, in rows of 3, across the top of the chocolate roll. Spread evenly.

2   Roll up like a jelly roll.

The best way to do this is to lift the long side of the roll nearest you by means of the wax paper. Flip it over once then, still using the wax paper, roll it once again. Then pull the top piece of wax paper toward you, which will leave the roll at the edge of the bottom sheet of paper. Roll with that piece of wax paper for the third and last time. Smooth your hands over the paper-covered roll to shape it. Then uncover the chocolate roll and let the paper lay flat. Don't worry if the roll cracks a bit, as you are going to sprinkle on more cocoa as a cosmetic.

3   Cover the top with a generous dusting of **cocoa**

Serve this on a long thin jelly roll board with no further embellishments. The best way to transfer the chocolate roll to the board is to lift the piece of wax paper on which it is resting and slide it onto the board. With a small sharp knife trim the paper around the edges of the board. When you have cut and passed the slices, sit back and enjoy the most enthusiastic and heartfelt compliments to your cooking that you will ever have.

Filets de Sole Duglère

Pommes de Terre Duchesse

MENU
28

Orange and Endive Salad

Mousse au Chocolat Basque

Suggested Wine: Chablis

Filets de Sole Duglère
(Fillets of Sole with Fresh Tomatoes)

(See recipe on page 150.)

Pommes de Terre Duchesse
(Duchess Potatoes)

Serves six

This is an excellent way to serve potatoes when you have a dish that they will enhance both by flavor and appearance. A little firmer than mashed potatoes, and a rich golden color because of the egg yolk added to them, Duchess Potatoes make an attractive picture frame when you pipe them around the serving platter. This is another of those touches that give a professional finish to dishes made right in your own kitchen. A tiny effort for an impressive result.

MARKETING LIST

Idaho potatoes
butter
eggs
salt
cayenne pepper

PREPARATION TRAY

potatoes, peeled and soaked

butter, melted

1 Soak for several hours in cold water:
> **4 Idaho potatoes** that have been peeled
> (This will rid them of excess starch.)

2 Cut potatoes in half across, put them in a heavy pan and cover with:
> **cold water**
> **1 teaspoon of salt**

3 Bring to a boil slowly.

4 Allow the water to boil gently until potatoes are just soft.

5 Drain them and return them to the empty pan.

6 Shake over a medium fire to dry.

7 Put into a mixer bowl and beat until smooth:
> boiled potatoes.

8 Add: **5 tablespoons (2½ ounces) of butter**
> **1 egg**
> **1 egg yolk**
> **1 scant teaspoon of salt**
> **a dash of cayenne**

9 When the mixture is light and smooth fill it into a pastry bag with a large star tube.

10 Pipe the duchess potatoes in scallops around the edge of a flat serving dish.

11 Sprinkle with **a little melted butter** and brown slightly under the broiler.

12 *Then* put your meat or fish in the center of the dish and run it under the broiler for the final browning. This will ensure that your potatoes get nicely browned without overdoing it on the sauce or glaze for the main part of the dish. Fish in particular cannot stay under the broiler for too long.

Orange and Endive Salad

Serves four to six

This is a delightfully fresh-tasting salad, and one that is rather out-of-the-ordinary as well. It is especially good with fish, pork or ham.

PREPARATION TRAY

endives, washed, dried and cut

orange rind, grated

oranges, sectioned

vinaigrette dressing

1 Carefully wash and dry: **6 Belgian endives**
2 Trim the base and cut them in half lengthwise.
3 Place them in a salad bowl.
4 Carefully grate just the thin outer skin from: **3 navel oranges**
5 Peel and section the 3 oranges.
6 Add the orange sections to the endive.
7 Add: about **2 tablespoons of the grated orange rind** to some vinaigrette salad dressing. (See recipe on page 69.)
8 Pour the dressing over the chilled salad just at serving time, and toss well.

MARKETING LIST

6 Belgian endives
3 large navel oranges
Vinaigrette dressing

Mousse au Chocolat Basque

(A Basque Recipe for Chocolate Mousse)

Serves six to eight

This is one of the most popular desserts served in my restaurant, *The Egg Basket*. Simple but delicious, it is presented there in small Japanese tea bowls, terra cotta on the outside with a black glaze interior. But you can use any small custard cups or pot de crème containers. We also add a rosette of whipped cream and a sprinkle of coarsely grated chocolate on top. Though I personally think it is better without.

MARKETING LIST

½ pound dark
   sweet chocolate
5 eggs
rum
salt
confectioners' sugar
Vanilla extract
heavy cream

PREPARATION TRAY

chocolate, measured and cut into small pieces

eggs, separated

heavy cream, whipped and flavored

---

1 Cut: **½ pound of dark, sweet chocolate** into small pieces to facilitate the melting. (Use an ice pick on a wooden board, as it might spoil the blade of a sharp knife.)

2 Put the chocolate pieces into a small deep heavy pan with: **6 tablespoons of water**
a pinch of salt

3 Stir over a very slow fire until the chocolate has dissolved. (It is of the utmost importance to melt chocolate at an extremely low temperature, as there is a high proportion of cocoa fat in it, and it tends to separate if there is too much heat. Should you, by mistake, get the pan too hot, simply add 1 or 2 tablespoons of ice water to the pan. Stir well, and the chocolate will blend together again and be smooth and shiny.)

4 Remove the melted chocolate to a bowl and stir in: **3 tablespoons of light rum**

339

5   Separate: **5 eggs**
Put the whites in a mixer bowl.
Put the yolks in a small bowl, being careful to keep them whole and unbroken, if possible. (If they break, it is hard to scrape all the egg yolk out of the bowl, and you may lose as much as half a yolk. But if they remain intact, they will slip out of the bowl, leaving no trace behind. This is important to remember any time you are using egg yolks that are not beaten.)

6   Then slide the yolks into the chocolate mixture and mix well.

7   Beat the whites, on the mixer, to soft peaks.

8   Remove from mixer, and add the chocolate mixture to the egg whites, mixing it all together well with a wire whisk.

9   Pour the mixture into a large pitcher, and use it to fill to the brim the small individual bowls or cups. (This is not only the neatest way to fill the containers, but pouring keeps the mousse light and airy.)

10   Put to set into the deep freeze for 2 hours, or into the refrigerator for 6 or 7 hours.

11   Whip in a metal bowl, over ice:
¾ cup of heavy cream
Beat it with a large wire whisk until it begins to hold its shape, then add:
1 teaspoon of vanilla extract
1 tablespoon of confectioners' sugar
Continue beating until the cream is thick.

12   Fill it into a pastry bag with a large rose tube.

13   Pipe a large rosette on the top of each chilled chocolate mousse.

14   You can grate some chocolate coarsely and sprinkle that on top of the cream, if you like.

These added flourishes are not really necessary, as I have said, and their inclusion would depend upon what had been served for the rest of the meal, and how calorie-conscious you and your guests are. True chocolate addicts would probably prefer to take their mousse straight.

340

MENU
29

Melon and Ginger

*Suprêmes
de Volaille Archiduc*

Potato Gnocchi

Coeur à la Crème

Suggested Wine: Montrachet

Melon and Ginger

Serves four

A lovely slice of melon is always a welcome beginning for a dinner, especially to the calorie-conscious whom we seem to have always with us these days. Just be certain the melon is ripe and sweet—not too far gone in mushy softness, nor yet too firm and tasteless. The powdered ginger is a rather different touch, and adds originality as well as flavor to an old favorite.

PREPARATION TRAY

cantaloupes, cut in half, seeded, put back together again and refrigerated

or

honeydew melon, cut in quarters, seeded, put back together and refrigerated

MARKETING LIST

2 Cantaloupes
or
1 honeydew melon
superfine granulated
sugar
powdered ginger

Wash the melons well, removing any labels that might be on them.

You can cut and seed them quite some time before serving if you put them together again and wrap them tightly in transparent wrap to hold them together in the refrigerator. The flesh dries out if it is exposed to air too long.

To serve: Use **½ a small cantaloupe or ¼ a honeydew melon** for each person.

Be sure the melon is well chilled.

Sprinkle each serving with a little:

> **superfine granulated sugar**
> **powdered ginger**

See how many of your guests can guess what it is that makes the melon taste so marvelously different.

Suprêmes de Volaille Archiduc
(Fillets of Chicken Breast Archduke)

Serves four

MARKETING LIST

4 half breasts of chicken, skinned and boned
Calvados
Salt
Cayenne pepper
mushrooms
salt butter
lemon juice
white peppercorns
boiled ham
dry sherry
truffle
fresh tarragon
garlic
Swiss gruyère cheese
flour
tomato paste
Dijon mustard
meat glaze
potato flour
Chicken Stock
dry white wine
red currant jelly
Can of artichoke bottoms
Parmesan cheese

One of the daintiest morsels you can set before a king—or your own family or guests, for that matter—is a breast of chicken that has been skinned, cut from the bone, and prepared with great delicacy. This is the ultimate, the supreme, of chicken, and the French aptly call such a chicken fillet a suprême. There are only two to a bird, but in these days when you can buy chicken breasts separately, it is not as prodigal a dish as it once was.

In this recipe the breasts are stuffed and served in a beautiful sauce, and even for those who are tired of "chicken every Sunday" this is a different and unusual aspect of the same old bird. It is one of the most satisfactory party dishes I know.

PREPARATION TRAY

breasts of chicken, stuffed and floured

chicken stock

Gruyère cheese, sliced thin

artichoke bottoms

Parmesan cheese, grated

butter, melted

truffles, sliced or mushroom caps, sautéed

1   Have your butcher skin and bone and split: **2 whole chicken breasts** (This will give you four fillets or *suprêmes*.)

2   Trim off any pieces of fat or membrane, using a small, very sharp knife.

3   The underside of the *suprême*, the side that lay next to the carcass, will not be as smooth and plump as the breast meat that was directly beneath the skin. You will see a long white tendon imbedded in the underside. Take a small sharp knife and carefully cut the flesh away from the tendon, pulling it as you cut until it comes out. Then flatten the flesh with the side of a large chef's knife. When you prepare these *suprêmes* you will see how easy the job is if you have a really sharp knife. With a dull blade you might botch the whole thing.

4   Now, lay the 4 *suprêmes*, plump side up, on your cutting board. Holding your hand on the rounded top, carefully cut a pocket parallel to your hand about half way through the *suprême*.

5   Open the *suprêmes* so they are spread flat on your cutting board.

6   Brush them with **a little Calvados**

7   Sprinkle with: **the tiniest bit of salt**
a little cayenne

8   Let them marinate so for about 5 minutes.

While they are standing, slice fairly thin: **4 ounces of mushrooms**

2   In a sauté pan heat:
3 tablespoons (1½ ounces) of salt butter

3   When it is foaming add:
the mushrooms, coating them well with the butter
2 teaspoons of lemon juice
a few grains of salt
a little freshly ground white pepper

4   Cook for 2 or 3 minutes only.

5   Add: **3 ounces of finely shredded boiled ham** (Because the ham is salty and you are using salt butter, you want to use very little salt otherwise.)
2 tablespoons of dry sherry
1 small shredded truffle (When opening a can of

344

truffles always decant them into a jar and cover with brandy. Keep them that way in the refrigerator for as long as you wish—or they last.)

2 teaspoons of freshly chopped tarragon

a smidgen of chopped garlic (I should say that a scant ¼ teaspoon would give the message.)

6   Remove from the fire and let these ingredients cool, then add:

3 ounces of coarsely shredded Swiss Gruyère cheese
(If you added it to the hot mushroom mixture, the cheese would melt and get sticky and stringy.)

1   Put a good tablespoon of the above stuffing into each *suprême*. Place it in the center of the pocket, leaving a margin around the edges. Fold over and seal the edges of the flesh carefully. Raw breast of chicken is rather gummy, and it will seal shut with a little pressure.

2   Dust the breasts lightly with **flour.** Clap them smartly between your palms, and they will retain just a fine even film of flour.

3   At this point you could wrap and refrigerate the *suprêmes* until you were ready to cook them. Chicken breasts must be cooked for a very short time only, and they are much better if served immediately. Otherwise they dry out and harden.

4   To cook, heat in a heavy sauté pan:

4 tablespoons (2 ounces—½ stick) of salt butter

5   When the butter turns a delicate golden tan, put in the *suprêmes*, smooth side down (the side that was under the skin) .

6   Cover with a flat lid and a weight, and brown. The butter should not be permitted to get so hot that it turns brown, and 3 or 4 minutes should be sufficient to brown one side of the chicken.

7   Remove the cover, turn over the *suprêmes*, and brown them on the other side, uncovered, for another 3 or 4 minutes. These tender pieces of chicken do not take long to cook, and you want them soft and juicy. Overcooking makes them dry and tough.

8   In a small pot pour: **¼ cup of Calvados**

9 Heat it, tip it toward the flame until it ignites, and pour it flaming over the *suprêmes*.

10 When the chicken has stopped blazing, remove the pieces from the pan to a warm plate.

11 Add to the pan, off the fire:
 1 level teaspoon of tomato paste
 1 level teaspoon of Dijon mustard
 ½ teaspoon of meat glaze (This will give your dish quite enough salt.)
 2 teaspoons of potato flour

12 When these ingredients have been mixed to a smooth paste with a small wire whisk, mix in:
 1¼ cups of good strong chicken stock (See recipe on page 353.)
 ¼ cup of dry white wine
 2 tablespoons of sherry
 1 teaspoon of red currant jelly
 ½ teaspoon of freshly ground white pepper

13 Stir over the fire until the sauce comes to a boil.

14 Reduce heat to a simmer, and put back the chicken breasts. Be sure the sauce does not boil, as that would toughen the chicken.

15 Cover the pan with wax paper, and place the lid on top. (Any moisture from condensation will then fall on the paper instead of into the sauce.)

16 Let the *suprêmes* simmer ever so gently for not more than 15 minutes.

To serve: Arrange the breasts down a flat *au gratin* dish. Place on top of each breast an **artichoke bottom.** Cover with a thin slice of **imported Swiss Gruyère cheese.** Put into a preheated 300° oven for 3 to 4 minutes, until the cheese envelops the chicken breast.

Coat the whole dish with the sauce, spooning it carefully with a large basting spoon.

Sprinkle with a little **freshly grated Parmesan cheese.** Dot with a little **melted butter**

Brown under a hot broiler for a few minutes.

You may garnish the *Suprêmes de Volaille* with fluted sautéed **mushrooms** or **slices of truffle**

Potato Gnocchi

Serves four to six

The Italians have been most inventive in their use of starches, as the whole wide range of pastas can testify. Spaghetti, macaroni, fettucine are fairly popular here, but we tend to overlook the possibilities of gnocchi, probably because it doesn't come prepackaged or already prepared. And it's a shame, really, because the different kinds of gnocchi are marvelous with certain dishes. And not at all difficult to make. This potato gnocchi, for example, would be excellent with roast pork, sauerbraten or other hearty dishes, and you will have the satisfaction of serving good old potatoes up in a brand new way.

MARKETING LIST

Idaho potatoes
salt
eggs
butter
flour
Chicken stock
Parmesan cheese

PREPARATION TRAY

gnocchi dough

chicken stock

Parmesan cheese, grated

butter, melted

au gratin dish, buttered

1 Peel but do not cut: **4 good Idaho potatoes**

    2 Put in a pan with: **cold water to cover**
       1 teaspoon of salt

    3 Bring the water to a boil, then let the potatoes simmer briskly until they are soft when pricked with an ice pick.

    4 Drain the water off.

    5 Return the pan to a low fire and shake it to absorb excess moisture from the potatoes.

    6 Put in a mixer bowl: the 4 cooked potatoes

    7 Beat them until smooth.

    8 Then beat in: **1 whole egg**
       1 egg yolk
       1½ tablespoons (¾ ounce) of butter

    9 When the mixture is smooth, remove it from the machine, and add enough **flour** so that you can roll the *gnocchi* dough without having it stick. (Mix in your flour a little at a time, and as soon as you feel that the mixture is no longer sticky, stop!)

   10 Lightly flour a board.

   11 Roll out the *gnocchi* dough into long sausage shapes about as thick around as your thumb.

   12 Cut it off into 3-cornered pieces. (On your first cut, slant the knife to the left, on the next to the right and so on until you have cut it all.)

1 Heat in a heavy pan: **6 cups of chicken stock** (See recipe on page 353.)

    2 When it is hot but not boiling, put in the *gnocchi*.

    3 Allow them to poach until they rise to the surface of the liquid.

    4 Remove the *gnocchi* with a slotted spoon and allow them to drain.

    5 Arrange the *gnocchi* down a buttered *au gratin* dish.

    6 Sprinkle them with: **a little melted butter**
       a little freshly grated Parmesan cheese

    7 Place under the broiler until the *gratin* (brown crust) forms.

Serve at once.

Coeur à la Crème
(Cream Cheese Hearts)

Cheese cloth
fresh cream cheese
fresh Vanilla bean
heavy Cream
Confectioners' sugar
red currant jelly
fresh strawberries
dry sherry
lemon
10 heart-shaped
   molds
(The Coeur à
la Crème baskets
are nicest, but
you can also use
the metal heart-
shaped molds
pierced with holes.)

Serves ten

Sweet fresh cream cheese is used in a number of delectable French desserts. One of the simplest and best, in my opinion, is coeur à la crème which comes to the table wrapped in muslin or cheesecloth, encased in a heart-shaped basket, and as fresh as a May morning.

I have found it much more satisfactory to make coeur à la crème in small individual molds rather than one large one, as the little ones drain better and are lighter.

This is a dessert that stars two of France's finest products —cream cheese and ripe red berries—both so excellent that they need no fuss or fanfare in their presentation. Fortunately for us it is possible to create a very creditable coeur à la crème with the ingredients available here. Try this recipe if you want an unusual dessert of great charm.

PREPARATION TRAY

cheesecloth, cut in squares the proper size

heavy cream, whipped

strawberry sauce

1   Put in a mixer bowl: **½ pound of cream cheese**
2   Beat until it is very light and fluffy.
3   Slowly add:
    ½ cup confectioners' sugar, and beat well
    a pinch of salt
    ½ a fresh vanilla bean (Slit it lengthwise with a sharp paring knife and scrape the tiny black seeds into the cream cheese mixture.)
4   Put in a large metal bowl, over another bowl of ice:
    1 pint of heavy cream

5 Whip with a large whisk until the cream holds its shape when it drops from the whisk.

6 Add whipped cream to the cream cheese mixture, and mix lightly but thoroughly with the whisk.

7 Cut 10 squares of cheesecloth (double thickness) large enough so that they come about 1½ inches beyond the mold when used as a lining.

8 Wring the cheesecloth out in ice water and carefully line the heart-shaped molds.

9 Fill well with the cheese mixture, and dome it up a little.

10 Carefully cover with the ends of the cheesecloth, and place the molds on a rack over a jelly roll pan into which they can drain.

11 Place in the refrigerator for 6 hours or overnight.

To serve: Since this dessert glorifies the country freshness of cream cheese and berries, it is a nice gesture to bring it to the table wrapped in cheesecloth, in its rustic little baskets. However, if you have made them in the tin molds, unmold them in the kitchen.

Fold back the cheesecloth, and turn each mold upside down on its dessert plate. Then, holding the cheesecloth down, lift up the mold, gently peel off the cheesecloth, and there will be a beautiful, creamy white heart.

Serve separately the following strawberry sauce:

1 Put in a small heavy saucepan: **¼ cup of dry sherry ¾ cup of red currant jelly**

2 Stir over a slow fire until jelly melts.

3 When the liquid has cooled, add to it: **1½ cups of sliced fresh strawberries** carefully coated with: **1 tablespoon of lemon juice**

Raspberries or sliced peaches can be used in place of strawberries, but always use the red currant jelly. And if you are feeling very grand, you can substitute 2 tablespoons of your precious framboise for the sherry. This is a particularly beautiful summer dessert, because it looks so cool and—since there is no cooking—so will you.

SOME BASIC PROCEDURES

Praline Powder

This delicious confection is made of ground-up nuts that have been roasted in boiling sugar, and there is nothing else in the world that quite approximates its burnt almond and caramel flavor.

A jar of the powder keeps in the refrigerator indefinitely, and is wonderful to have on hand as a flavoring for souf-flés, mousses, ice creams, frostings or a dessert topping.

MARKETING LIST

almonds –
not blanched
granulated sugar
Cream of Tartar

PREPARATION TRAY

jelly roll pan, lightly oiled

screw-top jar

1 In a heavy pan put:
   ¾ cup of almonds—not blanched
   1½ cups of granulated sugar
   ½ teaspoon of cream of tartar
2 Place the pan over a slow fire, stirring occasionally until the contents becomes a dark caramel.
3 Pour the syrup into a lightly oiled jelly roll pan.
4 When it sets, break it up into chunks and pulverize it in a blender or meat grinder with a fine blade.
5 Store the praline powder in a screw-top jar.

Tarragon Vinegar

It is not easy to find a good tarragon vinegar on the market, but it is easy to make one yourself. Salad dressings and certain sauces such as hollandaise can be only as good as what goes into them, and your vinegar is an important ingredient. So here's how!

Make a gallon at a time, and when it has matured, decant a pint or a quart for everyday use. You can keep adding fresh cider vinegar to the larger jar, and will have a never-ending supply of fine tarragon vinegar. (By "never-ending" I guess I really mean that you can keep it going for about three years. My editor is so literal!)

MARKETING LIST

A one gallon jar with a wide mouth.
enough fresh tarragon to fill it.
3 quarts of good cider vinegar

1 Wash your **fresh tarragon** thoroughly and leave it whole.
2 Dry very carefully—you don't want any water in the vinegar.
3 Stuff the jar fairly full of tarragon on the stalk. It should look a bit like a tropical hothouse.
4 Fill the jar with:
   a good cider vinegar (Beware of using the plain commercial vinegars. They are often far too acid. The cider vinegar is mellower.)
5 Seal the jar tightly and store it in a dark place for 3 months.
6 As you pour off vinegar to use, refill with more cider vinegar.

Incidentally, it is best to make this in summer when tarragon is plentiful and cheap. Otherwise it would be almost as costly to fill a gallon jar with tarragon as with rare orchids—though far more sensible.

How to Prepare a Soufflé Dish

1 Take a soufflé dish with straight sides and, using a pastry brush, coat the inside well with melted butter.
2 Next, tear off a length of wax paper long enough to go around the dish.

352

3 Fold it in half lengthwise.
4 With the pastry brush, butter one side of the folded paper.
5 Keep the buttered side of the paper facing inside, and wrap it once around the soufflé dish. If you rest the dish and the bottom of the paper on your table top, the cuff of paper will not pleat but will go around smoothly.
6 Make a slip knot in a length of white string and loop it over the paper cuff, tying it around the soufflé dish about 3 inches from the bottom.

For a sweet soufflé: Sprinkle the inside of the dish and the cuff with **granulated sugar.**

For a cheese or other savory soufflé: Sprinkle the inside of the dish and cuff with a light dusting of **bread crumbs.**

For a cold mousse: Do not butter the soufflé dish, but brush the wax paper with vegetable oil before tying it around the dish. Never brush with melted butter when something is to be chilled. The butter will chill and harden, and it will stick to your preparation. You want to be able to peel the oiled paper cuff off neatly when the cold mousse has set, leaving several inches of mousse standing above the rim of the dish.

Whether it is used for a cold mousse or a hot soufflé, the wax paper cuff enables you to have a spectacularly high-rising result . . . sometimes a bit of artful kitchen magic is needed to help nature along.

Basic Chicken Stock
About four cups.

The distinctive flavor of French sauces is in large part due to the stock or broth used in their preparation. Fonds de cuisine—foundations of the kitchen—is the term for these liquids, and indeed the most glorious dishes of the haute cuisine are firmly founded on the stock pot.

Since this is such an important and fundamental ingredient of so many recipes, it pays to take a little extra care in its preparation. Don't throw leftovers · indiscriminately into a pot of water, and don't expect mere bouillon cubes to give you the quality of real meat and bones. You will get out of your stock pot exactly what you put into it— cooking being very much like life in that and other respects.

Cooking in the grand manner necessitates having brown stock and white, made from veal, poultry, game and beef, as well as fish stock (or fumet) for fish and seafood sauces. I have simplified my recipes so that one basic chicken stock, and one basic fish stock (see recipe on page 52) work admirably for all of them. The addition of meat glaze—a highly concentrated paste that results when brown stock has been boiled down—enables us to make the brown sauces even when using this basic chicken stock.

Most chefs make their own meat glaze, but for our purposes one of the better beef extracts is convenient and very good. If you keep a jar of that in your refrigerator, and several 1-cup or 2-cup plastic containers of homemade chicken stock in your freezer you will have the foundation for a number of fine sauces.

If you want to have a more ambitious stock, you can make a pot-au-feu (see recipe on page 276) which permits you to have your stock and eat it too. But, as you will see, this basic chicken stock is simple to prepare and it makes a delicious contribution to your sauces. Make a batch every few weeks, so you will always have some on hand.

MARKETING LIST

6 chicken feet
6 chicken wings
onion
celery
carrot
bay leaf
peppercorns
salt

PREPARATION TRAY

chicken feet, blanched and peeled

onion, sliced

celery, sliced

carrot, sliced

plastic containers ready

354

1   Put in a sauce pan: **6 chicken feet**
2   Cover them with cold water.
3   Bring to a boil, then drain.
4   Rinse the chicken feet in cold water and peel off the scaly yellow outer skin.

1   In a sauce pan put: **6 chicken wings**
        6 chicken feet, blanched and peeled
        6 cups of cold water
2   Bring slowly to a boil, then reduced to a simmer.
3   Carefully skim off all the scum.
4   Add to the pan:
    2 ribs of celery, sliced
    1 small yellow onion, sliced
    ½ small carrot, sliced (too much of this vegetable makes your stock overly sweet)
    1 bay leaf
    6 black peppercorns
    2 teaspoons of salt
5   Simmer uncovered (so that the liquid will reduce and the stock will be stronger) for 1½ hours.
6   Allow to cool.
7   Strain into the plastic containers. (If you are only going to refrigerate instead of freeze the stock you can keep it in screw-top glass jars, but glass might crack when the liquid expands as it freezes.)
8   Before freezing, allow the stock to chill uncovered, and then remove any fat that has risen to the top.

As I said, this is an excellent basic stock for sauces. But if you want to make an aspic or a clear consommé, use the stronger recipes on page 276.

In any case, you will find that to have stock in the freezer is as comforting and convenient as having money in the bank. A Wall Street student of mine used to call it his "frozen assets," and he became quite miserly, cooking up quarts and quarts of stock just for the pleasure of seeing his freezer full of potential delicacies.

How to Clean and Prepare Mussels for Cooking

1 Put all your mussels in the kitchen sink. If there are any whose shells are open, and who do not shut when handled, discard them. And heed well this simple rule:
When a mussel is open, though not cooked, it is dead.
When a mussel is shut, though cooked, it is dead.
Open raw, or shut cooked are no good—throw those away.
Mussels frequently come into your kitchen absolutely covered with barnacles, bearded with seaweed, and quite gritty and sandy.

2 Put them into cold water with a strong solution (about 1 tablespoon per quart) of dry mustard. The mussels hate the mustard, so they keep tight shut. The solution loosens all the accumulation on their shells, and after they have soaked a few hours you can scrub them quite easily with a stiff brush, and scrape them with a small knife kept for this purpose—don't use a good paring knife!

3 When they are clean, soak them in a little clear cold water until you are ready to use them. You can refrigerate them, but always keep them in water.

4 If you do not plan to use the mussels until the next day, sprinkle a little dry oatmeal on the surface of the water. The mussels love oatmeal and they will open their shells a crack to eat it, growing fatter and fatter in the process. You know, that is the cheap restaurants' trick for fattening oysters.

5 Just before using them, drain the mussels and rinse them under fresh running water.

How to Truss Poultry

Chickens, squabs, ducks, geese—any poultry that is roasted or browned whole should be firmly tied up in the process. The trussing keeps wings and legs neatly in position, and makes the bird juicier, more compact and more attractive.

356

1   Place the poultry on its back with the drumsticks pointing toward you.
2   Push the legs well up alongside the breast.
3   Pull the wing tips to spread the wings out.
4   Use soft white string, and bring the string over the tips of the drumsticks, down around them, and then cross the two ends of the string between the drumsticks, making a figure 8.
5   Pull up the two ends of string, hook them under the lower tip of the keel bone and bring them up between the drumsticks and the breast.
6   Smooth the skin over the breast so it is plump and firm, and pull the ends of string tight enough to hold it so.
7   Now flip the chicken over and thread the two ends of the string through the second joint of each wing.
8   Fold the flap of skin from the neck down over the back. Tie it flat, pulling the string tight. Tie with a knot, and cut the string.
9   Fold back the first joint of each wing so that the wings are akimbo. They will then form a solid flat base for the bird to rest on when it is turned on its back.
10 Trim off any excess skin from the neck flap.
11 Turn the bird over and push in the rump (we children used to call it "the parson's nose" with a good deal of irreverent snickering).

This trussing can make even the scraggiest bird look round and plump, and when it is browned or roasted the juices are held in by the compactness of the flesh. Remove the string before serving and the poultry will still hold its shape.

How to Cut up Chicken for Casserole

A chicken that is browned whole and then cut up into pieces and finished in a sauce, retains far more of its flavor and good juices than a chicken cut up to begin with. Always brown your birds trussed and whole. Then remove the string, and for casserole dishes cut the poultry in the following manner:

1 Turn the bird on its side. Take a small, sharp carving knife and slit the skin between the thigh and the body. Continue cutting until you feel the backbone socket with the knife.
2 Carefully pull the leg joint back to loosen it.
3 Continue cutting, using a sawing motion toward the backbone, getting all the meat cut away from the carcass.
4 Remove the entire leg and thigh.
5 Cut in half at the joint.
6 Remove the knobs at the end of the drumstick.
7 Repeat with the other leg.
8 Take your knife and cut along one side of the keel of the breastbone to the bottom of the bone.
9 With kitchen shears or poultry shears cut through the breastbone from the neck to the bottom.
10 Turn the bird on its side again. Cut through the center of the ribs parallel to the breastbone.
11 Cut through the joint of each wing near the neck.
12 On the bias, cut each breast off in half, giving you one piece of breast with a wing and one without for each side.

You will have 8 pieces of chicken—four of breast and four of leg, plus the backbone on which no meat is left. The backbone does contain the oysters, however, and it gives extra flavor to your dish, so put it back to cook with the other pieces. If your dinner is not a formal one, serve the backbone with the other pieces of chicken. Some lucky bone lover will be delighted.

INDEX

INDEX

360

INDEX

INDEX

INDEX

INDEX

INDEX

INDEX

ABOUT THE AUTHORS

DIONE LUCAS, a diplomate of the famed École du Cordon Bleu in Paris, trained and worked under some of the great chefs of the Continent. As a young woman, she opened a cooking school and restaurant in London. In this country she operated her own restaurant, The Egg Basket, in New York, and taught her culinary arts and skills in her own famous Gourmet Cooking School.

Mrs. Lucas, known to millions across the country for her television demonstrations and on the Continent for her three world-wide teaching tours, was virtually responsible for this country's burgeoning interest in gourmet cooking.

DARLENE GEIS is a writer and editor who turned from paper and pen to pots and pans under Mrs. Lucas' tutelage—and then back again to paper and pen. She is the author of the definitive book on dinosaurs for young people, *Dinosaurs and Other Prehistoric Animals*, a number of popular teen-age novels, including *Design for Ann* and *The Mystery of the Thirteenth Floor*, as well as many magazine articles on a variety of subjects for adults. Mrs. Geis has been senior editor of Harry N. Abrams, Inc., for a number of years and is the editor of *The Joys of Wine*, *Wines of California*, and the *Los Angeles Times California Cookbook*.